感动一个国家

的

文字

艾柯 编译

天津教育出版社
TIANJIN EDUCATION PRESS

所有的人生而平等，这是造物主赋予人们的不可剥夺的权利，其中包括生存权、自由权和追求幸福的权利。

图书在版编目（CIP）数据

感动一个国家的文字／艾柯，编译.－天津：
天津教育出版社，2006.4
（美丽英文）
ISBN 7-5309-4671-4

I.感... II.艾... III.文学－作品综合集－美国
IV.I712.11

中国版本图书馆 CIP 数据核字（2006）第 028158 号

感动一个国家的文字

责任编辑	田昕
装帧策划	先知先行

作　者	艾柯 编译
出版发行	天津教育出版社
	天津市和平区西康路 35 号
	邮政编码 300051
经　销	全国新华书店
印　刷	河北省三河市南阳印刷有限公司
版　次	2006 年 5 月第 1 版
印　次	2006 年 5 月第 1 次印刷
规　格	32 开（787×1092 毫米）
字　数	180 千字
印　张	8.25
书　号	ISBN 7-5309-4671-4/I·186
定　价	18.80 元

CONTENTS

目录

第一卷　国家的神圣职责

CONTENTS
目 录

第二卷　　自由与平等的梦想

Contents

目 录

CONTENTS

目录

第三卷 不朽的精神殿堂

CONTENTS

目 录

CONTENTS

目 录

国家的神圣职责

第一卷

所有的人生而平等，这是造物主赋予人们的不可剥夺的权利，其中包括生存权、自由权和追求幸福的权利。正是为了保障这些权利，人们才建立了政府，而政府的正当权力，则是经被统治者同意授予的。任何形式的政府，一旦破坏了这些目标，人民就有权利去改变它或废除它，并重新建立一个新的政府。新政府所依据的原则及其组织权力的方式，务必使人民相信：唯有这样才能够获得安全和幸福。

"五月花号" 公约

The Mayflower Compact

In the name of God, Amen.

We whose names are underwritten, the loyal subjects of our dread sovereign Lord, King James, by the grace of God, of Great Britain, France and Ireland king, defender of the faith, etc., having undertaken.

For the glory of God, and advancement of the Christian faith, and honor of our king and country, a voyage to plant the first colony in the Northern parts of Virginia, do by these presents solemnly and mutually in the presence of God, and one of another, covenant and combine ourselves together into a civil body politic, for our better ordering and preservation and furtherance of the ends aforesaid and by virtue hereof to enact constitute, and frame such just and equal laws, ordinances, acts, constitutions, and offices, from time to time, as shall be thought most meet and convenient for the general good of the colony, unto which we promise all due submission and obedience.

In witness whereof we have here under subscribed our names at Cape-Cod the 11th of November, in the year of the reign of our sovereign lord, King James, of England, France, and Ireland the eighteenth, and of Scotland the fifty-fourth. Anno Domini 1620.

感动一个国家的文字

以上帝的名义，阿门。

我等签约人，信仰的捍卫者，蒙上帝保佑的大不列颠、法兰西和爱尔兰的国王詹姆斯国王陛下的忠顺臣民。

为了上帝的荣耀，为了增进基督教信仰，为了我们国王和国家的荣誉，我们远涉重洋，在弗吉尼亚北部开拓第一块殖民地。我们在上帝面前一起庄严地盟誓签约，自愿结成民众自治团体。为使上述目的得以顺利实施、维护和发展，也为了将来能随时依此而制定和颁布有益于殖民地全体民众利益的公正与平等的法律、法规、法案、宪章和公职，我们全体都保证遵守和服从。

据此于公元1620年11月11日，于英格兰、法兰西、爱尔兰十八世国王暨苏格兰五十四世国王詹姆斯陛下在位之年，我等在卡德角签署姓名如下。

历史链接

1620年11月11日，在经过66天的海上漂泊之后，"五月花号"帆船向北美大陆靠近。他们的目的地本来是哈德逊河口地区，但由于海上风浪险恶，他们错过了目标，于是就在现在的卡德角外的普利茅斯港抛锚。由于那时已是深秋，他们就决定在那里登陆。

在上岸之前，41名男乘客签订了一份公约，目的是为了建立一个大家都能受到约束的自治基础。在这份后来被称为《"五月花号"公约》的文件里，签署人立誓创立一个自治团体，这个团体是基于被管理者的同意而成立的，并且将依法治理这块土地上的一切事务。这份公约是由"五月花号"船上的每一个家长，每一个成年单身男子和大多数受雇佣的男仆所签署的，由于妇女那时没有政治权利，所以没有请她们签署。

1991年的《世界年鉴》评价该公约是"自动同意管理自己的一个协议，是美国的第一套成文法"，它预示了民主政治的许多理念。这份著名的文件也被人们称为"美国的出生证明"。

Chief Logan's Lament

洛根首领的哀辞

"I appeal to any white man to say, if ever he entered Logan's cabin hungry, and he gave him not meat; if ever he came cold and naked, and he cloathed him not. During the course of the last long and bloody war Logan remained idle in his cabin, an advocate for peace. Such was my love for the whites, that my countrymen pointed as they passed, and said, 'Logan is the friend of white man.' I had even thought to have lived with you, but for the injuries of one man. Colonel Cresap, the last spring, in cold blood, and unprovoked, murdered all the relations of Logan, not even sparing my women and children. There runs not a drop of my blood in the veins of any living creature. This called on me for revenge. I have sought it, I have killed many, I have fully glutted my vengeance, for my country I rejoice at the beams of peace. But do not harbour a thought that mine is the joy of fear. Logan never felt fear. He will not turn on his heel to save his life. Who is there to mourn for Logan?— Not one."

感动一个国家的文字

"我请求任何一位白人说说看，他有没有饿着肚子走进洛根家的小屋，而洛根没有给他肉吃；他有没有在又冷又没衣服穿时来到洛根家，而洛根没有给他衣服穿。在最近这次漫长而血腥的冲突中，洛根一直待在他自己的小屋里，他一直是位和平的倡导者。我对白人的爱就是如此。甚至我的同胞经过我家时都要指着我说：'洛根是白人的朋友。'如果不是因为一个人伤害了我，我甚至想过和你们搬在一起住。去年春天，克雷萨普上校残酷无情地杀害了洛根所有的亲人，甚至连我的女人和孩子也不放过。现在活着的人们中间，没有一个人的血管里流淌着我的血。这个事实呼唤我去复仇。为了寻求报复，我杀死了许多人，我已经复仇够了，为了国家，我很高兴看到和平的曙光。但不要以为我的高兴是出于害怕——洛根什么都不害怕。他不会为了保全自己的性命而临阵脱逃。谁将到那儿为洛根哀悼？——答案是：没有一个人。"

历史链接

　　1774年，居住在俄亥俄河流域的印第安人与白人之间发生了一系列血腥冲突。根据托马斯·杰斐逊在《弗吉尼亚纪事》(Notes on Virginia) 一书中的记载，事情的起因是白人对印第安人的抢劫行为非常愤怒，他们为了报复，派出士兵杀害了许多无辜的印第安人，其中包括"明戈"印第安人 (Mingo Indians) 首领洛根的家人，而洛根向来是把白人当做朋友对待的。

　　于是，在洛根的领导下，印第安人也发动了一场反对白人定居者的战争，他们杀死了许多无辜的白人，包括男人、妇女和儿童，并剥去了他们的头皮。1774年10月，印第安人被弗吉尼亚的民团打败。在这个决定性的战役之后，洛根拒绝和其他首领一起去向获胜的白人屈膝求饶。相反，他给弗吉尼亚皇家总督邓莫尔勋爵寄去这篇演讲。

　　据杰斐逊说，"这篇演讲成了当时所有人谈论的主题"。它先被刊登在《弗吉尼亚公报》上，后又被刊登在北美大陆各种报纸上，甚至连英格兰的报刊也广泛刊登了这篇演讲。

I That all men are by nature equally free and independent, and have certain inherent rights, of which, when they enter into a state of society, they cannot, by any compact, deprive or divest their posterity; namely, the enjoyment of life and liberty, with the means of acquiring and possessing property, and pursuing and obtaining happiness and safety.

II That all power is vested in, and consequently derived from, the people; that magistrates are their trustees and servants, and at all times amenable to them.

III That government is, or ought to be, instituted for the common

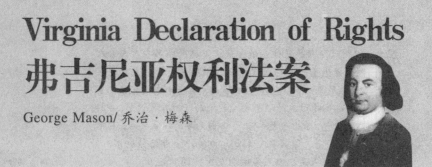

Virginia Declaration of Rights
弗吉尼亚权利法案

George Mason/ 乔治·梅森

一、人人生来自由、平等与独立，并享有某些天赋之人权，即当他们结合为一个社会时，他们不能凭任何契约剥夺其后裔的这些权利；这些权利，即享受生活与自由的权利，包括获取与拥有财产、追求和享有安全与幸福。

二、所有的权力都源自人民，因而也都属于人民；管理者是他们的受托人与仆人，无论什么时候都应服从于人民。

三、政府应当是为了保证人民、国家和社会的共同利益和安全而设立的；在不同形式的政府之间，最好的政府是能够提供最大幸

benefit, protection, and security of the people, nation or community; of all the various modes and forms of government that is best, which is capable of producing the greatest degree of happiness and safety and is most effectually secured against the danger of maladministration; and that, whenever any government shall be found inadequate or contrary to these purposes, a majority of the community hath an indubitable, unalienable, and indefeasible right to reform, alter or abolish it , in such manner as shall be judged most conducive to the public weal.

IV That no man, or set of men, are entitled to exclusive or separate emoluments or privileges from the community, but in consideration of public services; which, not being descendible, neither ought the offices of magistrate, legislator, or judge be hereditary.

V That the legislative and executive powers of the state should be separate and distinct from the judicative; and, that the members of the two first may be restrained from oppression by feeling and participating the burthens of the people, they should, at fixed periods, be reduced to a private station, return into that body from which they were originally taken, and the vacancies be supplied by frequent,

福和安全的政府，是能够最有效地防止弊政危险的政府。因此，当发现任何政府不合乎甚至违反这些宗旨时，社会大众享有不容置疑、不可剥夺和不能取消的权力并以公认为最有助于大众利益的方式，改革、变换或废除政府。

四、除非为了服务公众，任何个人或群体都无权从社会获取独占的或垄断的利益或特权；公共职位——行政长官、立法者和法官等职位不能世袭。

五、州的立法权、行政权应与司法权分立，并要有明确的界限；前两者的成员如能感受并分担人民的疾苦，就不至于压迫人民；他们应在规定的任职期限之后恢复平民身份，回到他们原来所在的机构，其空缺则通过经常的、确定

certain, and regular elections in which all, or any part of the former members, to be again eligible, or ineligible, as the laws shall direct.

VI That elections of members to serve as representatives of the people in assembly ought to be free; and that all men, having sufficient evidence of permanent common interest with, and attachment to, the community have the right of suffrage and cannot be taxed or deprived of their property for public uses without their own consent or that of their representatives so elected, nor bound by any law to which they have not, in like manner, assented, for the public good.

VII That all power of suspending laws, or the execution of laws, by any authority without consent of the representatives of the people is injurious to their rights and ought not to be exercised.

VIII That in all capital or criminal prosecutions a man hath a right to demand the cause and nature of his accusation to be confronted with the accusers and witnesses, to call for evidence in his favor, and to a speedy trial by an impartial jury of his vicinage, without whose unanimous consent he cannot be found guilty, nor can he be compelled to give evidence against himself ; that no man be deprived of his liberty except by the law of the land or the judgement of his peers.

IX That excessive bail ought not to be required, nor excessive fines imposed; nor cruel and unusual punishments inflicted.

X That general warrants, whereby any officer or messenger may be commanded to search suspected places without evidence of a fact committed, or to seize any person or persons not named, or whose offense is not particularly described and supported by evidence, are grievous and oppressive and ought not to be granted.

XI That in controversies respecting property and in suits be-

感动一个国家的文字......

的以及定期的选举来填补；在选举当中，将按照法律规定，确定以前的所有成员或部分成员是否仍符合连任的条件。

六、选举议会代表的各项选举，都应该自由进行；凡是能够证明与本社会有永久性共同利益关系并属于本社会的人都享有选举权；未经选举人本人或其代表同意，不能对选举人征税或剥夺其财产供公众使用；同样，选举人也不受任何未经他们以同样方式同意的法律的约束。

七、任何当局未经人民代表同意而中止法律或执行法律，都有损于人民的权利，都不得行使。

八、在一切有关可判死刑的案件或刑事诉讼中，人们有权了解对其起诉的理由和性质，有权与起诉人和证人对质，要求查证对其有利的证据，并有权要求来自其邻近地区的公正陪审团进行迅速审理；没有经过陪审团的一致同意，不能确认他有罪，也不能强迫他自证其罪；除非根据当地法律或由其他地位相同的公民所组成的陪审团裁决，不能剥夺任何人的自由。

九、不得要求人们缴纳过量的保释金或过重的罚金，也不得判处极其残酷的刑罚。

十、在没有获得犯罪事实的证据之前，对官员和执法人员签发一般搜捕令，使其搜查可疑地点，或拘捕未经指名或其罪行未经阐明且无确凿证据足以佐证之人，这种搜捕令为不可容忍并且是压制性的，绝对不能签发。

十一、在财产纠纷和公民之间的诉讼案件当中，应由陪审团进

tween man and man, the ancient trial by jury is preferable to any other and ought to be held sacred.

XII That the freedom of the press is one of the greatest bulwarks of liberty and can never be restrained but by despotic governments.

XIII That a well regulated militia, composed of the body of the people, trained to arms, is the proper, natural, and safe defense of a free state; that standing armies, in time of peace, should be avoided as dangerous to liberty; and that, in all cases, the military should be under strict subordination to, and be governed by, the civil power.

XIV That the people have a right to uniform government; and therefore, that no government separate from, or independent of, the government of Virginia, ought to be erected or established within the limits thereof.

XV That no free government, or the blessings of liberty, can be preserved to any people but by a firm adherence to justice, moderation, temperance, frugality, and virtue and by frequent recurrence to fundamental principles.

XVI That religion, or the duty which we owe to our Creator and the manner of discharging it, can be directed by reason and conviction, not by force or violence; and therefore, all men are equally entitled to the free exercise of religion, according to the dictates of conscience; and that it is the mutual duty of all to practice Christian forbearance, love, and charity towards each other.

感动一个国家的文字 . . . . .

行裁定，这一古老的审判程序比其他任何审判程序更加可取，它神圣不可侵犯，应予以保持。

十二、出版自由乃自由的重要保证之一，绝不能加以限制；只有专制政体才会限制出版自由。

十三、由受过军事训练的公民组成并且管理得当的民兵，是自由州正当、自然而安全的保障；在和平时期，应避免设置常常会危及自由的常备军；在任何情况下，军队都应严格服从文职权力，并受其领导。

十四、公民有权享有一个统一的政府。因此，在弗吉尼亚地区内，不得在弗吉尼亚政府之外另行设立任何政府。

十五、必须坚守公正、适度、节制和勤俭等品德，遵守各项基本法律，否则任何公民都不能拥有自由的政府，也无法享受上帝所赐的自由。

十六、宗教，亦即我们对创世主所负有的责任以及尽这种责任的方式，只能由理智和信念加以引导，不能诉诸暴力，因此，任何人都拥有按照良知的指示自由信仰宗教的平等权利；同样，所有人都有责任以基督的节制、博爱和仁慈对待他人。

历史链接

《弗吉尼亚权利法案》被认为是殖民地草拟宪法的先导，它也是一部有关天赋人权问题最著名的纲领性文件。这部法案诞生于《独立宣言》发表前一个月。作为宪法框架的一部分，它率先列举了一批公民权利。作者乔治·梅森是弗吉尼亚的一个大地主，他坚信"根植于人性之中的伟大权利"。

历史学家理查德·伯恩斯坦指出："权利"并非仅指那些不受政府干涉的个人权益，它还包括"正当之事"和行为准则。乔治·梅森因为重申有关个人权益与自由的原则，所以"在人类自由史上获得光荣地位"。

The Declaration of Independence

独立宣言

Thomas Jefferson／托马斯·杰斐逊

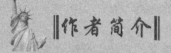 ‖作者简介‖

托马斯·杰斐逊（1743～1826），生于美国弗吉尼亚州，1762 年毕业于威廉与玛丽学院，1767 年取得律师资格。

杰斐逊于 1769 年进入殖民地议会，为反英运动领袖之一。1774 年发表的小册子《英属北美权利概要》(A Summary View of the Rights of British America) 为杰斐逊的重要作品，文中指出英国国会无权为殖民地制定法律。1775 年他随弗吉尼亚代表团出席在费城举行的第二次大陆会议，1776 年因起草《独立宣言》而名垂史册。《独立宣言》超越了一时一地的历史特殊意义，成为人类追求自身价值的伟大文献。

When in the Course of human events, it becomes necessary for one people to dissolve the political bands which have connected them with another, and to assume among the powers of the earth, the separate and equal station to which the Laws of Nature and of Nature's God entitle them, a decent respect to the opinions of mankind requires that they should declare the causes which impel them to the separation.

We hold these truths to be self-evident, that all men are created equal, that they are endowed by their Creator with certain unalienable Rights, that among these are Life, Liberty, and the pursuit of Happiness. That to secure these rights, Governments are instituted among Men, deriving their just powers from the consent of the governed. That whenever any Form of Government becomes destructive of these ends, it is the Right of the People to alter or to abolish it , and to institute new Government, laying its foundation on such principles and organizing its powers in such form, as to them shall seem most likely to effect their Safety and Happiness.

Prudence, indeed, will dictate that Governments long established should not be changed for light and transient causes; and accordingly all experience hath shewn, that mankind are more disposed to suffer,

人类发展过程中，一个民族在必须解除同另一个民族的联系，并按照自然法则和上帝的旨意，以独立平等的身份立于世界列国之林时，出于对人类舆论的尊重，有必要把促使他们独立的原因予以宣布。

我们认为下述真理是不言而喻的：所有的人生而平等，这是造物主赋予人们的不可剥夺的权利，其中包括生存权、自由权和追求幸福的权利。正是为了保障这些权利，人们才建立了政府，而政府的正当权力，则是经被统治者同意授予的。任何形式的政府，一旦破坏了这些目标，人民就有权利去改变它或废除它，并重新建立一个新的政府。新政府所依据的原则及其组织权力的方式，务必使人民相信：唯有这样才能够获得安全和幸福。

若审慎地考虑，一个成立已久的政府是不应当由于无关紧要和暂时的原因而予以更

13

while evils are sufferable, than to right themselves by abolishing the forms to which they are accustomed.

But when a long train of abuses and usurpations, pursuing invariably the same object evinces a design to reduce them under absolute Despotism, it is their right, it is their duty, to throw off such Government, and to provide new Guards for their future security. Such has been the patient sufferance of these Colonies; and such is now the necessity which constrains them to alter their former Systems of Government.

The history of the present King of Great Britain [George III] is a history of repeated injuries and usurpations, all having in direct object the establishment of an absolute Tyranny over these States. To prove this, let Facts be submitted to a candid world.

He has refused his Assent to Laws, the most wholesome and necessary for the public good.

He has forbidden his Governors to pass Laws of immediate and pressing importance, unless suspended in their operation till his Assent should be obtained, and when so suspended, he has utterly neglected to attend to them.

He has refused to pass other Laws for the accommodation of large districts of people, unless those people would relinquish the right of Representation in the Legislature, a right inestimable to them and formidable to tyrants only.

He has called together legislative bodies at places unusual, uncomfortable, and distant from the depository of their public Records, for the sole purpose of fatiguing them into compliance with his measures.

He has dissolved Representative Houses repeatedly, for opposing with manly firmness his invasions on the rights of the people.

换的。而且过去的所有经验也说明，人类更倾向于忍受尚能忍受的苦难，只要尚能忍受，人们都宁可选择忍受，而不愿去废除他们业已习惯的政府形式。

但是，当滥用职权和巧取豪夺的行为连绵不断、层出不穷，证明政府追求的目标是企图把人民置于专制主义统治之下时，人民就有权利，也有义务推翻这样的政府，并为自己未来的安全建立新的保障，这就是这些殖民地的人民一向忍受苦难，以及现在不得不起来改变原先政治制度的原因。

当今大不列颠国王（乔治三世）的统治历史，就是一部反复重演的伤天害理、巧取豪夺的历史。所有这些行径的唯一目的，就是要在各州之上建立一个独裁暴政。为证明这一点，就让以下的事实公诸全世界，让公正的世人做出评判：

他拒绝批准那些对公众利益最有益、最必要的法律。

他禁止他的总督们批准刻不容缓、极其重要的法律，要不就先行搁置这些法律直至征得他的同意；而这些法律被搁置后，他又对这些法律完全置之不理。

他拒绝批准方便广大地区人民的其他的法律，除非这些地区的人民情愿放弃自己在立法机构中的代表权；而代表权对人民来说是无比珍贵的，只有暴君才畏惧它。

他把各州立法团体召集到特别的、极不方便的、远离政府档案库的地方去开会，其唯一的目的就是使他们疲于奔命，不得不顺从他的旨意。

他一再解散议会，只因为议会坚决反对他侵犯人民的权利。

He has refused for a long time, after such dissolutions, to cause others to be elected; whereby the Legislative powers, incapable of Annihilation, have returned to the People at large for their exercise; the State remaining in the meantime exposed to all the dangers of invasion from without, and convulsions within.

He has endeavored to prevent the population of these States; for that purpose obstructing the Laws for Naturalization of Foreigners; refusing to pass others to encourage their migrations hither, and raising the conditions of new Appropriations of Lands.

He has obstructed the Administration of Justice, by refusing his Assent to Laws for establishing Judiciary powers.

He has made Judges dependent on his Will alone, for the tenure of their offices, and the amount and payment of their salaries.

He has erected a multitude of new offices, and sent hither swarms of officers to harass our people, and eat out their substance.

He has kept among us, in times of peace, Standing Armies, without the consent of our legislatures.

He has affected to render the Military independent of and superior to the Civil power.

He has combined with others to subject us to a jurisdiction foreign to our constitution and unacknowledged by our laws; giving his Assent to their Acts of pretended Legislation:

For quartering large bodies of armed troops among us;

For protecting them by a mock Trial from punishment for any Murders which they should commit on the Inhabitants of these States;

For cutting off our trade with all parts of the world;

For imposing taxes on us without our consent;

For depriving us in many cases of the benefits of trial by jury;

For transporting us beyond seas to be tried for pretended offences;

感动一个国家的文字

他在解散众议院之后，又长时期地不让人民另选新的议会；于是这项不可剥夺的立法权便归由普通民众来行使，致使在这期间各州仍然处于内乱外患的危险之中。

他竭力抑制各州的人口增长；为此目的，他为《外国人归化法》设置障碍，拒绝批准其他鼓励移民的法律，并提高了重新分配土地的条件。

他拒绝批准建立司法权力的法律，以阻挠司法机构的设置。

他迫使法官为了保住各自的任期、薪金的数额和支付而不得不置于他个人意志的支配之下。

他滥设新官员职位，委派大批官员到这里侵扰我们的人民，吞噬他们的财物。

他不经我们立法机关的同意，在和平时期就把常备军驻扎在我们各州。

他力图使军队独立于政权，并凌驾于政权之上。

他与某些人相互勾结，把我们置于一种既不符合我们的法规，也未经我们法律承认的管辖之下，并批准他们自拟的法案，目的是：

任其在我们这里驻扎大批武装部队；

不论这些人对我们各州居民犯下何等严重的谋杀罪，审判只是虚晃一枪，结果总让他们逍遥法外；

切断我们与世界各地的贸易；

未经我们同意便向我们强行征税；

在许多案件中剥夺我们的陪审权；

以莫须有的罪名押送我们去海外受审；

For abolishing the free system of English Laws in a neighbouring Province, establishing therein an Arbitrary government, and enlarging its Boundaries so as to render it at once an example and fit instrument for introducing the same absolute rule into these colonies;

For taking away our charters, abolishing our most valuable Laws and altering fundamentally the forms of our governments;

For suspending our own Legislatures, and declaring themselves invested with power to legislate for us in all cases whatsoever.

He has abdicated government here by declaring us out of his protection and waging war against us.

He has plundered our seas, ravaged our coasts, burnt our towns, and destroyed the lives of our people.

He is at this time transporting large armies of foreign mercenaries to complete the works of death, desolation and tyranny, already begun with circumstances of cruelty and perfidy scarcely paralleled in the most barbarous ages, and totally unworthy the head of a civilized nation.

He has constrained our fellow Citizens taken captive on the high seas to bear Arms against their country, to become the executioners of their friends and Brethren, or to fall themselves by their hands.

In every stage of these oppressions we have petitioned for redress in the most humble terms. Our repeated petitions have been answered only by repeated injury. A prince, whose character is thus marked by every act which may define a tyrant, is unfit to be the ruler of a free people.

Nor have we been wanting in attentions to our British brethren.

We have warned them from time to time of attempts by their legislature to extend an unwarrantable jurisdiction over us.

We have reminded them of the circumstances of our emigration and settlement here.

在邻近的地区废除保障自由的英国法律体制，在那里建立专制政权，并扩大其疆域，使其立即成为一个样板和合适的工具，以便进而把同样的专制统治引向我们这些殖民地；

取消我们的宪章，废除我们最珍贵的法律，并彻底改变我们各州政府的形式；

解散我们的议会，并宣称他们拥有代表我们的所有立法权。

他放弃设在这里的政府，宣称我们已不属他们保护之列，并向我们发动战争。

他掠夺我们的领海，践踏我们的海岸，焚烧我们的城市，屠杀我们的人民。

他此时正在运送大批外国雇佣兵，来从事其制造死亡、荒凉和暴政的勾当，其残忍与卑劣从一开始就连最野蛮时代的人也难以相比，他已完全不配当一个文明国家的元首。

他强迫我们在公海被他们俘虏的同胞拿起武器反对自己的国家，使他们成为残杀自己亲友的刽子手，或使他们死于自己亲友的手下。

在遭受这些压迫的每一阶段，我们都曾以最谦卑的言辞请求予以纠正；而我们一次又一次的请愿所得到的答复都只是一次又一次的伤害。一个君主，当他的每个行为都已打上暴君的烙印时，他已不配做自由人民的统治者。

我们从未对我们大不列颠的弟兄不予关照。

我们一再提醒他们，他们的立法机构企图把不合理的管辖权横加到我们头上。

我们也曾将此地移民和定居的种种实情告诉他们。

We have appealed to their native justice and magnanimity, and we have conjured them by the ties of our common kindred to disavow these usurpations, which would inevitably interrupt our connections and correspondence.

They too have been deaf to the voice of justice and of consanguinity. We must, therefore, acquiesce in the necessity, which denounces our Separation, and hold them, as we hold the rest of mankind, Enemies in War, in Peace Friends.

We, therefore, the representatives of the United States of America, in General Congress, Assembled, appealing to the supreme judge of the world for the rectitude of our intentions, do, in the name, and by the authority of the good people of these colonies, solemnly publish and declare. That these united colonies are, and of right ought to be free and independent states; that they are absolved from all Allegiance to the British crown, and that all political connection between them and the State of Great Britain is and ought to be totally dissolved; and that as free and independent states, they have full power to levy war, conclude Peace, contract alliances, establish Commerce, and to do all other Acts and Things which independent states may of right do.

And for the support of this Declaration, with a firm reliance on the protection of divine providence, we mutually pledge to each other our lives, our fortunes, and our sacred honor.

...

感动一个国家的文字 . . . . . .

我们诉求于他们天赋的正义之心和宽宏之念，恳请他们念及同种同宗的情谊，抵制那些掠夺行为以免影响我们之间的联系和友谊。

　　但是，他们对这种正义的、血肉之亲的呼吁置若罔闻。因此，我们只能不理睬他们对我们脱离的痛斥，并且以对待世界上其他民族的态度对待他们：和我们作战的即是敌人，和我们和平相处的就是朋友。

　　因此，我们，集合在大会中的美利坚合众国的代表们，以这些殖民地的善良人民的名义，并经他们授权，向全世界最崇高的正义人士呼吁，说明我们的严正意向，同时庄严宣布：我们这些联合起来的殖民地现在是，而且按公理也应该是，独立自由的国家；我们对英国王室效忠的全部义务，我们与大不列颠王国之间的一切政治联系全部断绝，而且必须断绝。作为独立自由的国家，我们完全有权宣战、讲和、结盟、通商和采取独立国家有权采取的一切行动。

　　为了拥护此项宣言，我们怀着神明保佑的坚定信心，以我们的生命、我们的财产和我们神圣的荣誉，互相宣誓。

　　……

历史链接

　　1775年4月，列克星敦民兵打响了北美独立战争的第一枪。同年5月，第二届大陆会议在费城召开。大会决定北美殖民地脱离英国而独立，并指定杰斐逊、富兰克林等五人起草北美独立宣言。经过商定，宣言起草委员会决定将这一重任委托给长于写作的杰斐逊。

　　从1776年6月11日到28日，杰斐逊满怀激情，写出了《独立宣言》的初稿，并提交大会批审，经过两天逐字逐句的讨论和修改，最后于1776年7月4日该宣言被通过。美利坚合众国从此正式诞生。

Common Sense
常　识

Thomas Paine／托马斯·佩恩

 ‖作者简介‖

　　托马斯·佩恩(1737～1809)，英国散文家、政论家。他出生于英格兰，才华出众，家境寒微，自学成才，学识广博，在自然科学和人文科学上都进行过深入研究，渴望重建公平的社会秩序。他于1774年移民到北美大陆，很快就被卷进北美独立的浪潮之中，他的代表作《常识》就是支持北美独立的伟大宣言。这本小册子发表后立即引起轰动，几个月之内就售出50万册。

...

　　The sun never shined on a cause of greater worth. It's not the affair of a city, a county, a province, or a kingdom; but of a continent — of at least one eighth part of the habitable globe. It's not the concern of a day, a year, or an age; posterity are virtually involved in the contest, and will be more or less affected even to the end of time, by the proceedings now. Now is the seed time of continental union, faith and honor. The least fracture now will be like a name engraved with the point of a pin on the tender rind of a young oak; the wound would enlarge with the tree, and posterity read it in full grown characters.

By referring the matter from argument to arms, a new era for politics is struck — a new method of thinking has arisen. All plans, proposals, etc. prior to the nineteenth of April, i.e.,to the commencement of hostilities, are like the almanacs of the last year; which though proper then, are superceded and useless now. Whatever was advanced by the advocates on either side of the question then, terminated in one and the same point, viz., a union with Great Britain; the only difference between the parties was the method of effecting it; the one proposing force, the other friendship; but it has so far happened that the first has failed, and the second has withdrawn her

……

阳光下从未有过如此伟大的事业，这不只是一个城市、一个县、一个省、一个国家的事，而是一个洲——至少占地球面积八分之一的事情。它不仅关系到一天、一年或一个时代，子孙后代实际上也卷入了这场斗争，直到最后都或多或少受到当前行动的影响。现在是把团结、信心和荣誉等美德播种在美洲大陆的时候。一点点的裂缝也会像用针尖刻在小橡树嫩皮上的名字一样，随着橡树长大而变大，后代看到的将是变大了的字符。

事情由争论转为诉诸武力，标志着一个政治新纪元的到来——一种新的思考方式诞生了。4 月 19 日以前，即敌对行动开始以前的计划、议案就像去年的年历，当时虽然实用，但现在已被取代，没有一点用处了。不管问题双方的倡导者当时提倡的是什么，最后都归结于同样一个问题上，即与大不列颠合并的问题。双方之间唯一不同的就是实行合并的办法：一方建议诉诸武力，另一方建议友好协商。但已经发生的

influence.

...

In this extensive quarter of the globe, we forget the narrow limits of three hundred and sixty miles(the extent of England) and carry our friendship on a larger scale; we claim brotherhood with every European Christian, and triumph in the generosity of the sentiment.

It is pleasant to observe by what regular gradations we surmount the force of local prejudices, as we enlarge our acquaintance with the world. A man born in any town in England divided into parishes, will naturally associate most with his fellow parishioners (because their interests in many cases will be common) and distinguish him by the name of neighbor; if he meets him but a few miles from home, he drops the narrow idea of a street, and salutes him by the name of townsman; if he travels out of the county and meet him in any other, he forgets the minor divisions of street and town, and calls him countryman, i.e., countryman: but if in their foreign excursions they should associate in France, or any other part of Europe, their local remembrance would be enlarged into that of Englishmen. And by a just parity of reasoning, all Europeans meeting in America, or any other quarter of the globe, are countrymen; for England, Holland, Germany, or Sweden, when compared with the whole, stand in the same place on the larger scale, which the divisions of street, town, and county do on the smaller ones; distinctions too limited for continental minds. Not one third of the inhabitants, even of this province, are of English descent. Wherefore, I reprobate the phrase of parent or mot her country applied to England only, as being false, selfish, narrow and ungenerous.

事实表明前者已失败，后者撤回了其影响。

……

在这片广阔的空间里，我们忘记了三百六十英里的狭小局限（英国的国土面积），在更宽的领域发展友谊；我们主张每一个欧洲基督教徒都是兄弟，而且为这种广阔的胸襟感到高兴。

当扩大交往范围之后，可以欣喜地看到，我们大大摆脱了地区偏见的束缚。一个出生在英国任何一个以教区划分的城市的人，自然跟他所在教区的教徒关系最密切（因为在很多情况下他们的利益是相同的），以邻居相称；如果他在离家才几英里的地方见到邻居，他会丢掉狭隘的街道观念，向他致意并称邻居是同市人；如果他出郡旅游，遇到邻居，他会忘记街道、城市小的划分，叫他老乡，即同乡；但如果出国旅行，他们在法国或任何别的欧洲国家见了面，他们的划分观念现在就扩大为英国人了。根据同样的推理，所有的欧洲人，在美国或地球其他任何地方见了面，都是老乡。因为英国、法国、荷兰、德国或瑞典，跟整个地球相比，在较大范围内占有的位置是相同的，其性质与划分的街道、城市和郡在较小范围内占有着相同的位置一样。对于我们美洲人来说，这种区分的局限性太强了；即便在一个省里，英国后裔也不到三分之一。因此，我强烈谴责把母国这个词只用来指代英国的行径，因为这是错误的、自私的、狭隘的、不大度的。

Farewell Address 告别演说

George Washington/乔治·华盛顿

‖作者简介‖

乔治·华盛顿(1732~1799)在领导美国独立战争取得胜利之后,成为第一任总统的不二人选,然后他勉强同意连任一届。但第二个任期绝非一次快乐野餐,华盛顿拒绝连任第三届总统。

1796年9月17日,华盛顿发表了他的告别辞。在一个还有国王、世袭首长和小暴君们统治的世界里,华盛顿把权力让给民选继任者的决定表明,美国的民主实验有了一个良好的开端。

Friends and Citizens,

The period for a new election of a citizen to administer the executive government of the United States being not far distant, and the time actually arrived when your thoughts must be employed in designating the person who is to be cloathed with that important trust, it appears to me proper, especially as it may conduce to a more distinct expression of the public voice, that I should now apprise you of the resolution I have formed, to decline being considered among the number of those, out of whom a choice is to be made.

...

The Unity of Government which constitutes you one people is also now dear to you. It is justly so; for it is a main pillar in the edifice of your real independence, the support of your tranquility at home,

感动一个国家的文字

your peace abroad; of your safety; of your prosperity; of that very Liberty which you so highly prize. But as it is easy to foresee that, from different causes and from different quarters, much pains will be taken, many artifices employed to weaken in your minds the conviction of this truth; as this is the point in your political fortress against which the batteries of internal and external enemies will be most constantly and actively (though often covertly and insidiously) directed, it is of infinite moment that you should properly estimate the immense value of your national union to your collective and individual happiness; that you should cherish a cordial, habitual and immoveable attachment to it; accustoming yourselves to think and speak of it as of the

各位朋友、同胞：

　　我们重新选举一位公民来主持美国政府的行政工作，已为期不远。此时此刻，大家必须独立思考决定将要把这一重任付托给谁。因此，我觉得我现在应当向大家声明，尤其是这样做有助于使公众意见得以更为明确的表达——我早已下定决心，谢绝将我列为候选人。

　　……

　　政府的统一，使大家结成一个民族，现在你们也珍视这种统一，这是理所当然的，因为你们真正的独立，仿佛一座大厦，而政府的统一，乃是这座大厦的主要柱石；它保证国内的安定，国外的和平；保证你们的安全，你们的繁荣以及你们如此重视的自由。然而不难预见，会有某些力量企图削弱大家心中对于这种真理的信念，滋生这些力量的原因不一样，来路也各不相同，但都挖空心思，千方百计地影响你们。之所以如此，是因为你们在政治中的一个重要堡垒就是统一，内外敌人的炮火，会持续不断地加紧（虽然常是秘密地与阴险地）轰击。因此，最重要的乃是大家应当正确估计民族团结对于集体和个人幸福所具有的重大价值；大家应当对它抱着诚挚的、持久的和坚定不移的忠诚；你们在思想上和交流中要习惯于把它当做大家政治安全和繁荣的保障；要谨慎地守护它。如果有人提到这种

palladium of your political safety and prosperity; watching for its preservation with jealous anxiety; discountenancing whatever may suggest even a suspicion that it can in any event be abandoned, and indignantly frowning upon the first dawning of every attempt to alienate any portion of our country from the rest, or to enfeeble the sacred ties which now link together the various parts.

...

As a very important source of strength and security, cherish public credit. One method of preserving it is to use it as sparingly as possible, avoiding occasions of expense by cultivating peace, but remembering also that timely disbursements to prepare for danger frequently prevent much greater disbursements to repel it, avoiding likewise the accumulation of debt, not only by shunning occasions of expense, but by vigorous exertion in time of peace to discharge the debts which unavoidable wars may have occasioned, not ungenerously throwing upon posterity the burden which we ourselves ought to bear.

...

Against the insidious wiles of foreign influence(I conjure you to believe me, fellow-citizens)the jealousy of a free people ought to be constantly awake, since history and experience prove that foreign influence is one of the most baneful foes of republican government. But that jealousy to be useful must be impartial; else it becomes the instrument of the very influence to be avoided, instead of a defense against it. Excessive partiality for one foreign nation and excessive dislike of another cause those whom they actuate to see danger only on one side, and serve to veil and even second the arts of influence on the other. Real patriots who may resist the intrigues of the favorite are liable to become suspected and odious, while its tools and dupes usurp the applause and confidence of the people, to surrender their interests.

信念在某种情况下可以被抛弃，即使那只是猜想，也应该表示反对。如果有人企图使我国的一部分跟其余部分脱离开来，或想削弱目前联系各部分的神圣纽带，在其萌芽阶段，就应该严厉地加以指责。

……

我们应当重视保存国家的财力，因为这是力量和安全极为重要的源泉。有一个保存财力的办法就是尽量少动用它，并维护和平以避免意外开支；同时要记住，未雨绸缪而及时拨款，往往可以避免弥补灾难时支付更大的款项。同样，我们要避免债台高筑，为此，不仅要节约开支，而且在和平时期还要尽力去偿还不可避免的战争所带来的债务，不要将我们自己应该承受的债务负担无情地留给后辈。

……

一个自由民族应当经常保持警觉，时刻提防外国势力的阴谋诡计（同胞们，请你们相信我），因为历史和经验表明，外国势力乃是共和政府最致命的敌人之一。不过要想做到有效的提防，必须不偏不倚，否则它会成为我们所要摆脱的势力的工具，而不是抵御那种势力的工具。对某一国家过度偏爱，对另一个国家过度偏恶，会使受到这种影响的国家只看到一方的危险，却掩盖甚至纵容另一方所施的诡计。当我们所喜欢的那个国家的爪牙和受其蒙蔽的人，利用人民的赞赏和信任诱骗人民放弃本身的利益时，那些可能抵制该国诡计的真正爱国志士，反而极易成为怀疑与憎恶的对象。

乔治·华盛顿 ▶

The great rule of conduct for us in regard to foreign nations is in extending our commercial relations, to have with them as little political connection as possible. So far as we have already formed engagements, let them be fulfilled with perfect good faith. Here let us stop.

...

It is our true policy to steer clear of permanent alliances with any portion of the foreign world; so far, I mean, as we are now at liberty to do it; for let me not be understood as capable of patronizing infidelity to existing engagements. I hold the maxim no less applicable to public than to private affairs, that honesty is always the best policy. I repeat it, therefore, let those engagements be observed in their genuine sense. But, in my opinion, it is unnecessary and would be unwise to extend them.

...

Though, in reviewing the incidents of my administration, I am unconscious of intentional error, I am nevertheless too sensible of my defects not to think it probable that I may have committed many errors. Whatever they may be, I fervently beseech the Almighty to avert or mitigate the evils to which they may tend. I shall also carry with me the hope that my country will never cease to view them with indulgence; and that, after forty five years of my life dedicated to its service with an upright zeal, the faults of incompetent abilities will be consigned to oblivion, as myself must soon be to the mansions of rest.

Relying on its kindness in this as in other things, and actuated by that fervent love towards it, which is so natural to a man who views in it the native soil of himself and his progenitors for several generations, I anticipate with pleasing expectation that retreat in which I promise myself to realize, without alloy, the sweet enjoyment of partaking, in the midst of my fellow-citizens, the benign influence of good laws under a free government, the ever-favorite object of my heart, and the happy reward, as I trust, of our mutual cares, labors, and dangers.

　　我们处理对外事务的最重要原则，就是在与它们发展商务关系时，尽可能避免涉及政治。我们已订的条约，必须忠实履行。但以此为限，不要再增加。

　　……

　　我们真正的对外政策，是避免同任何国家订立永久性的同盟合约。我的意思是我们现在可自由处理这种问题，但请不要误会，以为我赞成不履行现有的条约。我认为，诚实是最好的政策，这句格言不仅适用于私事，也适用于公务。所以我再重复说一句，那些条约应按照它的原意加以履行。但我觉得延长那些条约是不必要，也是不明智的。

　　……

　　虽然我在检讨自己任期内的施政时，没有发觉有故意的错误，但是我很明白自己的缺点，并不认为自己没有犯过错误。不管这些错误是什么，我真诚地祈求上帝免除或减轻这些错误所可能产生的后果。而且我也将怀着希望，愿我的国家永远宽恕这些错误。我秉持正直的热忱，献身于国家已经四十五年了，我希望自己因为能力薄弱而犯的过失，会随着我不久以后长眠地下而烟消云散。

　　在这方面和在其他方面一样，我必须仰赖祖国的仁慈，我热爱祖国，一直受到爱国之情的激励，这是一种很自然的感情，尤其是对一个视祖国为自己及历代祖先的故土的人来说。因此，我也欣欣地期待着，在我热切盼望的退休实现之后，我将和我的同胞们愉快地分享自由政府下完善的法律的温暖——这是我一直由衷向往的目标，我还相信，这也是我们相互关怀、共同努力和赴汤蹈火的丰厚酬报。

杰斐逊 首任就职演说
First Inaugural Address

Thomas Jefferson/ 托马斯·杰斐逊

‖作者简介‖

托马斯·杰斐逊(1743~1826),《独立宣言》和《弗吉尼亚宗教自由法案》的起草者、弗吉尼亚大学创建人, 也是美国第三任总统。

在1800年大选中, 他与阿伦·伯尔(1756~1836)在选举团获得了相同的73票。1801年2月, 众议院再度投票, 以超过半数票(36票)的结果确认杰斐逊为总统。在杰斐逊的任期内, 他以每英亩2.5美分的价格向拿破仑皇帝(1769~1821)购买了路易斯安那, 由此将美国领土扩大了两倍。

杰斐逊的就职标志着民主共和思想的兴起以及联邦主义的衰落。他也是第一位在美国首都华盛顿举行就职典礼的总统。

...

During the contest of opinion through which we have passed the animation of discussions and of exertions has sometimes worn an aspect which might impose on strangers unused to think freely and to speak and to write what they think; but this being now decided by the voice of the nation, announced according to the rules of the Constitution, all will, of course, arrange themselves under the will of the law, and unite in common efforts for the common good. All, too, will bear in mind this sacred principle, that though the will of the majority is in all

感 动 一个国家的文字......

cases to prevail, that will to be rightful must be reasonable; that the minority possess their equal rights, which equal law must protect, and to violate would be oppression. Let us, then, fellow-citizens, unite with one heart and one mind. Let us restore to social intercourse that harmony and affection without which liberty and even life itself are but dreary things. And let us reflect that, having banished from our land that religious intolerance under which mankind so long bled and suffered, we have yet gained little if we countenance a political intolerance as despotic, as wicked, and capable of as bitter and bloody persecutions. During the throes and convulsions of the ancient world, during the agonizing spasms of infuriated man, seeking through blood and slaughter his long-lost liberty, it was not wonderful that the agita-

......

我们经历了一段时期的辩论，当时，大家讨论得很热烈，竞相奔走。初识的人，对自由思考不习惯，不习惯把心中的想法自由地说出来或写出来，刚见这种情形时，可能面面相觑。而现在经全国的民众一致决定了，并根据宪法的规定加以公布，大家当然会在法律的意旨之下，妥善安排，并且团结一致，为共同利益而努力。大家也会记住一项神圣的原则，即大多数人的意志，虽然在任何情形下都应采用，但这种意志必须合理，才能切实可行；而且少数人也同样享有这些权利，必须受到法律的平等保护，如果加以侵犯，便是压迫。因此，我们应当团结起来，齐心协力，在相处中应恢复和睦与友爱。因为如果没有它们，自由，甚至生活本身，都将成为死气沉沉的事物。我们还应想到，我们已经把宗教上的偏执性摈弃于国度之外，这种偏执性已经使人类流血甚多、受苦良久。如果我们又鼓励政治上的偏执性，而且其专横与邪恶以及所造成的酷烈而血腥的迫害，与宗教裁判所导致的后果不相上下，那么，我们的进步微乎其微。当旧世界经历痛苦和激变时，当盛怒的人备受痛苦，想经由血腥与屠杀寻找他们丧失已久的自由时，那如滚滚浪涛般的震

tion of the billows should reach even this distant and peaceful shore; that this should be more felt and feared by some and less by others, and should divide opinions as to measures of safety. But every difference of opinion is not a difference of principle. We have called by different names brethren of the same principle. We are all Republicans, we are all Federalists. If there be any among us who would wish to dissolve this Union or to change its republican form, let them stand undisturbed as monuments of the safety with which error of opinion may be tolerated where reason is left free to combat it. I know, indeed, that some honest men fear that a republican government can not be strong, that this Government is not strong enough; but would the honest patriot, in the full tide of successful experiment, abandon a government which has so far kept us free and firm on the theoretic and visionary fear that this Government, the world's best hope, may by possibility want energy to preserve itself ? I trust not. I believe this, on the contrary, the strongest Government on earth. I believe it the only one where every man, at the call of the law, would fly to the standard of the law, and would meet invasions of the public order as his own personal concern. Sometimes it is said that man can not be trusted with the government of himself. Can he, then, be trusted with the government of others? Or have we found angels in the forms of kings to govern him? Let history answer this question.

Let us, then, with courage and confidence pursue our own Federal and Republican principles, our attachment to union and representative government. Kindly separated by nature and a wide ocean from the exterminating havoc of one quarter of the globe; too high-minded

感 动一个国家的文字

撼将会波及遥远而和平的彼岸。每个人对此事的感觉与恐惧的程度各异，对有关安全措施的意见也发生分歧，这没有什么好奇怪的。但是，意见的差异并非说明原则的差异。与我们遵守同一原则的弟兄们，曾被冠以各种各样的称号。我们都是共和党人，我们都是联邦同盟会员。如果我们当中有人想解散这一联邦，或者想改变它的共和体制，我们也不会干扰他们，这样做就为安全树立了标志，表明只要理智能够自由地进行对抗，即使是错误亦是可以容许的。我当然知道有些诚实的民众担心共和政府不够强大有力，但是一个诚实的爱国者，当这个世界寄以最美好希望的政府正在成功地进行试验之时，仅因一种理论上的、虚幻的疑惧，就以为这个政府可能连生存的能力都不够，就因此放弃这个一直确保我们自由和安全的政府吗？我想肯定不会。相反，我相信这个政府是世界上最强大的政府，在这个政府的管理下，无论什么人，一听到法律的召唤，就会飞奔而来响应法律的号召，而且会对处理侵犯公共秩序的行为，如同处理自己的私事一样。有时人们说，一个人想自我约束是不可靠的。那么，让别人去管理他们就能变得可靠吗？或者我们是否曾见过天使幻化成国王的身份来管理人们？我们让历史来回答这个问题。

因此，我们应该凭借着勇气和信心，继续维持我们自己那种联邦共和的原则，拥护联邦和代议制政府。由于自然环境和大洋的阻隔，我们幸免遭受全球四分之一地区那种毁灭性的浩劫；我们具有高尚的品格，对别人的堕落忍无可忍；我们拥有天赐沃土，足以养活千世万代的子孙；我们有一种观念，坚信在发挥我们自己的才能上，在取得我们自己勤劳的成果上，在深受我们同胞的尊敬与信赖上(这种尊敬与信赖不是由门第造成的，而是来自我们行为的结果和他们的体会)，都拥有同等的权利；我们有善良敦厚的宗教，虽然派别不同，可是所有教派都以正直、守信、节制、感恩和仁爱来感化人；我们承认和崇拜统领万物的上帝，

托马斯·杰斐逊 ▶

to endure the degradations of the others; possessing a chosen country, with room enough for our descendants to the thousandth and thousandth generation; entertaining a due sense of our equal right to the use of our own faculties, to the acquisitions of our own industry, to honor and confidence from our fellow-citizens, resulting not from birth, but from our actions and their sense of them; enlightened by a benign religion, professed, indeed, and practiced in various forms, yet all of them inculcating honesty, truth, temperance, gratitude, and the love of man; acknowledging and adoring an overruling Providence, which by all its dispensations proves that it delights in the happiness of man here and his greater happiness hereafter — with all these blessings, what more is necessary to make us a happy and a prosperous people? Still one thing more, fellow-citizens—a wise and frugal Government, which shall restrain men from injuring one another, shall leave them otherwise free to regulate their own pursuits of industry and improvement, and shall not take from the mouth of labor the bread it has earned. This is the sum of good government, and this is necessary to close the circle of our felicities.

About to enter, fellow-citizens, on the exercise of duties which comprehend everything dear and valuable to you, it is proper you should understand what I deem the essential principles of our Government, and consequently those which ought to shape its Administration. I will compress them within the narrowest compass they will bear, stating the general principle, but not all its limitations. Equal and exact justice to all men, of whatever state or persuasion, religious or political; peace, commerce, and honest friendship with all nations, entangling alliances with none; the support of the State governments in all their rights, as the most competent administrations for our domestic concerns and the surest bulwarks against antirepublican tendencies; the preservation of the General Government in its whole constitutional vigor, as the sheet anchor of our peace at home and safety abroad; a jealous care of the right of election by the people— a mild and safe corrective of abuses which are lopped by the sword of revolution where peaceable remedies are unprovided; absolute acquiescence in the decisions of the majority, the vital principle of republics, from which is no appeal but to force, the vital principle and immediate parent of despotism; a well-disciplined militia, our best reliance in peace and for the first moments of war till regulars may

上帝的所作所为证明，它乐于看见人类现世的幸福和死后更大的幸福——我们有了这些恩赐，还需要什么才能使我们的民族幸福欢欣呢?各位同胞,我们还需要一种事物,那就是一个睿智和简朴的政府,它防止人们相互为敌,它让人们自由地从事各自的工作,并不断取得进步,它对人们辛勤劳动的成果从不巧取豪夺。这些就是一个优良政府的重要条件,也是我们要取得完满幸福的生活所必需的条件。

　　同胞们,我就要开始执行这神圣的职责,这种职责包含你们所珍视的一切,因此,我认为你们应当了解,我所认为的良好政府的要旨是什么,以及构成我们施政方针的各个方面。下面我将向大家简单地陈述,只讲一般原则,而不讲其所有范畴:要给予人人平等和公正的待遇,不管其地位、宗教或政治信仰如何;跟所有的国家和平共处,相互通商,并保持真诚的友谊,但不跟任何国家结盟,以免引起争端;维护各州政府的所有权利,使之成为处理内政的最适宜的行政机构和抵制反对联邦共和趋势最有力的屏障;根据宪法保持全国政府的活力,作为对内和平与对外安全的最后堡垒;注重维护人民的选举权,因为独立战争时留下的弊端没有和平的补救办法,而对那些弊端,能采取的一种温和而安全的矫正手段就是人民的选举权;坚决服从多数人的决定,共和政体的主要原则就在于此,

relieve them; the supremacy of the civil over the military authority; economy in the public expense, that labor may be lightly burthened; the honest payment of our debts and sacred preservation of the public faith; encouragement of agriculture, and of commerce as its handmaid; the diffusion of information and arraignment of all abuses at the bar of the public reason; freedom of religion; freedom of the press, and freedom of person under the protection of the habeas corpus, and trial by juries impartially selected. These principles form the bright constellation which has gone before us and guided our steps through an age of revolution and reformation. The wisdom of our sages and blood of our heroes have been devoted to their attaimnent. They should be the creed of our political faith, the text of civic instruction, the touchstone by which to try the services of those we trust; and should we wander from them in moments of error or of alarm, let us hasten to retrace our steps and to regain the road which alone leads to peace, liberty, and safety···

若非如此，便只好诉诸武力，专制的主要原则和直接起源就在于此；保留纪律严明的民兵，作为和平时期和战争初期最好的依靠，以待接替正式军队；实行文权高于军权的政策；压缩政府开支，减轻人民的经济负担；如实清偿我们的债务，审慎地维护公众的信心；促进农业发展，鼓励以商辅农；传播知识并以公众理智的判断作为谴责所有弊端的依据；保障宗教自由及出版自由，并以人身保护令和公平选出的陪审团进行审判来确保人身自由。在独立战争时期和革新时期，这些原则成为照耀我们道路、指引我们前进步伐的星宿。我们先哲的智慧，我们英雄的鲜血，都曾为了实现这些原则而无私奉献。它们应当成为我们政治信念的纲领、公民教育的教科书、测验我们赋予信任者工作的试金石；如果一时的错误或惊惶导致违背了这些原则，我们应该赶快回头，重新走上这唯一的一条通往和平、自由和安全的大道……

感动一个国家的文字......

First Inaugural Address
林肯首任就职演说

Abraham Lincoln/ 亚伯拉罕·林肯

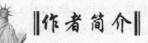

‖作者简介‖

　　亚伯拉罕·林肯(1809~1865年)，美国总统，共和党人。生于农民家庭，青年时代当过工人、石匠和店员，他先后任过州议员、律师和众议员。主张维护联邦统一，废除农奴制。在任期内他发表了《解放宣言》，提出"民有、民治、民享"的口号，并领导人民投入南北战争，重新统一了美国。1864年连任总统。1865年4月14日被南方奴隶主反对派指使的暴徒杀害。

　　This country, with its institutions, belongs to the people who inhabit it. Whenever they shall grow weary of the existing government, they can exercise their constitutional right of amending it, or their revolutionary right to overthrow it. I cannot be ignorant of the fact that many worthy and patriotic citizens are desirous of having the national Constitution amended. While I make no recommendation of amendments, I fully recognize the rightful authority of the people over the whole subject to be

39

exercised in either of the modes prescribed in the instrument itself; and I should under existing circumstances favor rather than oppose a fair opportunity being afforded the people to act upon it.···

The chief magistrate derives all his authority from the people, and they have conferred none upon him to fix terms for the separation of the states. The people themselves can do this also if they choose; but the executive, as such, has nothing to do with it. His duty is to administer the present government, as it came to his hands, and to transmit it, unimpaired by him, to his successor.

Why should there not be a patient confidence in the ultimate justice of the people? Is there any better or equal hope in the worm? In our present differences, is either party without faith of being in the right? If the Almighty Ruler of nations, with His eternal truth and justice, be on your side of the North, or on yours of the South, that truth, and that justice, will surely prevail, by the judgment of this great tribunal, the American people.

By the frame of the government under which we live, this same people have wisely given their public servants but little power for mischief; and have, with equal wisdom, provided for the return of that little to their own hands at very short intervals. While the people retain their virtue and vigilance, no administration, by any extreme of wickedness or folly, can very seriously injure the government in the short space of four years.

这个国家及其机构，属于居住在这里的人民。一旦他们对现存政府感到不能容忍，就可以行使他们的宪法权利去改组政府，或者行使革命权利去推翻它。我当然知道，许多可贵的、爱国的公民渴望宪法能得到修改。尽管我未提出修改宪法的建议，但我完全承认人民对整个问题所具有的合法权利，他们可以施行宪法本身所规定的两种方式中的任何一种；在目前情况下，我应该赞同而不是反对公平地为人民提供对此采取行动的机会……

总统的一切权力来自人民，但人民没有授权给他为各州的分离制造条件。如果人民有此意愿，那他们可以这样做，而对于总统来说，则不可能这样做。他的责任是管理交给他的这一届政府，并将它完整地移交给他的继任者。

为什么我们不能对人民所具有的最高的公正抱有坚韧的信念呢？世界上还有比这更好或一样好的希望吗？在我们目前的分歧中，难道双方都缺乏足够的自信吗？如果全能的主以其永恒的真理和公正支持北方这一边，或者支持南方这一边，那么，真理和公正必将通过美国人民这个伟大法庭的裁决而取得胜利。

就是这些美国人民，通过我们现有的政府结构，明智地只给他们的公仆很小的权力，使他们不能为害，并且同样明智地每隔很短的时间就把那小小的权力收回到自己手中。只要人民保持美德和警惕，无论怎样作恶和愚蠢的执政人员都不能在短短四年的任期内十分严重地损害政府。

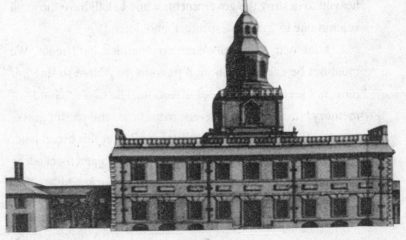

My countrymen, one and all, think calmly and well upon this whole subject. Nothing valuable can be lost by taking time. If there be an object to hurry any of you, in hot haste, to a step which you would never take deliberately, that object will be frustrated by taking time; but no good object can be frustrated by it. Such of you as are now dissatisfied still have the old Constitution unimpaired, and, on the sensitive point, the laws of your own framing under it; while the new administration will have no immediate power, if it would, to change either. If it were admitted that you who are dissatisfied hold the right side in the dispute, there still is no single good reason for pre-cipitate action. Intelligence, patriotism, Christianity, and a firm reliance on Him who has never yet forsaken this favored land are still competent to adjust, in the best way, all our present difficulty.

In your hands, my dissatisfied fellow countrymen, and not in mine, is the momentous issue of civil war. The government will not assail you. You can have no conflict, without being yourselves the aggressors. You have no oath registered in heaven to destroy the government; while I shall have the most solemn one to "preserve, protect, and defend" it.

I am loath to close. We are not enemies, but friends. We must not be enemies. Though passion may have strained, it must not break our bonds of affection. The mystic chords of memory, stretching from every battlefield, and patriot grave, to every living heart and hearthstone, all over this broad land, will yet swell the chorus of the Union, when again touched, as surely they will be, by the better angels of our nature.

感动一个国家的文字

我的同胞们，大家平静而认真地思考整个问题吧。任何宝贵的东西都不会因为从容对待而丧失。假使有一个目标火急地催促你们中的一位采取措施，而你决不能从容不迫，那么那个目标会因从容对待而落空；但是，任何好的目标是不会因为从容对待而落空的。现在感到不满意的人仍然有着原来的、完好无损的宪法，而且，在敏感问题上，你们有着自己根据这部宪法制定的各项法律，而新的一届政府即使想改变这两种情况，也没有直接的权力那样做。那些不满意的人在这场争论中即使被承认是站在正确的一边，也没有一点正当理由采取鲁莽的行动。理智、爱国主义、基督教精神以及对从不抛弃这片幸福土地的上帝的信仰，这些仍然能以最好的方式来解决我们目前的一切困难。

不满现状的同胞们，内战这个重大问题的关键掌握在你们手中，而不掌握在我手中。政府不会对你们发动攻击。你们不做挑衅者，就不会面临冲突。你们没有对天发誓要毁灭政府；我却要立下最庄严的誓言："坚守、维护和捍卫它"。

我不愿意结束我的讲话。我们之间不是敌人，而是朋友。我们一定不要相互为敌。尽管我们会感情冲动，但也不会反目成仇。那神秘的记忆之弦将延伸到每一个战场、每一个爱国将士的坟墓和我们广阔疆土上每一颗跳动的心以及每一个温暖的家庭；我们善良的天性必将再次拨动这根心弦，自豪地唱起联邦大合唱。

历史链接

在1860年的竞选纲领中，共和党明确宣布坚决反对奴隶制的扩张。因此共和党这次大选的胜利，意味着奴隶主把奴隶制扩大到西部去的希望完全破灭，这也意味着奴隶制面临灭亡。

为了挽救自己，奴隶主决定在林肯就职前发动叛乱。南卡罗来纳州等7个州先后宣布脱离联邦，并于1861年2月4日宣布成立另外一个名为"美利坚诸州同盟"的国家，将弗吉尼亚里士满定为首都，推举戴维斯为总统，内战一触即发。在这种情况下，林肯发表就职演说，为避免内战、维护国家统一而努力。

43

在葛底斯堡公墓的演说 Gettysburg Address

Abraham Lincoln／亚伯拉罕·林肯

Four score and seven years ago, our fathers brought forth upon this continent a new Nation, conceived in Liberty, and dedicated to the proposition that all men are created equal. Now, we are engaged in a great Civil War, testing whether that Nation, or any nation so conceived and so dedicated, can long endure. We are met on a great battlefield of that war. We have come to dedicate a portion of that field as a final resting-place for those who here gave their lives that Nation might live. It is altogether fitting and proper that we should do this.

But, in a larger sense, we cannot dedicate, we cannot consecrate, we cannot hallow this ground. The brave men, living and dead, who struggled here, have consecrated it far above our poor power to add or detract. The world will little note nor long remember what we say here, but it can never forget what they did here. It is for us,the living, rather to be dedicated here to the unfinished work which they who fought here have thus far so nobly advanced. It is rather for us to be here dedicated to the great task remaining before us; that from these honored dead, we take increased devotion to that cause for which they gave the last full measure of devotion; that we here highly resolve that these dead shall not died in vain; that this Nation, under God, shall have a new birth of freedom; and that government of the People, by the People, and for the People, shall not perish from the earth.

44

87 年前，我们的先辈们在这块大陆上创建了一个新的国家，它孕育于自由之中，奉行一切人生而平等的原则。现在我们正从事一场伟大的内战，以考验这个国家，或者任何一个孕育于自由和奉行上述原则的国家是否能够长久存在下去。我们聚集在这个伟大的战场上。烈士们为这个国家的生存而献出了自己的生命，我们聚集在这里，是要把这个战场的一部分奉献给他们作为最后的安息地。我们这样做是完全应该而且是非常恰当的。

但是，从广义上来说，我们不能奉献，不能圣化，更不能神化这块土地。那些曾在这里战斗过的勇士们，无论活着的或已死去的，已经将这块土地圣化了，这远远不是我们微薄之力所能增减的。今天我们在这里所说的话，全世界都不会太注意，也不会长久地记住，但那些勇士在这里的所作所为，全世界都会永远记得。换言之，我们这些依然活着的人，应该把自己奉献于那些勇士们已经向前推进但尚未完成的崇高事业。我们应该在这里把自己奉献于仍然摆在我们面前的伟大任务——我们要从那些光荣牺牲的勇士身上汲取更多的奉献精神，来完成他们投入毕生精力并为之献身的事业；我们要在这里下定决心，不能让那些勇士们白白牺牲；我们要使我们的祖国在上帝的保佑下得到自由的新生，要使这个民有、民治、民享的政府永世长存。

历史链接

在林肯当选总统后，南方各州相继宣布脱离联邦，内战爆发。1863 年 7 月 3 日，联邦军在宾西法尼亚州的葛底斯堡与南军激战，伤亡 2 万余人。为纪念阵亡将士，同年 11 月在葛底斯堡建起了国家公墓。本篇是林肯在公墓落成典礼上的致辞，虽不足 3 分钟，却是流传千古的佳作。

45

Ask Congress to Declare War Against Germany

要求国会对德国宣战

Woodrow Wilson/ 伍德罗·威尔逊

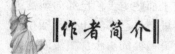

‖作者简介‖

伍德罗·威尔逊(1856~1924年)，美国政治家，生于美国牧师家庭，曾就读于四所大学，获哲学博士学位。1913~1921年任总统，任期内提出"新自由"口号，主张政治和经济的自由主义，曾表示对拉美国家采取"睦邻政策"。著有《国会政府》《华盛顿传》等作品。

…

It is a war against all nations. American ships have been sunk, American lives taken, in ways, which it has stirred us very deeply to learn of, but the ships and people of other neutral and friendly nations have been sunk and overwhelmed in the waters in the same way. There has been no discrimination. The challenge is to all mankind. Each nation must decide for itself how it will meet it. The choice we make for ourselves must be made with a moderation of counsel and a temperateness of judgment befitting our character and our motives as a nation. We must put excited feeling away. Our motive will not be revenge or the victorious assertion of the physical might of the nation, but only the vindication of right, of human right, of which we are only

感动一个国家的文字

a single champion.

When I addressed the Congress on the 26th of February last, I thought that it would suffice to assert our neutral rights with arms, our right to use the seas against unlawful interference, our right to keep our people safe against unlawful violence. But armed neutrality, it now appears, is impracticable. Because submarines are in effect outlaws when used as the German submarines have been used against merchant shipping, it is impossible to defend ships against their attacks as the law of nations has assumed that merchantmen would defend themselves against privateers or cruisers visible craft giving Chase upon the open sea. It is common prudence in such circumstances, grim necessity indeed, to endeavour to destroy them before they have shown their own intention. They must be dealt with upon sight, if dealt with at all. The German Government denies the right of neutrals to

……

　　这是一场想要征服整个世界的战争。美国的船只已经被击沉，许多美国人付出了生命。令人震惊的是其他友好中立国的许多船只和人员也都同样遭到袭击而沉入大海。这是对整个人类的挑战。每个国家都必须决定如何迎接这场挑战。我们为自己做出的选择，必须深思熟虑，判断适度，符合我们民族的性格和目的。我们必须把激愤的情绪放在一边。我们的目的不是为了报复，或是为了维护我们的国力，而是为了维护正义，人类的正义；我们只是维护人类正义的战士。

　　去年 2 月 26 日，我在国会讲话时曾想，用武力维护我们中立国的权利——保卫我们在海上的权利防止非法挑衅，保卫我们人员的安全，防止非法暴力——就足够了的。可现在看来，武装中立是不现实的。尽管国际法规定：商船有权保卫自己，反击在公海上追击自己的私掠船、巡洋舰和任何看得见的船只；利用潜水艇本来事实上是非法的，可是德国潜水艇却被用来袭击商船，商船怎能反击？在这种情况下，在这种严峻的时刻，只有在他们的意图暴露前就粉

use arms at all within the areas of the sea which it has proscribed, even in the defense of rights which no modern publicist has ever before questioned their right to defend. The intimation is conveyed that the armed guards which we have placed on our merchant ships will be treated as beyond the pale of law and subject to be dealt with as pirates would be. Armed neutrality is ineffectual enough at best; in such circumstances and in the face of such pretensions it is worse than ineffectual; it is likely only to produce what it was meant to prevent; it is practically certain to draw us into the war without either the rights or the effectiveness of belligerents. There is one choice we cannot make, we are incapable of making: we will not choose the path of submission and suffer the most sacred rights of our nation and our people to be ignored or violated. The wrongs against which we now array ourselves are no common wrongs; they cut to the very roots of human life.

With a profound sense of the solemn and even tragical character of the step I am taking and of the grave responsibilities which it involves, but in unhesitating obedience to what I deem my constitutional duty, I advise that the Congress declare the recent course of the imperial German government to be in fact nothing less than war against the government and people of the United States; that it formally accept the status of belligerent which has thus been thrust upon it, and that it take immediate steps not only to put the country in a more thorough state of defense, but also to exert all its power and employ all its resources to bring the government of the German Empire to terms and end the war.

...

It is a distressing and oppressive duty, gentlemen of the Congress, which I have performed in thus addressing you. There are, it may be, many months of fiery trial and sacrifice ahead of us. It is a fearful

感动一个国家的文字

thing to lead this great peaceful people into war, into the most terrible and disastrous of all wars, civilization itself seeming to be in the balance. But the right is more precious than peace, and we shall fight for the things which we have always carried nearest our hearts — for democracy, for the right of those who submit to authority to have a

碎他们的阴谋才是明智的；既然要反对他们，那就要在他们一出现就反对好了。在失去法律保护的海域内，中立国使用武装的权力还未曾被现代国际法专家置疑过，而德国政府根本否认这种自卫的权力。德国政府发出通告说，我们在商船上配有武装自卫人员是非法的，将作为海盗对待。其实，武装中立本来就是徒劳无益的；在这种情况下，在这样的要求面前，又岂止是徒劳呢？很可能本来打算阻止战争却引起了战争；但这实际上必然把我们拖入战争而又享受不到参战国的权利和实效。有一条我们不能选择的道路，我们根本也不会选择：那就是屈服的道路，也就是使我们的国家和民族最神圣的权利遭到无视和侵犯的道路。我们现在一致反对的侵权行为不是一般的侵权行为，是一个将断送人类生活源泉的侵权行为。

我深深意识到我采取的措施的庄严性和悲剧性，也深深意识到所承担的责任是沉重的；但我又要毫不犹豫地履行我的合法职责。我请求国会向人民宣告德国帝国主义政府近来的行为，实际上就是对美国政府和人民发动战争；因此美国被迫正式进入战争状态。美国之所以采取直接的行动，不仅是要保卫国家的安全，而且还是要使用一切力量和资源迫使德国帝国政府停止战争。

......

voice in their own governments, for the dominion of right by such a concert of free peoples as shall itself at last free. To such a task we can dedicate our lives and our fortunes, everything we are and everything that we have, with the pride of those who know that the day has come when America is privileged to spend her blood and her might for the principles that gave her birth and happiness and the peace which she has treasured. God helping her, she can do no other.

　　国会的先生们，我刚才向你们报告的是一项令人痛苦的任务。摆在我们面前可能是漫长岁月的严酷考验和牺牲。把这个和平伟大国家的人民引入战争，引入这场有史以来最可怕的灾难性战争是一件可怕的事；毕竟现在整个人类文明也似乎存亡未卜。但正义比和平更珍贵，我们将为了我们心头最珍贵的东西而战，即为了民主，为了拥护自己政府的人民的权利，为了各国自由人民协同一致行使权力以取得最终自由而战。为了这个任务，我们愿意献出自己的财产和生命，献出我们的一切。美国人珍惜赋予她生命、幸福与和平的原则。现在是她为此原则而奉献鲜血和力量的时候了，有上帝保佑，她别无选择。

历史链接　　1914年6月28日，第一次世界大战爆发。美国宣布中立。1915年5月7日，德国潜艇用鱼雷击沉英国商船，丧生者中有100多名美国平民。威尔逊一面发出警告，一面在交战双方中间斡旋和平。1917年初，在德国宣布恢复无限制的潜艇战后，威尔逊总统宣布和德国断交。1917年4月2日，在5艘美国商船被德国击沉后，他要求国会宣战。

罗斯福首任就职演说
First Inaugural Address

Franklin Roosevelt／富兰克林·罗斯福

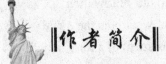

‖作者简介‖

　　富兰克林·罗斯福(1882~1945)，美国第32任总统，民主党人，著名的资产阶级政治家，出生于纽约。他生前颇孚众望，成为美国历史上唯一连任四届的总统。第二次世界大战中，他执行反对德、意、日法西斯侵略扩张的外交路线，引导美国加入了反法西斯阵营。他随之也成为该阵营的重要领袖之一。1945年4月，他因脑溢血而与世长辞。

President Hoover, Mister Chief Justice, my friends,

　　This is a day of national consecration, and I am certain that on this day my fellow Americans expect that on my induction in the Presidency I will address them with a candor and a decision which the present situation of our people impels. This is preeminently the time to speak the truth, the whole truth, frankly and boldly. Nor need we shrink from honestly facing the conditions, facing our country today. This great nation will endure as it has endured, will revive and will prosper so first of all, let me express my firm belief that the only thing we have to fear is fear itself-nameless, unreasoning, unjustified terror, which paralyzes needed efforts to convert retreat into advance. In every dark hour of our national life, a leadership of frankness and vigor has met with that understanding and support of the people themselves, which is essential to victory. And I am convinced that you will again give that support to leadership in these critical days.

...

Happiness lies not in the mere possession of money, it lies in the joy of achievement, in the thrill of creative efforts, the joy and moral stimulation of work no longer must be forgotten in the mad chase of evanescent profits. These dark days, my friends, will be worth all they cost us, if they teach us that our true destiny is not to be ministered on to, but to minister to ourselves, to our fellow men.

Recognition of the falsity of material wealth as the standard of success goes hand in hand with the abandonment of a false belief that public office and high political position are to be valued only by the standards of pride of place and personal profits, and there must be an end to our conduct in banking and in business, which too often has given to a sacred trust the likeness of callous and selfish wrong-doing. Small wonder that confidence languishes, for it thrives only on honesty on honor on the sacredness of our obligation, on faithful protection and on unselfish performance. Without them it cannot live.

Restoration calls, however, not for changes in ethics alone. This nation is asking for action, and action now.

Our greatest primary task is to put people to work. This is no unsolvable problem if we take it wisely and courageously. It can be accomplished in part by direct recruiting by the government itself, treating the task as we would treat the emergency of a war, but at the same time, through this employment, accomplishing greatly needed projects to stimulate and reorganize the use of our great natural resources.

...

These, my friends, are the lines of attack. I shall presently urge upon a new Congress in special session, detailed measures for their fulfillment, and I shall seek the immediate assistance of the 48 states.

感动一个国家的文字

胡佛总统、首席法官先生、朋友们：

对我们的国家而言，今天是一个神圣的日子。我肯定，同胞们都期待这一天，在我就职总统时，如当前形势下人民所要求的那样，坦诚而果敢地同他们讲话。那现在就是坦诚勇敢地讲出真话、实话的最好时机。我们不要因坦诚地面对国家今天的状况而退缩。这个伟大的国家会一如既往地承受起一切，它会复兴、繁荣起来。因此，首先让我表明我的坚定信念：我们所害怕的就是害怕本身——一种毫无理智、无任何根据的莫名恐惧，它会使我们为变后退为前进所做的种种努力化为泡影。在我国国民生活在黑暗中的时刻，坦率而有活力的领导都得到了人民的理解和支持，这是胜利的基本条件。我相信，在目前的危急时刻，他们会再次支持这个领导。

……

幸福并不是单纯地建立在金钱的占有上，在于取得成就后的欢悦，在于努力创造过程中的激情。一定不能忘记工作所带来的喜悦和激励，而去拼命地追求过眼云烟的金钱。在这些灰暗的日子里，能使我们意识到，我们真正的命运不是要别人来侍奉，而是要为自己和同胞们服务，那么，我们所付出的代价就是完全值得的。

认识到把物质财富作为衡量成功的标准是错误的，我们就要抛弃那些以个人地位的显赫及个人的收益作为衡量公职和高级政治地位的惟一标准的错误概念。我们必须在银行界和商界制止这一行为，它常常使人把圣洁的信托视为无情和自私的不良行为。信心减弱不足为奇，因为它只能依靠诚实、信誉、忠心和无私责任来维持。如果没有这些，信心就不可能存活。

复兴不仅仅是伦理观念上的改变。这个国家需要行动起来，现在就行动起来。

我们最大的、头等重要的工作就是让人民投入到工作中。只要我们把自己的智慧和勇气投入进去，就没有解决不了的问题。这部分可以由政府直接征募完成。对待这项任务就像对待一场紧急战争，但同时，通过这些人力，去完成更多急需的项目，以便刺激并重组博大的自然资源工程。

……

我的朋友，以上所言，就是实施方针。我马上敦促新国会的特别会议给予详细实施方案，同时，我会向 48 个州请求紧急支援。

Through this program of action, we address ourselves to putting our own national house in order, and making income balance outflow. Our international trade relations, though vastly important, are in point of time and necessity secondary to the establishment of a sound national economy. I favor as a practical policy the putting of first things first. I shall spare no effort to restore world trade by international economic readjustment, but the emergency at home cannot wait on that accomplishment.

The basic thought that guides these specific means of national recovery is not narrowly nationalistic. It is the insistence, as a first consideration upon the inter-dependence of the various elements in all parts of the United States of America — a recognition of the old and the permanently important manifestation of the American spirit of the pioneer. It is the way to recovery, it is the immediate way it is the strongest assurance that recovery will endure.

In the field of world policy I would dedicate this nation to the policy of the good neighbor. The neighbor who resolutely respects himself, and because he does so, respects the rights of others. The neighbor who respects his obligation, and respects the sanctity of his agreement, in and with, a world of neighbor.

If I read the temper of our people correctly we now realize what we have never realized before, our inter-dependence on each other, that we cannot merely take, but we must give as well. That if we are to go forward, we must move as a trained and loyal army willing to sacrifice for the good of a common discipline, because without such discipline, no progress can be made, no leadership becomes effective. We are all ready and willing to submit our lives and our property to such discipline because it makes possible a leadership which aims at the larger good. This, I propose to offer we are going to larger purposes, bind upon us, bind upon us all, as a sacred obligation with a unity of duty hitherto evoked only in times of armed strife.

通过这个行动计划，我们将致力于使国家体系恢复秩序，并使收入大于支出。我们的国际贸易，虽然很重要，但就目前在时间和必要性上，还次于对本国殷实经济的建立。我赞成，作为可实施的策略，首要事务一定要先行。虽然我将尽一切努力重新调整国际经济来恢复国际贸易，但我认为国内的紧急形势已无法等待这种重新协调的完成。

　　指导全国性复苏特殊措施的基本思想并不是狭隘的国家主义。首先要考虑的是坚持美国各部分之间的相互依赖性——这是对古老而永恒的美国精神先驱者的重视。这才是复苏之路，是最快之路，是复苏得以持久的最强有力的保证。

　　在国际政策领域里，我将使这个国家采取睦邻友好的政策。做一个果敢自重、尊重邻国的国家，做一个履行义务、尊重与他国协定的国家。

　　如果我能够准确地了解人民的心情的话，我想现在我们已意识到了我们从前从未意识到的问题，我们相互依存，我们不能只索取，还必须奉献。前进时，我们必须像一支经过训练的忠诚队伍，为了共同的准则而愿意牺牲。因为，如果缺乏这些准则，就无法取得进步，领导也不可能有效率。我们已做好了充分的准备，为了此准则愿意献出自己的生命和财产。因为它使领导谋求广大人民的福祉成为可能。我提议，为了更伟大的目标，我们所有的人，应该紧紧地团结在一起。这是一种神圣的义务，永远也不要停止，除非在战乱中。

With this pledge taken, I assume unhesitatingly, the leadership of this great army of our people dedicated to a disciplined attack upon our common problems. Action in this image, action to this end, is feasible under the form of government, which we have inherited from my ancestors. Our constitution is so simple, so practical, that it is possible always, to meet extraordinary needs, by changes in emphasis and arrangements without loss of a central form that is why our constitutional system has proved itself the most superbly enduring political mechanism the modern world has ever seen. It has met every stress of vast expansion of territory of foreign wars, of bitter internal strife, of world relations.

And it is to be hoped that the normal balance of executive and legislative authority will be fully equal, fully adequate to meet the unprecedented task before us. But it may be that an unprecedented demand and need for underlay action may call for temporary departure from that normal balance of public procedure.

We face the arduous days that lie before us in the warm courage of national unity in the clearest consciousness of seeking all and precious moral values, with the clean satisfaction that comes from the stem performance of duty by old and young alike, we aim at the assurance of a rounded, a permanent national life.

We do not distrust the future of essential democracy. The people of the United States have not failed. In their need, they have registered a mandate that they want direct, vigorous action. They have asked for discipline, and direction under leadership, they have made me the present instrument of their wishes. In the spirit of the gift, I take it.

In this dedication, in this dedication of a nation, we humbly ask the blessings of God, may He protect each and every one of us, may He guide me in the days to come.

有了这样的誓言，我保证毫不犹豫地领导我们的人民大军，投身于有条不紊地解决大家所普遍关心的问题中去。以这样的形象与目标行动，在我们从我们的先父手中接过的政府中是可行的。我们的宪法非常简单、可行。它通过对重点和整顿加以修正而不失中心思想，随时都可以应付特殊需要。这就是为什么我们的宪法体制已证明了我们是目前世界上最有适应能力的政治体制。它经历了巨大的疆土扩张、外战、内乱及国际关系所带来的压力。

同时我们还希望正常平衡的立法与执法当局做到充分平等，足以担当起前所未有的任务。但可能是空前的对次要行动的需求，会要求暂时抛开正常公共程序的平衡。

我们怀着全国民众团结一致给我们带来的热情和勇气，怀着寻求传统与珍贵的道德观念的清醒意识，带着不论老少都能坚守岗位得到满足而正视眼前这艰难的岁月。我们的目标是要保证国民生活的完美和长治久安。

我们根本不怀疑基本民主制度的未来。美国人民没有失败。他们在最需要的时候表达了他们想要直接有力行动的意志。他们要求纪律和领导指引方向，他们使我现在成为实现他们愿望的工具。我接受这份信任。

在举国上下奉献的时刻，我们谦卑地请求上帝赐福。愿上帝保护我们中的每一个人，愿上帝在未来的日子里指引我。

历史链接 在罗斯福首次就任总统的1933年初，正值经济大萧条的风暴席卷美国，到处是失业、破产、倒闭以及暴跌，到处可见美国的痛苦、恐惧与绝望。罗斯福却表现出一种压倒一切的自信，他在宣誓就职时发表了这篇富有激情的演说，告诉人们：我们唯一害怕的就是害怕本身。在1933年3月4日那个阴冷的下午，新总统的决心和乐观态度，点燃了举国同心同德的新精神之火。

要求对日本宣战
For a Declaration of War Against Japan

Franklin Roosevelt / 富兰克林 · 罗斯福

Mr.Vice president, Mr.Speaker, members of the Senate and the House of Representative,

Yesterday, December 7, 1941—a date which will Live in infamy—United States of America, was suddenly and deliberately attacked by naval and air forces of the Empire of Japan.

The United States was at peace with that nation, and, at the solicitation of Japan, was still in conversation with its government and its Emperor working towards the maintenance of peace in the Pacific.

Indeed, one hour after Japanese air squadrons had commenced bombing in the American island of Oahu. The Japanese Ambassador to the United States and his colleagues, delivered to our Secretary of States a formal reply to a recent American message. And while this reply stated that it seems useless to continue the existing diplomatic negotiations, it contained no threat or hint of war or of armed attack.

It will be recorded that the distance of Hawaii from Japan makes

感动一个国家的文字

it obvious that the attack was deliberately planned many days or even weeks ago. During the intervening time the Japanese Government has deliberately sought to deceive the United States by false statements and expressions of hope for continued peace.

The attack yesterday on the Hawaiian islands has caused severe damage to American naval and military forces. I regret to tell you that very many American lives have been lost. In addition, American ships have been reported torpedoed on the high seas between San Francisco and Honolulu.

副总统先生，议长先生，各位参议员和众议员：

昨天，1941 年 12 月 7 日将永远成为一个耻辱的日子——美利坚合众国遭到了日本帝国海空军部队蓄意的突然攻击。

美国同日本当时处于和平状态，同时，应日本的请求仍在同该国政府及天皇进行对话，期望能够维持太平洋区域的和平。

事实上，在日本空军中队开始轰炸美国的瓦胡岛之后一个小时，日本驻美大使及其同事还向我国国务卿提交了我国最近致日本书的正式复函。虽然该复函声称继续目前的外交谈判似乎无必要，却并未包含有关战争或武装攻击的威胁与暗示。

应该记录在案的是，夏威夷岛距日本的距离说明此次袭击显然是多日甚至数周前就早已蓄意谋划好的。在此谋划过程中，日本政府还通过有关希望维护和平的虚假声明和表达蓄意欺骗了合众国。

昨天夏威夷群岛所遭受的攻击，给美国海陆部队造成了严重的损害。我遗憾地告诉诸位：许多美国人失去了生命。此外，据报告，美国船只在旧金山与檀香山之间的公海上也遭到鱼雷袭击。

Yesterday, the Japanese government also launched an attack against Malaya.

Last night, Japanese forces attacked Hong Kong.

Last night, Japanese forces attacked Guam.

Last night, Japanese forces attacked the Philippine Islands.

Last night, the Japanese attacked Wake Island.

And this morning, the Japanese attacked Midway Island.

Japan has therefore undertaken a surprise offensive extending throughout the Pacific area. The facts of yesterday and today speak for themselves. The people of the United States has already formed their opinions and well understand the implications to the very life and safety of our nation.

As Commander-in-Chief of the Army and Navy, I have directed that all measures be taken for our defense. But always, let our whole nation remember the character of the onslaught against us.

No matter how long it may take us to overcome this premeditated invasion, the American people in their righteous might will win through to absolute victory.

I believe that I interpret the will of Congress and of the people when I assert that we will not only defend ourselves to the uttermost, but will make it very certain that this form of treachery shall never again endanger us.

Hostilities exist, there is no blinking the fact that our people, our territory, and our interest are in grave danger.

昨日，马来亚也遭到日军的袭击。

昨夜，香港遭到日本的袭击。

昨夜，关岛遭到日本的袭击。

昨夜，菲律宾群岛遭到日军袭击。

昨夜，威克岛遭到日军袭击。

今晨，中途岛遭到日本袭击。

如此，日本在整个太平洋区域发动了全面突袭。昨天和今天的形势让事实不言自明。合众国人民已经对此有了自己的看法，并清楚地认识到这是关系着我们国家安全及生存的问题。

作为陆海军总司令，我已下令采用一切手段进行防卫。整个国家都将永远记住针对我们的这次袭击的性质。

无论击败这次有预谋的进犯需要多长时间，美国人民都将凭借正义的力量赢得绝对胜利。

现在，我断言我们不但能确保自身的安全，也能够确保这种背信弃义的行为永远不会再对我们有所危害。我相信，我这样说是代表了国会和人民的意愿。

兵临城下，无须讳言。我们的人民、我们的领土以及我们的利益已陷入极度危急的境地。

▲炮火中的珍珠港

With confidence in our armed forces, with the unbounding deter-mination of our people, we will gain the inevitable triumph, so help us God.

I ask that the Congress declare that since the unprovoked and dastardly attack by Japan on Sunday, December 7, 1941, a state of war has existed between the United States and the Japanese Empire.

有了对我们武装力量的信赖，有了我们人民无比坚定的决心，胜利必定属于我们，愿上帝赐福于我们。

我要求国会宣布：鉴于日本于 1941 年 12 月 7 日星期日无故对我国进行卑鄙怯懦的袭击，美国自此同日本已处于交战状态。

罗斯福总统对日宣战 ◀

历史链接： 1941 年 12 月 7 日夏威夷时间 7 点 55 分，日本的 183 架飞机，向珍珠港发动偷袭，美国的太平洋舰队几乎全军覆没。第二天罗斯福在国会发表本篇演说，美国国会当天通过了向日本宣战的决定。

感动一个国家的文字 . . . . . .

自由与平等的梦想

第二卷

100年前，一位伟大的美国人——今天我们就站在他的雕像下——正式签署了《解放宣言》。这项重要法令的颁布，如一座伟大的灯塔，照亮了当时挣扎于不义之火焚烤下的数百万黑奴的希望；它像欢快的破晓曙光，结束了黑人陷于囹圄的漫漫长夜。

致白人传教士
To The White Missionary

Red Jacket/ 红夹克

‖作者简介‖

红夹克(约1758～1830)，北美塞内卡族首长，曾为英军效力，接受红色号衣，故名"红夹克"，后倒戈支持美国独立战争。本篇是他在6个部落首长联席会议上对白人传教士的回答，是印第安人抵制白人文化的代表作。

Brother, this council fire was kindled by you. It was at your request that we came together at this time. We have listened with attention to what you have said. You requested us to speak our minds freely. This gives us great joy; for we now consider that we stand upright before you and can speak what we think. All have heard your voice and all speak to you now as one man. Our minds are agreed.

Brother, you say you want an answer to your talk before you leave this place. It is right you should have one, as you are a great distance from home and we do not wish to detain you. But first we will look back a little and tell you what our fathers have told us and what we have heard from the white people.

Brother, listen to what we say. There was a time when our fore-

感动一个国家的文字

fathers owned this great island. Their seats extended from the rising to the setting sun. The Great Spirit had made it for the use of Indians. He had created the buffalo, the deer, and other animals for food. He had made the bear and the beaver. Their skins served us for clothing. He had scattered them over the country and taught us how to take them. He had caused the earth to produce corn for bread. All this He had done for His red children because He loved them. If we had some disputes about our hunting-ground they were generally settled without the shedding of much blood.

兄弟，是你点燃了这次会议之火。也是在你的要求下，我们各方人士此时此刻会聚在这里。我们刚才仔细聆听了你的讲话，你希望我们畅所欲言，这使我们感到分外高兴，因为今天我们是怀着坦诚的心情与你见面的，并希望说说我们的心里话。我们如同一个人般听了你的发言，现在又如同一个人般对你说话。我们的意见是一致的。

兄弟，你说在离开这里之前希望听到对你的讲话的反应。你说得对，你应该得到这样一个反应，因为你不远千里来到这里，我们也无意强留。首先让我们稍稍回顾一下过去。我想请你了解我们的父辈是如何对我们说的，而我们又从白人那里听到了什么。

兄弟，请听我们说吧。我们的祖先曾经拥有这片广袤无垠的土地。他们的足迹从日出之地一直延伸到日落之地。伟大的神灵创造了这片土地，供我们印第安人享用。他创造了野牛、麋鹿和其他动物作为我们的食物。他创造了熊及河狸，以其毛皮作为我们的衣裳。他使这些动物遍布大地，并教导我们捕捉的技巧。他还让土地长出五谷，作为我们的食粮。伟大的神灵所做的一切，都是为了他的红皮肤孩子们，因为他爱他们。即使我们的孩子之间为了猎物而互有争执，这些争执也总会在不需怎么流血的情况下得以平息。

But an evil day came upon us. Your forefathers crossed the great water and landed on this island. Their numbers were small. They found friends and not enemies. They told us they had fled from their own country for fear of wicked men and had come here to enjoy their religion. They asked for a small seat. We took pity on them, granted their request, and they sat down among us. We gave them corn and meat; they gave us poison in return.

The white people, brother, had now found our country. Tidings were carried back and more came among us. Yet we did not fear them. We took them to be friends. They called us brothers. We believed them and gave them a larger seat. At length their numbers had greatly increased. They wanted more land; they wanted our country. Our eyes were opened and our minds became uneasy. Wars took place. Indians were hired to fight against Indians, and many of our people were destroyed. They also brought strong liquor among us. It was strong and powerful, and has slain thousands.

Brother, our seats were once large and yours were small. You have now become a great people, and we have scarcely a place left to spread our blankets. You have got our country, but are not satisfied; you want to force your religion upon us.

Brother, continue to listen. You say that you are sent to instruct us how to worship the Great Spirit agreeably to His mind; and, if we do not take hold of the religion which you white people teach we shall be unhappy hereafter. You say that you are right and we are lost. How do we know this to be true? We understand that your religion is written in a Book. If it was intended for us, as well as you, why has not the Great Spirit given to us, and not only to us, but why did He not give to our forefathers the knowledge of that Book, with the means of understanding it rightly, we only know what you tell us about it. How

感动一个国家的文字

但是，罪恶的一天突然降临。你的祖先们远涉重洋，登上了这块大陆。那时他们的人数并不多，在这里，你们遇上的是朋友，而不是敌人。他们告诉我们，他们逃离自己的祖国是出于对邪恶之徒的恐惧，而来到这儿是为了继续自己的宗教信仰。他们请求得到一隅之地。我们怀着对他们的怜悯，同意了他们的请求。于是，他们同我们坐在了一起。我们给予他们的是谷物，是肉食，而他们回报的却是毒药。

兄弟，你们白人看上了我们的家园。消息不断地传回去，越来越多的白人如潮水般涌来。可是我们并不害怕他们，我们仍将他们视为朋友，他们也称我们为弟兄。于是，我们相信了他们，并给予他们更多的土地。最后，他们的人数剧增，他们还需要更多的土地，他们甚至想占有我们整个家园。我们困惑，我们不安。于是战争爆发了。他们雇佣印第安人去跟印第安人战斗，我们中的很多人就此遭到杀戮。白人们还带来了烈酒，这些烈酒使我们成千上万的同胞失去了生命。

兄弟，我们的领地曾经是那样广大，而你们的曾是那样狭小。现在，你们成了一个庞大的民族，而我们的生存之地却所剩无几，甚至我们连铺开毯子的地方都没有。你们夺走了我们的家园，却仍不知足，你们还想将自己的宗教强加在我们头上。

兄弟，请继续听我说。你说自己被派到这里来，是为了教导我们怎样敬神，并按照神的旨意行事，如果我们不信奉你们白人要求我们去信奉的宗教，将再也得不到幸福。你还说，你们是正义而高贵的，我们却深陷于迷茫和堕落中。可是，我们又如何证明你的话就是真理呢？我们知道你们的宗教是写在一本书上的，如果这本书既是为我们而写，也是为你们而写，为什么伟大的神灵没有把它赐予我们？为什么伟大的神灵既不直接如实地让我们的祖先知晓那本书的内容，又不赋予他们正确理解那本书的方法？我们所知道的仅

shall we know when to believe, being so often deceived by the white people?

Brother, you say there is but one way to worship and serve the Great Spirit. If there is but one religion, why do you white people differ so much about it? Why not all agreed, as you can all read the Book?

Brother, we do not understand these things. We are told that your religion was given to your forefathers and has been handed down from father to son. We also have a religion which was given to our forefathers and has been handed down to us, their children. We worship in that way. It teaches us to be thankful for all the favors we receive, to love each other, and to be united. We never quarrel about religion.

Brother, the Great Spirit has made us all, but He has made a great difference between His white and His red children. He has given us different complexions and different customs. To you He has given the arts. To these He has not opened our eyes. We know these things to be true. Since He has made so great a difference between us in other things, why may we not conclude that He has given us a different religion according to our understanding? The Great Spirit does right. He knows what is best for His children; we are satisfied.

Brother, we do not wish to destroy your religion or take it from you. We only want to enjoy our own.

Brother, you say you have not come to get our land or our money, but to enlighten our minds. I will now tell you that I have been at your meetings and saw you collect money from the meeting. I can not tell what this money was intended for, but suppose that it was for your

仅是你们所告诉的。我们总是受到白人的欺骗，又怎么知道什么时候该相信，什么时候不该相信？

兄弟，你说礼拜和侍奉全能的神灵只有一种方式。既然只存在一种信仰，为什么你们白人的所作所为与之截然不同？既然你们个个都熟读《圣经》，你们自己又为什么不照着《圣经》说的去做？

兄弟，这些事情我们通通不明白。我们只知道你们的宗教先被赋予你们的祖先，然后又代代相传。我们也有自己的宗教，它也被赋予我们的祖先，并一直传到我们，再传给我们的孩子们。它教导我们要为我们所受到的一切恩惠而对神灵充满感激之情，要相互热爱，团结一心。我们就是以这样的方式表达对宗教的信仰，我们从来不为信仰而纷争。

兄弟，伟大的神灵创造了我们全体，但他也在他的白皮肤孩子和红皮肤孩子之间制造了巨大差别。他给予我们不同的肤色，不同的习俗。伟大的神灵给予你们各种各样的艺术，而在这方面，他却至今未使我们开眼。我们知道那些艺术是真实的。既然神灵在其他方面也造就了这种巨大差别，我们为什么就不能按照这种理解得出这么一个结论——神灵给予我们印第安人一种不同的宗教？全能的神灵是对的。他知道对他的孩子们来说什么是最好的，我们为此感到满足。

兄弟，我们不想摧毁你们的宗教，也不想从你们身边夺走它。我们只是希望能信仰自己的宗教。

兄弟，你说你来此地并非为了我们的土地和金钱，而是为了启迪我们的心灵。我现在可以告诉你，我曾经出席过你主持的集会，亲眼看到你在收钱。我不能肯定这些钱将派什么用场，也许是为了

minister; and, if we should conform to your way of thinking, perhaps you may want some from us.

Brother, we are told that you have been preaching to the white people in this place. These people are our neighbors. We are acquainted with them. We will wait a little while and see what effect your preaching has upon them. If we find it does them good, makes them honest, and less disposed to cheat Indians, we will then consider again of what you have said.

Brother, you have now heard our answer to your talk, and this is all we have to say at present. As we are going to part, we will come and take you by the hand, and hope the Great Spirit will protect you on your journey and return you safe to your friends.

给你们的牧师。推而论之,假如我们接受了你们的思维方式,你或许也会向我们索取钱财。

兄弟,我听说你一直在这里给白人们讲道。那些白人都是我们的邻居,我们对他们非常熟悉。你的说教到底会对他们产生什么样的效果,我们将拭目以待。如果我们发现你的布道对他们确有益处,使他们变得诚实,不再老是欺骗印第安人,我们将重新考虑你所说的一切。

兄弟,现在你终于听到了我们对你讲话的反应。我们目前所能说的就是这些。我们将会全心照顾你,因为你即将离开我们。愿神灵保佑你一路平安,顺利地回到你的朋友们中间去。

Yonder sky that has wept tears of compassion upon my people for centuries untold, and which to us appears changeless and eternal, may change. Today is fair. Tomorrow it may be overcast with clouds. My words are like the stars that never change. Whatever Seattle says, the great chief at Washington can rely upon with as much certainty as he can upon the return of the sun or the seasons.

无数个世纪以来，浩渺苍天曾为我的族人洒下同情之泪；这人们看似永恒不易的苍天，实际上是会改变的：今天和风煦日，明日则可能乌云密布。但我的话却犹如天空亘古的恒星，永不变更。华盛顿的大酋长可以像信赖日月季节更替一般，相信西雅图所说的话。

西雅图酋长谈话

The "Alternate Statement" of Chief Seattle

Chief Seattle/ 西雅图酋长

西雅图首长（1786～1866），杜瓦米许族印第安人，勇武且善于领导，以首长身份统治德奥米什（Dwamish）和苏卡米什（Suquamish）等6个部落。西雅图早年受法国传教士的影响，信仰天主教。他的父亲与当地白人建立了友好关系，而他多年来一直维护着这种关系。1855年他与白人签订了《埃利澳特港条约》，并建立印第安人保留地，当时美国政府要将当地土人驱逐到"保留地"定居。本文就是西雅图在美国政府压力下的答复。

The white chief says that Big Chief at Washington sends us greetings of friendship and goodwill. This is kind of him for we know he has little need of our friendship in return. His people are many. They are like the grass that covers vast prairies. My people are few. They resemble the scattering trees of a storm-swept plain. The great, and I presume — good, White Chief sends us word that he wishes to buy our lands but is willing to allow us enough to live comfortably. This indeed appears just, even generous, for the Red Man no longer has rights that he need respect, and the offer may be wise also, as we are no longer in need of an extensive country.

There was a time when our people covered the land as the waves of a wind-ruffled sea cover its shell-paved floor, but that time long since passed away with the greatness of tribes that are now but a mournful memory. I will not dwell on, nor mourn over, our untimely decay, nor reproach my paleface brothers with hastening it, as we too may have been somewhat to blame.

Youth is impulsive. When our young men grow angry at some real or imaginary wrong, and disfigure their faces with black paint, it denotes that their hearts are black, and that they are often cruel and relentless, and our old men and old women are unable to restrain them. Thus it has ever been. Thus it was when the white man began to push our forefathers ever westward. But let us hope that the hostilities between us may never return. We would have everything to lose and nothing to gain. Revenge by young men is considered gain, even at the cost of their own lives, but old men who stay at home in times of war, and mothers who have sons to lose, know better.

Our good father in Washington — for I presume he is now our father as well as yours, since King George has moved his boundaries further north — our great and good father, I say, sends us word that if we do as he desires he will protect us. His brave warriors will be to

华盛顿的大酋长托白人酋长向我们致以友好的问候与祝愿。我们应该感谢他们的好意，因为我们知道他不需要我们的友情作为回报。他的子民众多，如广袤平原上无边的青草；我的族人寥寥，如风雨狂虐过后平原上稀拉树木。这位了不起的——我想也是仁慈的——白人酋长传话给我们，他愿意在为我们保留足够的土地过安逸生活的前提下，购买我们的土地。这看起来的确很合理，甚至该说是慷慨的，因为红种人已经没有要求受尊重的权利了；这个提议也许还是英明的，因为这么辽阔的国土对我们来说已经没有意义了。

曾几何时，我们的族人曾密密麻麻地布满了整片土地，就像随风涌浪的海水掩盖着满是贝壳的海底。但那个时代早已一去不复返了，部族曾经的辉煌只留给我们忧伤的回忆。我不愿再纠缠于我们部落过早的衰落，不愿再为此哀叹，也不愿将此归咎于白种兄弟，因为我们自己多少也有值得埋怨的地方。

年轻一代总是容易冲动。我们年轻的族人被或真实或虚幻的冤屈所激怒，用黑漆把脸涂黑，其实同时他们也抹黑了自己的心，变得残酷无情，而我们这些上了岁数的老人们又无力约束他们。然而，尽管一直都是如此，尽管自从白人把我们往西驱逐以来一直都是如此，但还是让我们寄希望于彼此之间的仇恨能够永远泯灭。仇恨能让我们失去一切，却毫无所得。对年轻人来说，可能复仇本身就是一种收获，即使那会让他们失去生命，但是那些在战时固守家园的老人，以及可能在战争中失去儿子的母亲们，懂得更多事情的真相。

我们在华盛顿的好父亲——自从乔治国王将他的边界线向北大举推进之后，我已经把他当成我们的，也是你们的父亲了——我说，我们了不起的好心肠的父亲传话来说，他会保护我们，唯一的条件就是我们要按他说的去做。他神武的勇士将为我们筑起护卫之墙，他神奇的战舰会驻满

73

us a bristling wall of strength, and his wonderful ships of war will fill our harbors, so that our ancient enemies far to the northward — the Haidas and Tsimshians, will cease to frighten our women, children, and old men. He in reality he will be our father and we will be his children.

But can that ever be? Your God is not our God! Your God loves your people and hates mine! He folds his strong protecting arms lovingly about the paleface and leads him by the hand as a father leads an infant son. But, He has forsaken His Red children, if they really are His.

Our God, the Great Spirit, seems also to have forsaken us. Your God makes your people wax stronger every day. Soon they will fill all the land. Our people are ebbing away like a rapidly receding tide that will never return. The white man's God cannot love our people or He would protect them. They seem to be orphans who can look nowhere for help. How then can we be brothers? How can your God become our God and renew our prosperity and awaken in us dreams of returning greatness?

If we have a common Heavenly Father He must be partial, for He came to His paleface children. We never saw Him. He gave you laws but had no word for His red children whose teeming multitudes once filled this vast continent as stars fill the firmament. No, we are two distinct races with separate origins and separate destinies. There is little in common between us.

To us the ashes of our ancestors are sacred and their resting place is hallowed ground. You wander far from the graves of your ancestors and seemingly without regret.

Your religion was written upon tablets of stone by the iron finger of your God so that you could not forget. The Red Man could never comprehend or remember it. Our religion is the traditions of our

我们的港口。这样一来，我们北边的宿敌——海达人和辛姆希人——再也不能威胁到我们的妇孺老弱。如此这般，他作为父亲，我们作为孩子就成了事实了。

但这可能吗？你们的上帝并不是我们的上帝；你们的上帝爱护你们的子民，却憎恨我的族人。他以他那有力的臂弯慈爱地环绕保护着白人，就像父亲指引新生儿般指引着他们，但是他却遗弃了他的红皮肤的孩子——如果我们真的能称做他的孩子的话。

我们的上帝，那伟大的神灵，好像也已经遗弃了我们。你们的神让你们的人民一天天强大起来，很快就能占据整个大地，而我的族人却衰落得如急退的潮水一去不回了。白人的神不会爱护我们的同胞，不然他为何不保护他们，而让他们像孤儿一样求助无门？既然如此，我们怎能成为兄弟呢？你们的神又怎能成为我们的神，让我们重振雄风并唤醒我们重返昔日鼎盛时期的梦想呢？

假如我们真的有着同一位天父的话，那他也必定偏心，因为他只照看着他那白皮肤的儿子，我们却从来见不到他；他教给你们律法，对他红皮肤的儿子却无话要说，尽管他们曾经如繁星占满苍穹般遍布着整个大陆。不，我们是两个截然不同的种族，起源不同，命运也各异。我们之间几乎毫无共同点。

在我们看来，祖先的骨灰是神圣的，他们的安息之所也是圣地，而你们却似乎可以毫无哀痛感地远离祖先墓地。

你们的宗教，是你们的神恐怕你们遗忘，以铁指书写在石板之上的。红种人对此既不能领会也难以记住；我们的宗教传自我们的

ancestors — the dreams of our old men, given them in solemn hours of the night by the Great Spirit; and the visions of our sachems, and is written in the hearts of our people.

Your dead cease to love you and the land of their nativity as soon as they pass the portals of the tomb and wander away beyond the stars. They are soon forgotten and never return. Our dead never forget this beautiful world that gave them being. They still love its verdant valleys, its murmuring rivers, its magnificent mountains, sequestered vales and verdant lined lakes and bays, and ever yearn in tender fond affection over the lonely hearted living, and often return from the happy hunting ground to visit, guide, console, and comfort them···

···

Our departed braves, fond mothers, glad, happy hearted maidens, and even the little children who lived here and rejoiced here for a brief season, will love these somber solitudes and at eventide they greet shadowy returning spirits.

And when the last Red Man shall have perished, and the memory of my tribe shall have become a myth among the White Men, these shores will swarm with the invisible dead of my tribe, and when your children think themselves alone in the field, the store, the shop, upon the highway, or in the silence of the pathless woods, they will not be alone. In all the earth there is no place dedicated to solitude. At night when the streets of your cities and villages are silent and you think them deserted, they will throng with the returning hosts that once filled them and still love this beautiful land. The White Man will never be alone.

Let him be just and deal kindly with my people, for the dead are not powerless. Dead, did I say? — There is no death, only a change of worlds.

感动一个国家的文字 . . . . . .

祖先——伟大的神灵于夜晚的神圣时刻，以梦的方式赐予我们族中长者，经过酋长们的洞察，铭刻在我们族人的心底。

你们的亡者一旦踏上墓地的大门，便不再爱护你们，也不再爱护曾经的故国家园。从此飘忽于群星之外，很快就被生者遗忘，也永不再回来。我们的逝者却永远不会遗忘这个曾赐予他生命的美丽世界。他们依然爱恋着青翠的峡谷，潺潺的河流，雄伟的大山，以及幽静的溪谷和碧绿的湖泊海湾，并且以最温柔体贴的情感牵挂着内心孤寂的生者，一次次地从他们极乐的狩猎之地回来，探望他们，指引他们，安抚他们……

……

我们已逝的勇士，多情的母亲，欢欣的少女，甚至还有仅仅在这里生长嬉戏过一段短短的美好岁月的孩子们，都热恋着这一片黯淡荒寂的土地，并在夜幕降临之时，迎接那些蒙蒙的族人之魂飘然而归。

当最后一个红种人逝去，我们部落的回忆在白人心中已经成为神话之时，这里的海岸仍将聚集着我们族人无形的灵魂；当你们的后代以为他们是独自在田野、库房、商店、公路或者寂静的树林之中流连时，他们也绝非孤身一人。大地之上没有任何地方是真正孤寂的，夜深人静，当你们城镇或村庄的街道悄然入梦，也许你会以为此刻它们都是荒无生命的。其实不然，街上将挤满了回归故园的亡魂。他们曾生活在这里，至今仍然热爱这片美丽的故土。有他们相伴，白人永远不会感到孤单。

愿他公正友善地对待我的族人，因为死者并不是无能为力的。我说他们是死者吗？不，世上并没有"死亡"一说——他们只是去了另外一个世界。

不自由，毋宁死

Give Me Liberty, Or Give Me Death

Patrick Henry/ 帕特里克·亨利

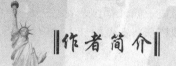 ‖作者简介‖

　　帕特里克·亨利(1736～1799)，美国革命时期杰出的政治家、演说家，曾任律师、弗吉尼亚州议员。本篇演说发表于1775年3月23日弗吉尼亚州第2届议会上，在美国革命文献史上占有重要地位。

Mr. President,

No man thinks more highly than I do of the patriotism, as well as abilities, of the very worthy gentlemen who have just addressed the House. But different men often see the same subject in different lights; and, therefore, I hope that it will not be thought disrespectful to those gentlemen, if, entertaining as I do, opinions of a character very opposite to theirs, I shall speak forth my sentiments freely and without reserve. This is no time for ceremony. The question before the House is one of awful moment to this country. For my own part I consider it as nothing less than a question of freedom or slavery; and in proportion to the magnitude of the subject

感动一个国家的文字

ought to be the freedom of the debate. It is only in this way that we can hope to arrive at truth, and fulfill the great responsibility which we hold to God and our country. Should I keep back my opinions at such a time, through fear of giving offence, I should consider myself as guilty of treason towards my country, and of an act of disloyalty towards the majesty of heaven, which I revere above all earthly kings.

Mr. President, it is natural to man to indulge in the illusions of hope. We are apt to shut our eyes against a painful truth, and listen to the song of that Siren, till she transforms us into beasts. Is this the part of wise men, engaged in a great and arduous struggle for liberty? Are we disposed to be of the number of those who, having eye, see not, and having ears, hear not, the things which so nearly concern their

议长先生：

没有谁比我更加敬佩这些在议会上发言的先生们的爱国热情和才干了。但是，对待一个问题每个人都会有不同的看法。因此，假如我持有的观点与他们恰恰相反，并且无所顾忌毫不保留地表达出来，希望不会被认为对他们有何不敬之意。现在已经没有时间让我们讲客套了。议会所面临的问题是我们的国家正处于危难之际。我个人认为，最严重的一点就是关系到我们是独立自主还是被奴役的大问题。事关重大，应该准许人们畅所欲言。如此，我们才有望阐明事实，完成上帝和国家托付的重任。此时此刻，如果因为害怕冒犯他人而保持缄默，我会认为自己是在叛国，是对比世上所有君王更令人敬畏的天主的不忠。

议长先生，人类天生就容易沉迷于希望的幻想之中。痛苦的现实来临时，我们往往会紧闭双眼不敢面对，宁可倾听海妖的歌声，直到我们被变成野兽为止。这是聪明人在追求自由的艰苦卓绝的奋斗中所应该做的吗？我们难道愿意做那些对关系着能否获得拯救这样重大的事情视而不见、听而不闻的人吗？就我而言，不管这会带给我多大的精神折磨，我都愿意了解全部的事实和最糟糕的结果，

temporal salvation? For my part, whatever anguish of spirit it may cost, I am willing to know the whole truth; to know the worst and to provide for it.

I have but one lamp by which my feet are guided; and that is the lamp of experience. I know of no way of judging of the future but by the past. And judging by the past, I wish to know what there has been in the conduct of the British ministry for the last ten years, to justify those hopes with which gentlemen have been pleased to solace themselves and the House? Is it that insidious smile with which our petition has been lately received? Trust it not, sir; it will prove a snare to your feet. Suffer not yourselves to betray with a kiss. Ask yourself how this gracious reception of our petition comports with these war-like preparations, which cover our waters and darken our land. Are fleets and armies necessary to a work of love and reconciliation? Have we shown ourselves so unwilling to be reconciled, that force must be called into win back our love? Let us not deceive ourselves, sir. These are the implements of war and subjugation; the last arguments to which kings resort. I ask gentlemen, sir, what means this martial array, if its purpose be not to force us to submission? Can gentlemen assign any other possible motives for it? Has Great Britain any enemy, in this quarter of the world, to call for all this accumulation of navies and armies? No, sir, she has none. They are meant for us; they can be meant for no other. They are sent over to bind and rivet upon us those chains which the British ministry have been so long forging. And what have we to oppose to them? Shall we try argument? Sir, we have been trying that for the last ten years. Have we anything new to offer on the subject? Nothing. We have held the subject up in every light of which it is capable; but it has been all in vain. Shall we resort to entreaty and humble supplication? What terms shall we find which have not been already exhausted? Let us not, I beseech you, sir, de-

并为此做好准备。

经验是指导我前进的惟一明灯；过去是判断未来的唯一依据。因此，我想知道英国政府在过去十年中有何作为，使得各位有理由信心十足心甘情愿地来安慰自己也安慰议会？是因为他们最近接受我们的请愿时所露出的狡诈的笑容吗？先生们，别相信这些笑容，事实会证明这只是一个圈套。别被人家的一个吻给出卖了！大家想想，他们如此仁慈地接受我们的请愿，而同时又在我们的水域、我们的土地上大规模地备战，这是多么不协调呀！难道爱护与和解用得着出动他们的战舰和军队吗？难道我们的爱需要用武力才能挽回吗？先生们，别再自欺欺人了！这些只是战争和征服的手段，是国王最后的托词。请问各位，如果这些军事装备不是用来迫使我们归顺的，那它们是用来干什么的呢？哪位先生能告诉我，这还有什么别的意图吗？难道在这个地方，大不列颠王国还有其他敌人需要用这些庞大的海陆军队来对付吗？不，先生们，没有其他敌人了！这些就是用来对付我们的！它们是英国政府早就造好，用来囚禁我们的锁链。我们能用什么来反抗呢？争辩吗？先生们，我们已经和他们争辩十年了！再还有什么话可说吗？我们所能做的都做过了，然而一切都只是徒劳。难道我们还要卑躬屈膝，摇尾乞怜吗？我们已经用尽了一切办法。所以，先生们，我恳请你们别再自欺欺人了！为了避免这一场即将来临的风暴，我们已经尽力而为了。我们请愿过，我们抗议过，我们也乞求过，我们曾跪倒在国王的御座前，哀

ceive ourselves longer. Sir, we have done everything that could be done, to avert the storm which is now coming on. We have petitioned; we have remonstrated; we have supplicated; we have prostrated ourselves before the throne, and have implored its interposition to arrest the tyrannical hands of the ministry and Parliament. Our petitions have been slighted; our remonstrance have produced additional violence and insult; our supplications have been disregarded; and we have been spurned, with contempt, from the foot of the throne. In vain, after these things, may we indulge the fond hope of peace and reconciliation. There is no longer any room for hope. If we wish to be free — if we mean to preserve inviolate those inestimable privileges for which we have been so long contending—if we mean not basely to abandon the noble struggle in which we have been so long engaged, and which we have pledged ourselves never to abandon until the glorious object of our contest shall be obtained, we must fight! I repeat it, sir, we must fight! An appeal to arms and to the God of Hosts is all that is left us!

They tell us, sir, that we are weak; unable to cope with so formidable an adversary. But when shall we be stronger? Will it be the next week, or the next year? Will it be when we are totally disarmed, and when a British guard shall be stationed in every house? Shall we gather strength by irresolution and inaction? Shall we acquire the means of effectual resistance, by lying supinely on our backs and hugging the delusive phantom of hope, until our enemies shall have bound us hand and foot? Sir, we are not weak if we make a proper use of those means which the God of nature hath placed in our power. Three millions of people, armed in the holy cause of liberty, and in such a country as that which we possess, are invincible by any force which our enemy can send against us. Besides, sir, we

求他制止政府和国会的专制暴行。我们的请愿遭到蔑视，我们的抗议带来的是变本加厉的暴力和侮辱，我们的乞求换来的是不屑一顾，我们在天子脚下被轻蔑地一脚踢开！事已至此，我们还能沉迷于和平友好的美好幻想之中吗？已经不再有任何希望了！假如我们渴望自由——假如我们真要维护为之奋斗已久的神圣权利不受侵犯——假如我们不至于卑鄙到想放弃我们抗争已久，发誓不达目的决不罢休的伟大角逐，那么，我们必须战斗！我再重复一遍，先生们，我们必须战斗！除了诉诸武力，求助于战神，我们别无选择！

先生们，他们说我们势单力薄，无力抵抗如此强劲的对手。但是，我们什么时候能变得更加强大呢？下周？还是明年？难道非要等到我们被彻底解除武装，家家户户都被英军占领的时候吗？难道优柔寡断，毫无作为能为我们积聚力量吗？难道我们能高枕而卧，要等到束手就擒之时，才能找到退敌的良策吗？先生们，只要我们懂得如何利用造物主赐予我们的力量，我们就绝不弱小。我们拥有300万为神圣的自由而武装起来的人民，我们拥有这样一方国土，这就是敌人任何武力都不可战胜的力量！况且，先生们，我们并非孤军作战。公正之神与我们同在，并主宰着一切国家的命运，并会唤起朋友们为我们进行战斗。先生们，战斗需要的不只是强大的力量，还需要机警、积极和勇敢，何况我们已经别无选择了。即使我们卑

shall not fight our battles alone. There is a just God who presides over the destinies of nations, and who will raise up friends to fight our battles for us. The battle, sir, is not to the strong alone; it is to the vigilant, the active, the brave. Besides, sir, we have no election. If we were base enough to desire it, it is now too late to retire from the contest. There is no retreat but in submission and slavery! Our chains are forged! Their clanking may be heard on the plains of Boston! The war is inevitable—and let it come! I repeat it, sir, let it come!

It is in vain, sir, to extenuate the matter. Gentlemen may cry Peace, Peace — but there is no peace. The war is actually begun! The next gale that sweeps from the north will bring to our ears the clash of resounding arms! Our brethren are already in the field! Why stand we here idle? What is it that gentlemen wish? What would they have? Is life so dear, or peace so sweet, as to be purchased at the price of chains and slavery? Forbid it, Almighty God! I know not what course others may take; but as for me, give me liberty, or give me death!

怯懦弱，想抽身而出，也已经太晚了。我们无路可退，回首只是屈从和被奴役！囚禁我们的枷锁早已铸成，镣铐的铿锵声回荡在波士顿平原的上空！战争已经在所难免——那就让它来吧！先生们，我再说一遍，让它来吧！

先生们，不用再徒劳地试图缓和事态。各位可以高喊和平——但和平并不存在。事实上战争已经打响！很快，从北方席卷而来的风暴就将带来隆隆的炮声！我们的弟兄们已经奔赴战场！为何我们还在此袖手旁观？各位先生究竟想要什么？又能得到什么？莫非生命如此珍贵，和平如此美好，竟值得我们以镣铐和奴役为代价来获得？全能的主啊，快阻止他们吧！我不知道别人将选择怎样的道路，但对我来说，不自由，毋宁死！

The Emancipation Proclamation
解放宣言

Abraham Lincoln/亚伯拉罕·林肯

Whereas, on the 22nd day of September, A.D. 1862, a proclamation was issued by the President of the United States, containing, among other things, the following, to wit:

" That on the 1st day of January, A.D. 1863, all persons held as slaves within any State, or designated part of a State, the people whereof shall then be in rebellion against the United States, shall be then, thenceforward, and forever free; and the Executive Government of the United States, including the military and naval authority thereof, will recognize and maintain the freedom of such persons, and will do no act or acts to repress such persons, or any of them, in any efforts they may make for their actual freedom.

公元1862年9月22日，联邦总统公布了一项宣言，内容如下：
"从公元1863年1月1日起，如果任何一州或州内指定地区仍保留有奴隶，当地人民将被视为是反叛合众国政府的。所有被定为奴隶者都应获得自由，并永远享有自由的权利。合众国政府，包括陆、海军当局，承认并维护上述人员的自由。对于这些人为争取真正自由而做出的努力，政府和当局不采取任何压制行动。

85

" That the Executive will, on the 1st day of January aforesaid, by proclamation, designate the States and parts of States, if any, in which the people thereof, respectively, shall then be in rebellion against the United States; and the fact that any State or the people thereof shall on that day be in good faith represented in the Congress of the United States by members chosen thereto at elections wherein a majority of the qualified voters of such States shall have participated shall, in the absence of strong countervailing testimony, be deemed conclusive evidence that such State and the people thereof are not then in rebellion against the United States. "

Now, therefore, I, Abraham Lincoln, President of the United States, by virtue of the power in me vested as Commander-In-Chief of the Army and Navy of the United States in time of actual armed rebellion against the authority and government of the United States, and as a fit and necessary war measure for supressing said rebellion, do, on this 1st day of January, A.D.1863, and in accordance with my purpose so to do, publicly proclaimed for the full period of one hundred days from the day first above mentioned, order and designate as the States and parts of States wherein the people thereof, respectively, are this day in rebellion against the United States the following, to wit:

" Arkansas, Texas, Louisiana(except the parishes of St. Bernard, Palquemines, Jefferson, St. John, St. Charles, St. James, Ascension, Assumption, Terre Bone, Lafourche, St. Mary, St. Martin, and Orleans, including the city of New Orleans), Mississippi, Alabama, Florida, Georgia, South Carolina, North Carolina, and Virginia (except the forty-eight counties designated as West Virginia, and also the counties of Berkeley, Accomac, Northhampton, Elizabeth City, York, Princess Anne, and Norfolk, including the cities of Norfolk and Portsmouth), and which excepted parts are for the present left precisely as if this proclamation were not issued. "

感动一个国家的文字

And by virtue of the power and for the purpose aforesaid, I do order and declare that all persons held as slaves within said designated States and parts of States are, and henceforward shall be, free; and that the Executive Government of the United States, including the military and naval authorities thereof, will recognize and maintain the freedom of said persons.

"从 1863 年 1 月 1 日起，如果在任何一州或地区有反叛合众国者，总统将会认定并宣布其为反叛合众国政府之州或地区。而由多数合格选民选出代表，并将富有诚意地加入合众国国会的州，如果无其他有力反证，该州及其人民将被确认为不反叛合众国政府的。"

现在，我，亚伯拉罕·林肯，合众国总统，在合众国政府及其权威受到武装叛乱威胁之际，根据合众国陆、海军总司令的职权，为剿灭叛乱而必须采取适当的军事手段，在 1863 年 1 月 1 日即上次为此目的而发表宣言满 100 天之际，正式宣布并认定下列各州、州内部分地区及其人民反叛合众国政府，他们为：

阿肯色州、得克萨斯州、路易斯安那州（以下地区除外：圣伯纳、帕拉奎明斯、杰弗逊、圣约翰、圣查理士、圣詹姆士、阿克森、阿森姆逊、特里本、拉孚切、圣玛丽、圣马丁和奥尔良各教区、包括新奥尔良市）、密西西比州、亚拉巴马州、佛罗里达州、佐治亚州、南卡罗来纳州、北卡罗来纳州及弗吉尼亚州（西弗吉尼亚的四十八个县以及柏克莱县、阿康玛克县、诺斯汉姆顿县、伊丽莎白市、约克、安公主与诺福克县，包括诺福克市及普茨茅斯市除外）。同时明确规定，目前对上述除外的各地区仍然保持本宣言公布前的原状。

根据上述目的以及我本人的权力，我正式命令并宣布：在上述各州及州内部分地区，所有被称为奴隶者，从现在起，获得自由，并永远享有自由的权利。合众国政府，包括陆、海军当局，承认及维护上述人员的自由。

And I hereby enjoin upon the people so declared to be free to abstain from all violence, unless in necessary self-defence; and I recommend to them that, in all case where allowed, they labor faithfully for reasonable wages.

And I further declare and make known that such persons of suitable condition will be received into the armed service of the United States to garrison forts, positions, stations, and other places, and to man vessels of all sorts in said service.

And upon this act, sincerely believed to be an act of justice, warranted by the Constitution upon military necessity, I invoke the considerate judgment of mankind and the gracious favor of Almighty God.

我在此告诫上述宣布获得自由的人员，除了迫不得已的自卫外，应避免使用任何暴力；同时奉劝他们，只要条件允许，在任何条件下都应该勤恳地工作，以取得合理的薪金。

我还要宣布，上述人员如符合条件，可以应征入伍，守卫堡垒要塞、据点兵站及其他地方，亦可在各种军舰上服役。

我真诚地认为，依照宪法规定，必要时动用军事行动保证宣言得以实施，这是正义之举。我请求人们对此行动予以谅解，请求全能的上帝慈悲赐福。

历史链接

南北战争初期联邦政府军失利，为扭转战局，林肯决定以革命方式进行斗争。1862年9月22日，林肯召开内阁会议，公布预告性《解放宣言》。1863年元旦，林肯以总统身份，依据宪法所授予的合众国陆海军总司令的职权颁布了《解放宣言》，此举使大批黑人奴隶参加联邦军队。但《解放宣言》不适用于没有参加叛乱的边界蓄奴州，对这些州的奴隶解放仍按1862年4月国会决议，采取自愿的、逐步的、有偿的方式实行。而且《解放宣言》是作为军事措施颁布的，没有以宪法的形式固定下来。直到1865年和1868年，国会分别通过了宪法第13、14条修正案，才正式废除奴隶制。

感动一个国家的文字

在法庭上的最后陈述
Last Statement to the Court

John Brown／约翰·布朗

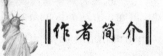

作者简介

约翰·布朗(1800～1859)，一位狂热的废奴主义者，生于康涅狄格州的托灵顿。

I have, may it please the Court, a few words to say.

In the first place, I deny everything but what I have long admitted: of a design on my part to free slaves. I intended certainly to have made a clean thing of that matter, as I did last winter, when I went into Missouri and there took slaves without the snapping of a gun on either side, moving them through the country, and finally leaving them in Canada. I designed to have done the same thing again on a larger scale. That was all I intended. I never did intend murder or treason, or the destruction of property, or to excite or incite slaves to rebellion, or to make insurrection.

I have another objection, and that is that it is unjust that I should suffer such a penalty. Had I interfered in the manner which I admit, and which I admit has been fairly proved—for I admire the truthfulness and candor of the greater portion of the witnesses who have

89

testified in this case — had I so interfered in behalf of the rich, the powerful, the intelligent, the so-called great, or in behalf of any of their friends, either father, mother, brother, sister, wife or children, or any of that class, and suffered and sacrificed what I have in this interference, it would have been all right. Every man in this Court would have deemed it an act worthy of reward rather than punishment.

This Court, acknowledges, too, as I suppose, the validity of the law of God. I see a book kissed, which I suppose to be the Bible, or at least the New Testament, which teaches me that all things whatsoever I would that men should do to me, I should do even so unto them. It teaches me, further, to remember them that are in bonds as bound with them. I endeavored to act up to that instruction. I say I am yet too young to understand that God is any respecter of persons. I believe that to have interfered as I have done, as I have always freely admitted I have done, in behalf of His despised poor, I did no wrong, but right. Now, if it is deemed necessary that I should forfeit my life for the furtherance of the ends of justice, and mingle my blood further with the blood of my children and with the blood of millions in this slave country whose rights are disregarded by wicked, cruel, and unjust enactments, I say, let it be done.

Let me say one word further. I feel entirely satisfied with the treatment I have received on my trial. Considering all the circumstances, it has been more generous than I expected. But I feel no consciousness of guilt. I have stated from the first what was my intention, and what was not. I never had any design against the liberty of any person, nor any disposition to commit treason or incite slaves to rebel or make any general insurrection. I never encouraged any man to do so, but always discouraged any idea of that kind.

Let me say, also, in regard to the statements made by some of those who were connected with me, I hear it has been stated by some

感动一个国家的文字 . . . .

of them that I have induced them to join me. But the contrary is true.
I do not say this to injure them, but as regretting their weakness. Not
one but joined me of his own accord, and the greater part at their own
expense. A number of them I never saw, and never had a word of
conversation with, till the day they came to me, and that was for the
purpose I have stated.

Now, I have done.

如果法庭允许，我有几句话想说：

首先，除了一直以来我都供认不讳的解放奴隶计划外，我否认任何的事。我确实很想像去年冬天那样，把事情痛痛快快地解决了。当时我进入密苏里，在那里和对方一枪也没有打，就把奴隶带走了，穿越这个国家，最后把他们留在加拿大。我计划把这样的事情再大规模地做一次。我想做的就是这些。我从来就没有过谋杀、叛国或破坏别人财产的念头，还有所谓集训、煽动奴隶反叛或举行暴动之类的事。

我还有另外一项抗议，那就是，我受到这样的惩处是不公正的。如果我干涉此事是以我所承认的方式进行，而且不可否认我所采取的方式已经被公正地证实了——因为我钦佩大部分为本案作证的人持真诚坦率的态度——如果我干预此等事，并且在这干预中受害，是为了富人、有权势的人、有谋略的人、所谓的大人物，或是为了他们的哪个朋友，父母也好、兄弟姐妹也好、妻子儿女也好，或任何与此相类似的人，而牺牲了我的一切，那就没事了。本法庭的每个人就会认为这么一个行动值得嘉奖，而不是要给予处罚。

我想，本法庭也承认上帝的法规是正当可行的。我看到一本书被人们亲吻着，我想这本书是《圣经》或者至少是一本《新约全书》，它给予我教诲，我如果希望人们怎样对待我，我就要以这样的方式对待人。它还教诲我，要铭记那些被奴役的人们，就好像你也和他们一样被奴役。按照这一教诲，我竭尽全力地行动着。我说，我还太年轻，难以理解上帝为什么不一视同仁。我相信：就像我曾经做过的那样——我总是坦率地承认我做的事——为上帝那些受人鄙视的可怜的孩子们采取干预措施，是正确而不是错误的。现在，如果为了推动正义的目标，有必要让我不得不付出生命，必须把我和我的孩子们的鲜血，以及在这个奴隶制国家里，被邪恶残忍、毫无人道的法律所剥夺了权利的千百万人的血混合在一起，我说，那就这么做吧！

让我再说一句。关于对我的审判，我感到完全满意。考虑到诸多情况，它比我所预想的要宽容多了。但我并不觉得自己是个罪人。我一开始就陈述了我的意图是什么，而不是什么。我从未谋划要反对任何人的自由，从未企图去叛国，从未煽动奴隶反叛或举行大规模的暴动。我从未唆使任何人这么做，相反，我总是规劝人们摈弃这念头。

对于那些与我有关的人所作的陈述，我也有几句话要说。我听说他们中有些人说我诱使他们加入团伙。但事实恰恰相反。我这样说不是为了伤害他们，而是对他们的软弱深表遗憾。他们中没有一个人不是自愿加入我的队伍，而且大部分人还自己承担费用。他们中的许多人来找我之前，我从未与他们谋面，也从未与他们说过一句话，而他们来找我，就是为了我所陈述的那个意图。

现在，我说完了。

历史链接

1856年，布朗获悉赞成奴隶制的人洗劫了堪萨斯的劳伦斯城，他非常愤慨。布朗和他的同伴将五个赞成奴隶制的殖民者从他们家中拖出来砍死。这个事件被称为"波塔沃托米大屠杀"，它导致更多暴力事件发生，致使200多人丧生。1858年，布朗在密苏里又指挥了一次袭击。在那儿，他杀死一个奴隶主，解放了11个奴隶，并带着这些奴隶一起逃到加拿大。1859年10月，约翰·布朗占领了在弗吉尼亚哈泼斯渡口的美国军工厂。在随后与州及联邦军队的一场血战中，这些袭击者们被捕了。布朗于1859年11月2日被判决犯有叛国罪、谋杀罪和煽动叛乱罪，布朗在法庭宣布对他的判决时对法庭发表的陈述，第二天就在《纽约先驱报》登出。在他被处决的那一天，整个北方的人民都把他当做圣人和英雄，向他致敬。

感动一个国家的文字......

Prospectus for *The Liberator*

《解放者》报发刊词

William Lloyd Garrison/ 威廉·劳埃德·加里森

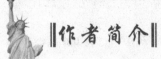

‖作者简介‖

威廉·劳埃德·加里森 (1805~1879)，生于马萨诸塞州，当过新闻记者、职业改革家，他的一生为废奴主义运动、争取妇女权利运动和平主义运动等四处奔走呼号。1831年，他创办了《解放者》报来推进废奴主义事业，他抨击奴隶制的罪恶，呼吁立即解放黑奴。加里森是个杰出的雄辩家，总能一语中的地谴责社会的罪恶。

In the month of August, I issued proposals for publishing "The Liberator" in Washington City; but the enterprise, though hailed in different sections of the country, was palsied by public indifference. Since that time, the removal of the Genius of Universal Emancipation to the Seat of Government has rendered less imperious the establishment of a similar periodical in that quarter.

During my recent tour for the purpose of exciting the minds of the people by a series of discourses on the subject of slavery, every place that I visited gave fresh evidence of the fact, that a greater revolution in public sentiment was to be effected in the free States — and particularly in New-England—than at the South.I found contempt more bitter, opposition more active, detraction more relentless, prejudice more stubborn, and apathy more frozen, than among slave-owners themselves. — Of course, there were individual exceptions to the

contrary. This state of things afflicted, but did not dishearten me. —
I determined, at every hazard, to lift up the standard of emancipation
in the eyes of the nation, within sight of Bunker Hill and in the birth-
place of liberty.— That standard is now unfurled; and long may it
float, unhurt by the spoliations of time or the missiles of a desperate
foe—yea, till every chain be broken, and every bondman set free! Let
Southern oppressors tremble — let their secret abettors tremble — let
their Northern apologists tremble — let all the enemies of the perse-
cuted blacks tremble.

I deem the publication of my original *Prospectus* unnecessary,
as it has obtained a wide circulation. The principles therein inculcated
will be steadily pursued in this paper, excepting that I shall not array
myself as the political partisan of any man. In defending the great
cause of human rights, I wish to derive the assistance of all religions
and of all parties.

Assenting to the" self-evident truth" maintained in the American
Declaration of Independence, "that all men are created equal, and
endowed by their Creator with certain inalienable rights — among
which are Life, Liberty and the pursuit of Happiness, "I shall strenu-
ously contend for the immediate enfranchisement of our slave
population. In Park-Street Church, on the Fourth of July, 1829, I
unreflectingly assented to the popular but pernicious doctrine of gradual
abolition. I seize this moment to make a full and unequivocal recantation,
and thus publicly to ask pardon of my God, of my country, and of my
brethren the poor slaves, for having uttered a sentiment so full of
timidity, injustice, and absurdity. A similar recantation, from my pen,
was published in the Genius of *Universal Emancipation* at Baltimore,

八月份，我在华盛顿发布了出版《解放者》的倡议。虽然在全国不同的地方，都对此事业表示了不同程度的热烈响应，但公众的漠不关心却使之陷入瘫痪状态。从那时起人们就认为，既然《世界解放精神》杂志已经被转移到政府所在地，那么就没有必要立马再在那里创一份相类似的期刊。

这些日子以来，为了激发公众的意识，我到处奔波，发表了一系列关于奴隶问题的演讲。所到之处，我总能获得一些新的例证，即：在自由州，更为巨大的、新一轮的公众革命热情将被重新掀起，尤其是在新英格兰，这种情形比南方诸州更为激烈。我发现在这些地方的反应，比起奴隶主们自己的情绪，那些原本轻蔑的更加不屑一顾，那些反对人士更加积极，那些刻薄贬损斥责的更加无情，而原本就有偏见的则更加固执己见，而漠不关心的也更加冷漠。当然，这里也还会有例外的情形出现。我为这种现状烦恼，却绝不会垂头丧气。我已决定冲破一切艰难险阻，面向近在眼前的邦克山，脚踏这片孕育着自由的土地，让解放的战旗在我们民族的心目中高高飘扬。这面战旗如今已经延展开来，并且将久久地飘扬。岁月的流逝不能损耗她的半点英姿，即使是在敌人疯狂绝望的射击中她也毫发未伤——是的，直至每一根锁链都被毁坏，每一个奴隶都获得自由！让南方的压迫者们瑟瑟发抖吧！让他们的幕后的帮凶们发抖吧！让北方那些为他们狡辩的人们发抖吧！让所有残酷迫害黑人的敌人们发抖吧！

我认为发表我的《发刊词》是不必要的，因为它已经被民众广泛知晓。里面所宣扬的原则将在这份报纸中贯彻执行。但我要声明的是，我将不会为任何党派的观点而游说。在这捍卫人权的伟大事业中，我希望得到所有教派和党派的支持。

我赞同《独立宣言》中主张的"清者自清"的真理，即"人生来平等；他们的创造者赋予他们某些确信无疑、不容剥夺的权利——包括生存权、自由权以及追求幸福的权利"。因此我要为奴隶即将得到自由而努力奋斗。1829年7月4日，我在公园街教堂发表了演说。当时我说我同意那种大众认同的、但又有些不妥的关于一步步地废除奴隶制的观点，现在我认为我当时的观点考虑不周。此刻，

in September, 1829. My conscience is now satisfied.

I am aware that many object to the severity of my language, but is there not cause for severity? I will be as harsh as truth, and as uncompromising as justice. On this subject, I do not wish to think, or to speak, or write, with moderation. No! No! Tell a man whose house is on fire to give a moderate alarm; tell him to moderately rescue his wife from the hands of the ravisher; tell the mother to gradually extricate her babe from the fire into which it has fallen; —but urge me not to use moderation in a cause like the present. I am in earnest—I will not equivocate—I will not excuse—I will not retreat a single inch— AND I WILL BE HEARD. The apathy of the people is enough to make every statue leap from its pedestal, and to hasten the resurrection of the dead.

It is pretended, that I am retarding the cause of emancipation by the coarseness of my invective and the precipitancy of my measures. The charge is not true. On this question of my influence—humble as it is—is felt at this moment to a considerable extent, and shall be felt in coming years —not perniciously, but beneficially—not as a curse, but as a blessing; and posterity will bear testimony that I was right. I desire to thank God, that he enables me to disregard "the fear of man which bringeth a snare", and to speak his truth in its simplicity and power. And here I close with this fresh dedication:

感动一个国家的文字

我要利用这个机会对我的话做一下更正，而且彻底地收回，并且当着公众的面，祈求上帝原谅我、国家原谅我、苦难的奴隶同胞们原谅我，原谅我当时的话多么怯懦、多么不公正和多么荒谬。1829 年 9 月巴尔的摩《普遍解放精神》报上，也同样刊登过关于要收回我的话的内容。只有这样，我的良心才得以安宁。

我知道有很多人对我激烈的言辞表示反对，但表示严肃认真的态度有错吗？我愿如真理般冷酷，如绝不妥协的正义那样坚持。在这个问题上，我不慢条斯理地思考、发言和写文章。不！不！你们可以向一个家中着了火的人温文尔雅地汇报情况，叫他慢慢地从死神手里把妻子抢回来，让做母亲的悠哉游哉地把火坑中的婴儿救出来——但是目前，你们不要奉劝我应该在这个事业中采取谦逊有礼的态度。我有着一颗诚挚的心——我不会说含糊其辞的话——我不会找任何借口——我将寸步不让——人们将听到我的呼喊声。人们冷漠的态度足以让每座雕像跳下它们的底座，足以促进死者更快地复活。

有人说，我在这场解放事业中，用满口粗俗谩骂的言辞和激烈唐突的手段，不过是装腔作势罢了。这样的控告是不真实的。我在这件事情上的影响力——虽然微不足道——此时此刻却已经造成了相当的威慑。在以后的日子里，我的影响将会扩大，它将是有益而不是有害的；是祈福的话语而不是诅咒的话语。我们的子孙后代将会证明我是正确的。我虔诚地感谢上帝，他使我不顾"落入天罗地网的恐惧"，使我能传播他那朴实而强大的真理。在这里，我愿以一首诗来结束我的演讲：

"Oppression! I have seen thee, face to face,
And met thy cruel eye and cloudy brow,
But thy soul-withering glance I fear not now —
For dread to prouder feelings doth give place
Of deep abhorrence! Scorning the disgrace
Of slavish knees that at thy footstool bow,
I also kneel — but with far other vow
Do hail thee and thy herd of hirelings base —
I swear, while life-blood warms my throbbing veins,
Still to oppose and thwart, with heart and hand,
Thy brutalising sway — till Afric's chains
Are burst, and Freedom rules the rescued land —
Trampling Oppression and his iron rod:
Such is the vow I take — SO HELP ME GOD!"

"压迫！我已当面见过你的面目，
见过你残酷的眼神与阴沉沉的额头；
但我已经不再害怕你那让人畏惧的眼神——
因为恐惧会让人产生一种极为讨厌的情绪，
它对跪倒在你脚下
那颜面丧尽的耻辱不屑一顾。
我是跪下了——但绝不奴颜媚骨，
我发誓，当我跳动的脉搏被滚滚热血温暖，
依然以赤胆忠心和双手来反抗和挫败
你那残暴的统治——直到冲破了非洲的锁链，
自由之子光临这片获救的土地——
踏平压迫和它的铁棒：
这就是我的誓言——愿上帝保佑我！"

I Have a Dream
我有一个梦想

Martin Luther King／马丁·路德·金

‖作者简介‖

马丁·路德·金 (1929～1968)，美国著名的黑人民权运动领袖，被誉为近百年来八大最具有说服力的演说家之一。金出身于亚特兰大黑人牧师家庭，15 岁时进入大学，先后获得文学士、神学士及博士学位。金一生曾三次被捕，三次被行刺。1964 年获诺贝尔和平奖。1968 年 4 月 4 日，金在田纳西州孟菲斯被一白人青年雷伊枪杀身亡，年仅 39 岁。

I am happy to join with you today in what will go down in history as the greatest demonstration for freedom in the history of our nation.

Five score years ago, a great American, in whose symbolic shadow we stand today, signed the *Emancipation Proclamation*. This momentous decree came as a great beacon light of hope to millions of Negro slaves who had been seared in the flames of withering injustice. It came as a joyous daybreak to end the long night of captivity.

But one hundred years later, we must face the tragic fact that the Negro is still not free. One hundred years later, the life of the Negro is still sadly crippled by the manacles of segregation and the chains of discrimination. One hundred years later, the Negro lives on a lonely island of poverty in the midst of a vast ocean of material prosperity. One hundred years later, the Negro is still languishing in the corners of American society and finds himself an exile in his own land. So we have come here today to dramatize an appalling condition.

In a sense, we have come to our nation's Capital to cash a check. When the architects of our republic wrote the magnificent words of the Constitution and the *Declaration of Independence*, they were signing a promissory note to which every American was to fall heir. This note was a promise that all men would be guaranteed the inalienable rights of Life, Liberty, and the pursuit of Happiness.

It is obvious today that America has defaulted on this promissory note insofar as her citizens of color are concerned. Instead of honoring this sacred obligation, America has given the Negro people a bad check; a check which has come back marked "insufficient funds". But we refuse to believe that the bank of justice is bankrupt. We refuse to believe that there are insufficient funds in the great vaults of opportunity of this nation. So we have come to cash this check — a check that will give us upon demand the riches of freedom and the security of justice. We have also come to this hallowed spot to remind America of the fierce urgency of now. This is no time to engage in the luxury of cooling off or to take the tranquilizing drug of gradualism. Now is the time to make real the promises of Democracy. Now is the time to rise from the dark and desolate valley of segregation to the sunlit path of racial justice. Now is the time to open the doors of

我很高兴今天和你们一起，为争取自由，参加这次将永垂我国史册的最伟大的示威集会。

一百年前，一位伟大的美国人——今天我们就站在他的雕像下——正式签署了《解放宣言》。这项重要法令的颁布，如一座伟大的灯塔，照亮了当时挣扎于不义之火焚烤下的数百万黑奴的希望；它像欢快的破晓曙光，结束了黑人陷于囹圄的漫漫长夜。

然而，整整一百年过去了，我们却仍然得面对这个悲惨的现实：黑人依然得不到自由；整整一百年过去了，黑人依然被种族隔离的镣铐和种族歧视的锁链羁绊着，举步维艰；整整一百年过去了，在物质繁荣的汪洋大海之中，黑人却依然独自生存在贫穷的孤岛之上；整整一百年过去了，黑人依然在美国社会的阴暗角落里向隅而泣，在自己的土地上却依然流离失所。因此，我们今天来到这里，把这种骇人听闻的情况公布于众。

在某种意义上，我们今天来首都是为了兑现一张支票。我们共和国的缔造者在撰写美国宪法以及独立宣言的壮丽篇章时，就签署了一张支票，并规定每个美国人都有权继承。这张支票承诺，所有的人——不论白人还是黑人——都拥有不可剥夺的生存、自由，以及追求幸福的权利。

显然，今天美国拒绝向她的有色公民承兑这张支票。美国拒不履行这项神圣的义务，却退给黑人同胞一张空头支票，一张标明"现金不足"的空头支票。但是，我们决不相信正义的银行会破产，我们决不相信这个国家装满机遇的巨大宝库居然会出现现金不足的窘

opportunity to all of God's children. Now is the time to lift our nation from the quicksands of racial injustice to the solid rock of brotherhood.

It would be fatal for the nation to overlook the urgency of the moment and to underestimate the determination of the Negro. This sweltering summer of the Negro's legitimate discontent will not pass until there is an invigorating autumn of freedom and equality. Nineteen sixty-three is not an end, but a beginning. Those who hope that the Negro needed to blow off steam and will now be content will have a rude awakening if the nation returns to business as usual. There will be neither rest nor tranquility in America until the Negro is granted his citizenship rights. The whirlwinds of revolt will continue to shake the foundations of our nation until the bright day of justice emerges.

But there is something that I must say to my people who stand on the warm threshold which leads into the palace of justice. In the process of gaining our rightful place we must not be guilty of wrongful deeds. Let us not seek to satisfy our thirst for freedom by drinking from the cup of bitterness and hatred.

We must forever conduct our struggle on the high plane of dignity and discipline. We must not allow our creative protest to degenerate into physical violence. Again and again we must rise to the majestic heights of meeting physical force with soul force. The marvelous new militancy which has engulfed the Negro community must not lead us to distrust of all white people, for many of our white brothers, as evidenced by their presence here today, have come to realize that their destiny is tied up with our destiny and their freedom

况。因此，我们来兑现这张支票——兑现
这张承诺一经要求将给我们以宝贵的自由和
正义的保障的支票。此外，我们来到这个神圣
之地，还为了要提醒美国，事情的解决已经迫在眉睫，
再没时间让我们奢言冷静，或拿渐进主义当镇静剂了。
现在是实现民主诺言的时候了；现在是走出阴暗荒芜的种
族隔离深谷，踏上种族平等的阳光大道的时候了；现在是向上帝所
有的孩子打开机遇大门的时候了；现在是把我们的国家从种族不平
等的流沙中托起，安放在手足之情铸就的磐石之上的时候了。

　　低估此事的紧迫性，或者低估黑人的决心，将给这个国家带来
不堪设想的后果。自由平等的朗朗秋日不到来，黑人合理愤怒的炙
人酷暑就不会过去。1963年不是此事的结束，而仅仅是一个开始。
如果这个国家依然无动于衷，我行我素，那么，那些曾希望黑人只
需发泄怒火就会心平气和的人就会猛醒。黑人一天得不到他的公民
权利，美国就休想获得片刻安宁。抗争的飓风将继续摇动着国家的
基石，直至光明璀璨的正义之日浮现眼前。

　　但是，我有一些话要告诫站在通向正义殿堂温暖门槛上的同胞
们。在争取合法地位的过程中，我们切不可因一步踏错而犯罪；我
们切不可因对自由的渴望，而痛饮仇恨的苦酒。

　　我们应该在斗争中永远表现出我们崇高的尊严和纪律。我们不
能容忍我们富于创造的抗争沦为粗野的暴动。我们应该一次次地把
自己提升到用灵魂的力量对抗对手的有形暴力的崇高境界。这场已
经席卷了整个黑人社会的非凡斗争，不应该把我们引入不信任所有

is inextricably bound to our freedom. We cannot walk alone.

And as we walk, we must make the pledge that we shall march ahead. We cannot turn back. There are those who are asking the devotees of civil rights,"When will you be satisfied?" We can never be satisfied as long as the Negro is the victim of the unspeakable horrors of police brutality.

We can never be satisfied as long as our bodies, heavy with the fatigue of travel, cannot gain lodging in the motels of the highways and the hotels of the cities.

We cannot be satisfied as long as the Negro's basic mobility is from a smaller ghetto to a larger one.

We can never be satisfied as long as our children are stripped of their selfhood and robbed of their dignity by signs stating "For Whites Only".

We can never be satisfied as long as a Negro in Mississippi cannot vote and a Negro in New York believes he has nothing for which to vote. No, no, we are not satisfied, and we will not be satisfied until justice rolls down like waters and righteousness like a mighty stream.

I am not unmindful that some of you have come here out of great trials and tribulations. Some of you have come fresh from narrow jail cells. Some of you have come from areas where your quest for freedom left you battered by the storms of persecution and staggered by the winds of police brutality. You have been the veterans of creative suffering. Continue to work with the faith that unearned suffering is redemptive.

Go back to Mississippi, go back to Alabama, go back to South Carolina, go back to Georgia, go back to Louisiana, go back to the slums and ghettos of our Northern cities, knowing that somehow this situation can and will be changed. Let us not wallow in the valley of despair.

感动一个国家的文字

白人的歧途——因为许多白人兄弟已经看到：我们彼此的命运紧紧相连，我们彼此的自由密不可分——今天，他们来参加我们这个集会就是对此最好的证明。我们不能独自前行。

而一旦开始行动，我们就必须确保勇往直前，我们无路可退。有人问献身于民权运动的人："你们什么时候才能满意？"我们永不满意，只要黑人仍然是不堪形容的警察野蛮暴行的牺牲品。

历经跋涉后，我们仍然不能为自己疲倦的身躯在公路上的客栈和城市里的旅馆找到一席之地。

我们永不满意，假如黑人的基本活动范围只是从窄小的贫民窟变成一个稍大的黑人居住区。

我们永不满意，假如我们的孩子仍然会看到"白人专用"的告示——那些剥夺了他们人格，践踏了他们自尊的告示。

我们永不满意，假如密西西比州的黑人依然不能投票，而纽约的黑人依然认为自己的投票毫无意义。不，我们并不满意，也永远不可能满意，除非正义如泉奔涌，公正如潮澎湃。

我不会忘记，你们中有些人经过重重磨难才能来到这里，有人刚刚从狭小的牢笼里放出，有人来自追求自由却惨遭迫害暴雨捶打和警察暴力飓风肆虐的地区。你们是久经磨难的老兵。那么，继续奋斗下去吧，要坚信：总有一天，无辜受难的人们终会得到拯救。

回到密西西比去吧，回到阿拉巴马去吧，回到南卡罗来纳去吧，回到佐治亚去吧，回到路易斯安那去吧，回到我们北方城市中的贫民窟和黑人居住区去吧。要知道，这种处境是可以而且一定能够改变的。我们切莫再沉湎于绝望的深谷之中。

105

I say to you today, my friends, that in spite of the difficulties and frustrations of the moment, I still have a dream. It is a dream deeply rooted in the American dream.

I have a dream that one day this nation will rise up and live out the true meaning of its creed: "We hold these truths to be self-evident: that all men are created equal."

I have a dream that one day on the red hills of Georgia the sons of former slaves and the sons of former slave-owners will be able to sit down together at a table of brotherhood.

I have a dream that one day even the state of Mississippi, a desert state, sweltering with the heat of injustice and oppression, will be transformed into an oasis of freedom and justice.

I have a dream that my four little children will one day live in a nation where they will not be judged by the color of their skin but by the content of their character.

I have a dream today.

I have a dream that one day the state of Alabama, whose governor's lips are presently dripping with the words of interposition and nullification, will be transformed into a situation where little black boys and black girls will be able to join hands with little white boys and white girls and walk together as sisters and brothers.

I have a dream today.

I have a dream that one day every valley shall be exalted, every hill and mountain shall be made low, the rough places will be made plain, and the crooked places will be made straight, and the glory of the Lord shall be revealed, and all flesh shall see it together.

This is our hope. This is the faith with which I return to the South. With this faith we will be able to hew out of the mountain of despair a

朋友们，今天我要告诉你们，尽管此刻困难挫折重重，但我仍然有一个梦想。这个梦深深扎根于伟大的美国之梦。

　　我有个梦想：总有一天这个国家奋然而起，实现其信条的真谛："我们认为这些真理不言自明，每个人生来就是平等的。"

　　我有个梦想：总有一天在佐治亚州的红土山坡上，昔日奴隶的儿子与昔日主人的儿子能够如兄弟手足般同榻而坐。

　　我有个梦想：总有一天就算是密西西比这样一个被不公正与种族压迫的热潮所统治着的荒漠之州，也能转变成一方自由和正义的绿洲。

　　我有个梦想：总有一天我的四个孩子将生活在一个不是以他们的肤色，而是以他们内在品质来评价他们的国度中。

　　今天，我有一个梦想。

　　我有个梦想：总有一天阿拉巴马州——该州州长今天仍在喋喋不休地说着不同意也不执行联邦法令的话语——能有所不同，黑人的小男孩与小女孩能够和白人的小男孩与小女孩如兄弟姐妹般地携手同行。

　　今天，我有一个梦想。

　　我有个梦想：总有一天我们会填平所有的峡谷，夷平所有的山丘，崎岖之地将变为坦荡的平原，曲折之路将变为笔直的大道；主的荣光将会显现，芸芸众生同声赞叹。

　　这是我们的渴望，也是将随我返回南方去的信念。靠着这个信念，我们就能把绝望之山开凿成希望之石。靠着这个信念，我们就

stone of hope. With this faith we will be able to transform the jangling discords of our nation into a beautiful symphony of brotherhood. With this faith we will be able to work together, to pray together, to struggle together, to go to jail together, to stand up for freedom together, knowing that we will be free one day.

This will be the day when all of God's children will be able to sing with a new meaning, "My country 'tis of thee, sweet land of liberty, of thee I sing. Land where my fathers died, land of the pilgrim's pride, from every mountainside, let freedom ring."

And if America is to be a great nation, this must become true.

So let freedom ring from the prodigious hilltops of New Hampshire. Let freedom ring from the mighty mountains of New York. Let freedom ring from the heightening Alleghenies of Pennsylvania!

Let freedom ring from the snowcapped Rockies of Colorado!

Let freedom ring from the curvaceous peaks of California!

But not only that; let freedom ring from Stone Mountain of Georgia!

Let freedom ring from Lookout Mountain of Tennessee!

Let freedom ring from every hill and every molehill of Mississippi. From every mountainside, let freedom ring.

When we allow freedom ring, when we let it ring from every village and every hamlet, from every state and every city, we will be able to speed up that day when all of God's children, black men and white men, Jews and Gentiles, Protestants and Catholics, will be able to join hands and sing in the words of the old Negro spiritual,"Free at last! Free at last! Thank God almighty, we are free at last!"

能把我们国家里种族争斗的不和谐之音，转谱成一曲兄弟般友爱的动人交响曲。靠着这个信念，我们就能共同工作，共同祈盼，共同战斗，共同昂首入狱，共同维护自由。我们已经知道，总有一天，我们会获得自由。

当这一天到来之时，上帝所有的子民都能以全新的意义高唱：我的祖国，亲爱的自由之邦，我为你歌唱。这是祖先安息的故园，这是朝圣者为之自豪的土地。让自由之声在每一座山峰回响！

当美国要成为真正伟大的国家，这一切必将成真。

因此，让自由之声在新罕布什尔州的巍峨高峰回响！让自由之声在纽约州的雄伟山脉中回响！让自由之声在宾夕法尼亚州高耸的阿勒格尼山峰回响！

让自由之声在科罗拉多州白雪皑皑的洛基山回响！

让自由之声在加利福尼亚州的柔美群峰回响！

不，不仅如此，让自由之声在佐治亚州的石山回响！

让自由之声在田纳西州的远眺山峰回响！

让自由之声在密西西比州的每一座山冈，每一座丘陵回响！

让自由之声在每一处山坡回响！

当我们让自由之声回响时，当我们让自由之声在每一个山村，每一处村寨，每一个州，每一座城回响时，我们就能让这一天早日降临。到那时，上帝所有的孩子——白人与黑人，犹太人与非犹太人，基督教徒与天主教徒——携手同唱那首古老的黑人圣歌："终于自由了！终于自由了！感谢全能的上帝，我们终于自由了！"

The Seneca Falls Declaration of Sentiments and Resolutions

塞尼卡福尔斯感伤宣言与决议

Elizabeth Cady Stanton/伊丽莎白·凯蒂·斯坦顿

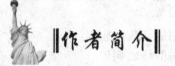 **||作者简介||**

伊丽莎白·凯蒂·斯坦顿（1815~1902），美国女权运动的伟大领袖，1848年7月19日至20日，她与其她四位妇女筹划召开一次会议，"讨论社会、公民、宗教状况和妇女的权利问题"。在斯坦顿的领导下，小组起草了一个模仿《独立宣言》的《感伤宣言》。大约100名妇女和男士聚会纽约的塞尼卡福尔斯，讨论、修改并接受了她们的《宣言》。比起普遍蔑视妇女权利，尤其是蔑视妇女投票权的舆论来，她们要进步得多。

1. Declaration of Sentiments

When, in the course of human events, it becomes necessary for one portion of the family of man to assume among the people of the earth a position different from that which they have hitherto occupied, but one to which the laws of nature and of nature's God entitle them, a decent respect to the opinions of mankind requires that they should declare the causes that impel them to such a course.

We hold these truths to be self-evident: that all men and women are created equal; that they are endowed by their Creator with certain inalienable rights; that among these are life, liberty, and the pursuit of happiness; that to secure these rights governments are instituted, deriving their just powers from the consent of the governed. Whenever any form of government becomes destructive of these ends, it is the right of those who suffer from it to refuse allegiance to it, and to insist upon the institution of a new government, laying its foundation on such principles, and organizing its powers in such form, as to them shall seem most likely to effect their safety and happiness. Prudence, indeed, will dictate that governments long established should not be changed for light and transient causes; and accordingly all experience hath shown that mankind are more disposed to suffer, while evils are sufferable, than to right themselves by abolishing the forms to which they are accustomed. But when a long train of abuses and usurpations,

1. 感伤宣言

在有关人类事务的发展进程中，当一部分人类家庭不得不依照自然法则和上帝的旨意，在人们之间接受妇女今非昔比的地位时，为了尊重人类的舆论，必须把妇女迫不得已而做出这样决定的原因予以宣布。

我们认为以下的真理是不可否认的：男人与妇女生而平等；造物者赋予她们某些不容剥夺的权利，其中有生命权、自由权和追求幸福的权利，政府的建立就是为了保障这些权利，而政府所拥有的正当权力，是经过被统治者的同意而产生的——不管哪种形式的政府要来破坏这些目标，受到伤害的人民就有权利拒绝对它忠诚，从而要求重新建立一个政府；莫基这个新政府的原则和它权力的组织方式，要建立在人民确认的基础上，只有这样才是最可能保障他们获得安全和幸福的。为了慎重起见，成立多年的政

pursuing invariably the same object, evinces a design to reduce them under absolute despotism, it is their duty to throw off such government, and to provide new guards for their future security. Such has been the patient sufferance of the women under this government, and such is now the necessity which constrains them to demand the equal station to which they are entitled. The history of mankind is a history of repeated injuries and usurpations on the part of man toward woman, having in direct object the establishment of an absolute tyranny over her. ···

···

Now, in view of this entire disfranchisement of one-half the people of this country, their social and religious degradation — in view of the unjust laws above mentioned, and because women do feel themselves aggrieved, oppressed, and fraudulently deprived of their most sacred rights, we insist that they have immediate admission to all the rights and privileges which belong to them as citizens of the United States.

In entering upon the great work before us, we anticipate no small amount of misconception, misrepresentation, and ridicule; but we shall use every instrumentality within our power to effect our object. We shall employ agents, circulate tracts, petition the State and National legislatures, and endeavor to enlist the pulpit and the press in our behalf. We hope this Convention will be followed by a series of Conventions embracing every part of the country.

2. Resolutions

Whereas, The great precept of nature is conceded to be, that "man shall pursue his own true and substantial happiness",Blackstone in his Commentaries remarks, that this law of Nature being coeval

感动一个国家的文字 . . . . . .

府不应该因为那些轻微和暂时性的原因而被变更。过去的一切经验也表明，人们对于任何尚且能忍受的苦难，都愿意忍受，而无意为了自身的利益就废除他们习惯多时的政府。但是，当一连串滥用职权和强行剥夺的行为在一个共同目标的驱使下发生时，就表明政府企图要用专制的政策来统制妇女。既然这样，她们就有义务推翻这个政府，并为她们未来的安全建立新的保障。在过去，妇女就是这样逆来顺受的，现在则成了为什么现在她们不得不要求自己有权得到地位的原因。人类的历史是一部男人对妇女进行不间断地伤害与掠夺的历史，这种行为的直接目的是对妇女建立绝对的暴政专制。……

……

现在，完全没有选举权的人数已经占据了全国人口的一半。她们在社会、宗教上都受到不公正的待遇。面对上面这些不公正的法律条文，和妇女实实在在感受到的冤屈和压迫，以及最神圣的权力被人蒙骗的事实，我们坚决要求立刻赋予所有妇女作为美国公民应当拥有的权利和特权。

在我们伟大的工作开始时，我们预测将会遭遇扑面而来的误解、谣传和嘲讽。不过，我们仍将全力以赴来实现我们的目标，我们将聘请代理人，大范围地宣传，向政府和立法机构请愿，努力争取教会与新闻界的支持。我们希望此次大会后，在全国各地将会相继召开一系列的会议。

2.决议

鉴于"人类必须追求真正意义上的幸福"被一致认为是自然的伟大法则，布莱克斯通在评论中指出，这是一条与人类共存亡的自然法则，是上帝亲赋的法则；理所当然也比任何其他法则具有更高的约束性。在全世界，所有国家里，无论何时，这条法则都具有约

with mankind, and dictated by God himself, is of course superior in obligation to any other. It is binding over all the globe, in all countries and at all times; no human laws are of any validity if contrary to this, and such of them as are valid, derive all their force, and all their validity, and all their authority, mediately and immediately, from this original; therefore,

Resolved, That such laws as conflict, in any way with the true and substantial happiness of woman, are contrary to the great precept of nature and of no validity, for this is "superior in obligation to any other".

Resolved, That all laws which prevent woman from occupying such a station in society as her conscience shall dictate, or which place her in a position inferior to that of man, are contrary to the great precept of nature, and therefore of no force or authority.

Resolved, That woman is man's equal — was intended to be so by the Creator, and the highest good of the race demands that she should be recognized as such.

Resolved, That the women of this country ought to be enlightened in regard to the laws under which they live, that they may no longer publish their degradation by declaring themselves satisfied with their present position, nor their ignorance by asserting that they have all the rights they want.

Resolved, That inasmuch as man, while claiming for himself intellectual superiority does accord to woman moral superionty, it is preeminently his duty to encourage her to speak and teach, as she has an opportunity, in all religious assemblies.

Resolved, That the same amount of virtue, delicacy, and refinement of behavior that is required of woman in the social state, should also be required of man, and the same transgressions should be visited with equal severity on both man and woman.

感动一个国家的文字 . . . . . .

束性。任何人类的法则如果与之相矛盾，都不具有任何效力。只有那些间接地或直接地从这一根源衍生的法律才具有效力和权威。

决议认为，不管什么形式，只要是与妇女真正意义上的幸福相冲突的法律，都是与自然的伟大法则相违背的，都是无效的，因为"自然的伟大法则的约束性是建立在所有其他法则之上的"。

决议认为，一切阻挡妇女获取道义作为谋取必要社会地位的法律，一切主张男尊女卑的法律，都是与自然的伟大法则背道而驰的，因而也是不具备任何法律效力或权威的。

决议认为，造物主的旨意是男女平等，人类道义善心的最高境界是争取男女平等。

决议认为，应当开化我国的妇女，让她们了解那些制约她们生活的法律，这样她们就不会对妇女目前的地位表示心满意足，从而表现出自己的低能，她们也不会声称自己已经拥有想要的一切权利，从而表现出自己的愚昧。

决议认为，既然男人宣称他在智商上相对优越，并且承认妇女在道德方面相对优越，那么男人的一个显而易见的责任就是，正如容许妇女在所有宗教团体中有机会做到的那样，鼓励妇女畅所欲言、为人师表。

决议认为，在社会上，在道德和行为举止文明礼仪等方面，对男士提出的要求也应当和妇女一样。男女犯下的罪若性质相同，应当受到同样的严厉制裁。

伊丽莎白·凯蒂·斯坦顿
与苏姗·B.安东尼 ▶

115

Resolved, That the objection of indelicacy and impropriety, which is so often brought against woman when she addresses a public audience, comes with a very ill-grace from those who encourage, by their attendance, her appearance on the stage, in the concert or in feats of the circus.

Resolved, That woman has too long rested satisfied in the circumscribed limits which corrupt customs and a perverted application of the Scriptures have marked out for her, and that it is time she should move in the enlarged sphere which her great Creator has assigned her.

Resolved, That it is the duty of the women of this country to secure to themselves their sacred right to the elective franchise.

Resolved, That the equality of human rights results necessarily from the fact of the identity of the race in capabilities and responsibilities.

Resolved, therefore, That being invested by the creator with the same capabilities, and the same consciousness of responsibility for their exercise, it is demonstrably the right and duty of woman, equally with man, to promote every righteous cause by every righteous means; and especially in regard to the great subjects of morals and religion, it is self-evidently her right to participate with her brother in teaching them, both in private and in public, by writing and by speaking, by any instrumentalities proper to be used and in any assemblies proper to be held; and this being a self-evident truth growing out of the divinely implanted principles of human nature, any custom or authority adverse to it, whether modern or wearing the hoary sanction of antiquity, is to be regarded as a self-evident falsehood, and at war with mankind.

Resolved, That the speedy success of our cause depends upon the zealous and untiring efforts of both men and women, for the overthrow of the monopoly of the pulpit and for the securing to women an equal participation with men in the various trades, professions, and commerce.

妇女在公开场合发表演说，常常招致某些人无礼的攻击，而这些人却以亲临现场的方式怂恿妇女登台演出、举行音乐会或在马戏院登台献艺。决议认为，这种攻击是极不得体的。

决议认为，妇女对于各种限制已经处于长期的麻木状态。这些限制的设置是败落的习俗和对《圣经》的肆意曲解造成的。现在妇女即将步入一片更为广阔的天地，一片伟大的造物主恩赐给她的天地。

决议认为，保障妇女神圣的选举权是本国妇女的职责。

决议认为，每个人的能力与责任相同这一事实必然产生人权平等的结果。

因此，决议认为，既然造物主赋予男女同等的能力和维护这些能力的同等责任感，所以显而易见，男女有着相同的权利和责任，来采取一切公正的手段促进所有正义事业的进行，在道德和宗教这些重大的问题上更是如此。毋庸置疑，妇女有权同她的兄弟一样能够在私下和公开的场合，发表文章和演讲，在任何合法的集会上运用任何合理的手段，开诚布公地宣讲。这是无可争议的真理，它诞生于人类本性的神圣原则中，任何与之相违背的习俗和权威，不论是现代的还是已经磨损发白的古老法则，都将被看做是不容争辩的谬误，是与人类利益相违背的。

决议认为，我们事业成功进程的加快，取决于男人与妇女的执著的热情和努力，推翻教会的独裁，确保让妇女在各行各业享有与男子同样的参与权。

Women's Right to Vote
妇女的选举权

Susan B. Anthony／苏珊·B.安东尼

‖作者简介‖

　　苏珊·B.安东尼（1820~1906），出生于马萨诸塞州，她曾经做过小学教师。身为一个独身妇女，她强烈地意识到妇女需要政治和经济上的独立。1851年，她遇到当时女权主义运动的另一领袖伊利莎白·凯蒂·斯坦顿，她们成了工作中的伙伴，终身保持着这一关系，而她们的合作关系决定了美国女权主义运动的进程。

　　在1872年的总统大选中，安东尼带领一群纽约州的妇女到当地投票地点参加投票。因为当时妇女投票是非法的，所以她被逮捕并于1873年6月被传讯。在此之前，她前往纽约州北部的大部分地区进行以下的演讲，说明剥夺妇女的选举权是不合理的。但她最终被判有罪并加以罚款，不过她拒付罚金，而且也没有人向她索取。

Friends and fellow citizens,

　　I stand before you tonight under indictment for the alleged crime of having voted at the last presidential election, without having a lawful right to vote. It shall be my work this evening to prove to you that in this voting, I not only committed no crime, but, instead, simply exercised my citizen's rights, guaranteed to me and all United States citizens by the National Constitution, beyond the power of any state to deny.

感动一个国家的文字

The preamble of the Federal Constitution says,

"We, the people of the United States, in order to form a more perfect union, establish justice, insure domestic tranquillity, provide for the common defense, promote the general welfare, and secure the blessings of liberty to ourselves and our posterity, do ordain and establish this Constitution for the United States of America."

It was we, the people; not we, the white male citizens; nor yet we, the male citizens; but we, the whole people, who formed the Union. And we formed it, not to give the blessings of liberty, but to secure them; not to the half of ourselves and the half of our posterity, but to the whole people—women as well as men. And it is a down-right mockery to talk to women of their enjoyment of the blessings

朋友们，公民们：

今天晚上，我带着罪名站在你们面前。在上次总统选举时，我因为没有合法选举权投了票而被指控为有罪。今天晚上我将向你们解释，在这次选举中我不但没有犯罪，相反我只是行使了我的公民权，行使了《合众国宪法》赋予给我和全体美国公民的公民权。《合众国宪法》是任何州都无法否定的根本大法。

《合众国宪法》的序言说：

"我们，美国的人民，为了形成更完美的统一，建立正义，确保国内安定，提供正常防御，促进公众的幸福和保证我们自己和我们子孙后代的自由，特此建立这部《美利坚合众国宪法》。"

是我们，人民；不是我们，男性白人公民；也不是我们，男性公民；而是我们整个人民，形成统一的联邦。我们成立统一的联邦，不是给予自由，而是保证自由；自由不是我们当中的一半人和我们的子孙后代当中的一半人享受，而是全体人民——男人们和女人们享受。因而当妇女被剥夺了确保她们自由权利的唯一手段——选举

of liberty while they are denied the use of the only means of securing them provided by this democratic- republican government—the ballot.

…

For any state to make sex a qualification that must ever result in the disfranchisement of one entire half of the people is to pass a bill of attainder, or an ex post facto law, and is therefore a violation of the supreme law of the land. By it the blessings of liberty are forever withheld from women and their female posterity. To them this government has no just powers derived from the consent of the governed. To them this government is not a democracy. It is not a republic. It is an odious aristocracy; a hateful oligarchy of sex; the most hateful aristocracy ever established on the face of the globe; an oligarchy of wealth, where the rich govern the poor. An oligarchy of learning, where the educated govern the ignorant, or even an oligarchy of race, where the Saxon rules the African, might be endured; but this oligarchy of sex, which makes father, brothers, husband, sons, the oligarchs over the mother and sisters, the wife and daughters, of every household — which ordains all men sovereigns, all women subjects, carries dissension, discord, and rebellion into every home of the nation.

Webster, Worcester, and Bouvier all define a citizen to be a person in the United States, entitled to vote and hold office.

The only question left to be settled now is: Are women persons? And I hardly believe any of our opponents will have the hardihood to say they are not. Being persons, then, women are citizens; and no state has a right to make any law, or to enforce any old law, that shall abridge their privileges or immunities. Hence, every discrimination against women in the constitutions and laws of the several states is today null and void, precisely as is every one against Negroes.

感动一个国家的文字 . . . . . .

权——的时候，却对她们谈什么自由之幸福，完全是彻头彻尾的讽刺。

．　……

对于任何一个国家来说，如果把性别规定为一种限制条件，它必将造成整整一半的人民被剥夺公民权。这样做就等于通过一项剥夺逃犯或死囚的政治权利的议案，即一项溯及已往的法律，因此这是对这个国家的最高法律的亵渎。根据这种做法，自由从妇女和她们的女性后代身上被夺走了。她们认为，如果得不到被统治者的允许，这个政府没有正当的权力；她们认为，这个政府不是民主政府，不是共和政府，它是个臭名昭著的独裁政府，是令人憎恨的性别寡头政权，是地球上最令人憎恨的独裁政权。人们可以忍受一个财富寡头政权——富人统治穷人的政权，可以忍受一个知识寡头政权——有学问的人统治没有学问的人的政权，　但是一个性别寡头统治，一个由各个家庭的父亲、兄弟、丈夫、儿子组成的寡头统治，一个使男人成为君主、女人成为臣民的寡头统治，将会把分裂、混乱和反叛带入这个国家的每个家庭之中。

韦氏词典、乌斯特词典和波维尔词典都把公民定义为美国的一个人，一个被赋予了选举权和参政权的人。

现在摆在我们面前并需要解决的唯一问题是：女人是人吗？我很难相信，反对我们的任何一个人会硬着心肠说女人不是人。那么既然是人，女人也就是公民，因此任何州都无权制定或执行任何剥夺她们公民特权或豁免权的法律。所以在几个州的宪法和法律中，那些歧视妇女的法律统统都是无效的，正如歧视黑人的法律是无效的一样。

Statement to the Court
对法庭的声明

Eugene Victor Debs／尤金·维克托·德布斯

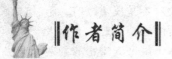

尤金·维克托·德布斯(1855~1926)，美国工人运动领导人，1898年协助创立美国社会党，并于1900年成为该党总统候选人。

德布斯和其他社会党人反对美国卷入第一次世界大战。由于他严厉批评威尔逊政府，于1918年6月以违犯1917年间谍法被捕。在德布斯发表了以下这篇讲话后，法官判他10年徒刑。

Your Honor, years ago I recognized my kinship with all living beings, and I made up my mind that I was not one bit better than the meanest on earth. I said then, and I say now, that while there is a lower class, I am in it, and while there is a criminal element I am of it, and while there is a soul in prison, I am not free.

I listened to all that was said in this court in support and justification of this prosecution, but my mind remains unchanged. I look upon the Espionage Law as a despotic enactment in flagrant conflict with democratic principles and with the spirit of free institutions…

感动一个国家的文字......

Your Honor, I have stated in this court that I am opposed to the social system in which we live; that I believe in a fundamental change—but if possible by peaceable and orderly means.

...

In this country—the most favored beneath the bending skies—we have vast areas of the richest and most fertile soil, material resources in inexhaustible abundance, the most marvelous productive machinery on earth, and millions of eager workers ready to apply their labor to that machinery to produce in abundance for every man, woman, and child—and if there are still vast numbers of our people who are the victims of poverty and whose lives are an unceasing struggle all the way from youth to old age, until at last death comes to their rescue and lulls these hapless victims to dreamless sleep, it is not the fault of the Almighty: It cannot be charged to nature, but it is due

阁下，若干年以前我认识到与所有生物都有亲属关系，并依此断定我不比世界上最卑贱的人好到哪里去。当时我是这么说的，现在也还这样说：只要还有底层社会存在，我就是其中一员；只要还有罪犯的元素，我就是它的构成之一；只要还有人被囚禁在牢狱中，我就不是自由人。

我在法庭上听了支持这一起诉和为之辩护的所有证词，但我的想法始终如一。在我看来，间谍法是与民主原则和自由制度的精神公然对抗的蛮横法令……

阁下，我在法庭上已经说过，我对我们现在的社会制度持反对态度；我坚信有必要做彻底的改变——尽可能采用和平的、有礼有节的手段。

……

我们这个国家有着优越的条件：我们土地辽阔而且富饶肥沃，我们有着取之不尽的原料资源，我们的机器设备是世界上生产力最强大的，为了我们国家的每个公民、每个儿童都能够享受这机器带来的利益，工人们使用这些机器制造出大量的产品。而如果我国继

entirely to the outgrown social system in which we live that ought to be abolished not only in the interest of the toiling masses but in the higher interest of all humanity.

I believe, Your Honor, in common with all Socialists, that this nation ought to own and control its own industries. I believe, as all Socialists do, that all things that are jointly needed and used ought to be jointly owned—that industry, the basis of our social life, instead of being the private property of a few and operated for their enrichment, ought to be the common property of all, democratically administered in the interest of all.

I am opposing a social order in which it is possible for one man who does absolutely nothing that is useful to amass a fortune of hundreds of millions of dollars, while millions of men and women who work all the days of their lives secure barely enough for a wretched existence.

This order of things cannot always endure. I have registered my protest against it. I recognize the feebleness of my effort, but, fortunately, I am not alone. There are multiplied thousands of others who, like myself, have come to realize that before we may truly enjoy the blessings of civilized life, we must reorganize society upon a mutual and cooperative basis; and to this end we have organized a great economic and political movement that spreads over the face of all the earth.

There are today upwards of sixty millions of Socialists, loyal, devoted adherents to this cause, regardless of nationality, race, creed, color, or sex. They are all making common cause. They are spreading with tireless energy the propaganda of the new social order. They are waiting, watching, and working hopefully through all the hours of the day and the night. They are still in a minority. But they have learned how to be patient and to bide their time. The feel — they

续有大量的人民沦为贫穷的殉葬品，一辈子疲于奔命，直到死亡来解脱他们，让他们的心不再痛苦，让这些不幸的被害者进入没有梦魇的长眠之中——那么，这样的罪过不是上帝造成的，不是自然造成的，而是我们畸形的社会制度造成的，这种社会制度应该被灭亡，这不仅是为劳动大众谋利，也是为所有的人类谋利。

阁下，我同其他社会党人一致认为，这个国家应当拥有并控制它自己的工业。我与其他社会党人都认为，全民应当共同拥有一切人们所需要和使用的东西——工业作为社会生活的基础，不应成为少数人的私有财产，为他们积累财富而运转，工业应成为全民所有的共同财产，为了全民的利益应当对其实行民主化的管理。

我反对这样的社会秩序，它让一个对社会毫无贡献的人成为亿万富翁，而让百万劳苦大众在贫困线上挣扎。

这种秩序不会永久长存。我已表达了我的抗议。我承认自己的努力不值一提，但值得庆幸的是我并非孤军作战。千千万万的人有着和我一样的意识，我们必须在共同合作的基础上建立社会，只有这样才能真正享受幸福的文明生活；为了这个目标，我们已组织起一个在全球内开展的伟大的经济政治运动。

如今社会党人已超过六百万，他们虽然国籍、种族、宗教、肤色、性别都各不相同，但都忠贞不渝地对待这一事业。他们正为共同的事业而行动。他们广泛宣传新的社会秩序，没有任何倦怠。他们等待着，观察着，充满了希望夜以继日地工作。虽然他们还是少数派，但他们知道该如何耐心地等待时机来临。他们感觉到——他

know, indeed—that the time is coming, in spite of all opposition, all persecution, when this emancipating gospel will spread among all the peoples, and when this minority will become the triumphant majority and, sweeping into power, inaugurate the greates social and economic change in history.

In that day we shall have the universal commonwealth — the harmonious cooperation of every nation with every other nation on earth···

Your Honor, I ask no mercy and I plead for no immunity. I realize that finally the right must prevail. I never so clearly comprehended as now the great struggle between the powers of greed and exploitation on the one hand and upon the other the rising hosts of industrial freedom and social justice.

I can see the dawn of the better day for humanity. The people are awakening. In due time they will and must come to their own.

When the mariner, sailing over tropic seas, looks for relief from his weary watch, he turns his eyes toward the southern cross, burning luridly above the tempest—vexed ocean. As the midnight approaches, the southern cross begins to bend, the whirling worlds change their places, and with starry finger — points the Almighty marks the passage of time upon the dial of the universe, and though no bell may beat the glad tidings, the lookout knows that the midnight is passing and that relief and rest are close at hand. Let the people everywhere take heart of hope, for the cross is bending, the midnight is passing, and joy cometh with the morning.

I am now prepared to receive your sentence.

们明白无误——虽然有很大的阻力，历经迫害，但这样的一天越来越近，解放的福音将恩及普天下的人民：这一少数派就会成为胜利的多数派，掌握政权，进行历史上最伟大的社会和经济变革。

到那时我们将实现世界联邦——国与国之间携手并肩，融洽合作……

阁下，我不乞求你们的宽恕，但我要为你们的软弱无助而辩护。我早就意识到：真理终将战胜谬误！我从来都没有像现在这样清醒地理解这样伟大的斗争——一方面是贪婪与剥削的权力横行；另一方面是正处于上升阶段的大量的工业自由与社会正义。

我能够看到人类博爱的黎明即将来临，人民正在觉醒。到时，他们将心甘情愿而且不得不爆发本能的欲求。

当我们的祖先漂洋过海，精疲力竭却还渴求信仰的时候，他们把目光转向了这片广袤的土地。那里，在狂暴的海洋上，烈火熊熊。当午夜来临，南部的热土开始伏首静卧。生生不息的世界斗转星移。万能的上帝在宇宙的刻度盘上拨弄星辰，调离时间。尽管从没有钟声敲打兴奋的潮汐，但是企望者却知道午夜正在消逝，苦难的解脱近在咫尺。让世界的每个角落的人们都布满希望吧，因为莽原静卧，子夜逝去，喜悦将伴着黎明姗姗而来。

现在，我已经准备好了接受你的审判。

Civil Disobedience

论公民的不服从

Henry David Thoreau / 亨利·大卫·梭罗

‖作者简介‖

亨利·大卫·梭罗（1817~1862），杂文家、诗人、自然主义者、改革家和哲学家。他出生于马萨诸塞州的康科德，毕业于哈佛大学，曾担任数年中学校长。

1846年7月，梭罗居住在瓦尔登湖边时，当地的警官找到他，叫他支付投票税。尽管数年来他已经行使了这项权利，但是梭罗拒绝支付税款。当夜，警官把他关在康科德的监狱里。第二天，梭罗的姨母帮他缴清税款，他便获释了。不过，他表明了他的观点：他不能向一个容许奴隶制存在并且侵略他国（墨西哥）的政府交税。他于1849年发表了下面这篇演说稿，为自己的行为进行辩护。

当时，这篇文章没有引起什么反响。但是到了十九世纪末，这篇文章却成为公认的经典之作，并赢得国际性的声誉。列夫·托尔斯泰、圣雄甘地、马丁·路德·金等人都对它推崇备至。

I heartily accept the motto, "That government is best which governs least; "and I should like to see it acted up to more rapidly and systematically. Carried out, it finally amounts to this, which also I believe," That government is best which governs not at all;" and when men are prepared for it, that will be the kind of government which the will have. Government is at best but an expedient; but most governments are usually, and all governments are sometimes, inexpedient. The objections which have been brought against a standing army, and they are many and weighty, and deserve to prevail, may also at last be brought against a standing government. The standing army is only an arm of the standing government. The government itself, which is only the mode which the people have chosen to execute their will, is equally liable to be abused and perverted before the people can act through it. Witness the present Mexican war, the work of comparatively a few individuals using the standing government as their tool; for in the outset, the people would not have consented to this measure.

This American government—what is it but a tradition, though a recent one, endeavoring to transmit itself unimpaired to posterity, but each instant losing some of its integrity? It has not the vitality and force of a single living man; for a single man can bend it to his will. It

　　我由衷地赞同这一名言——最少管事的政府是最好的政府。我还希望看到它能被迅速而彻底地得到执行。我相信，在它执行后，其最终结果将是——最好的政府是不进行任何管理的政府。只要人们对此有所期待，他们就会得到这样的政府。政府充其量不过是一种权宜之计，而大部分政府通常是不明智的，甚至有时所有政府都是不明智的。公民们对设置常备军的反对意见很多、很强烈，而且理应占主导地位，这种意见最终可能转变为反对常设政府，因为常备军队只不过是常设政府的一支胳臂。政府本身也只不过是由人民选择来执行他们意志的形式，在人民来不及通过它来执行意志之前，它同样也很容易被滥用。请看看当前的墨西哥战争，它是少数人将常设政府当做工具的结果，因为一开始人民就不同意采取这种做法。

　　目前的美国政府——它不过是一种传统形式，尽管其历史短暂，但它却竭力使自己完整地届届相传，可是每届政府却都会丧失掉一些自身的诚实和正直。除此之外它还能是什么呢？它的朝气和力量还顶不上一个活人，因为一个人就能随心所欲地摆布它。对于人民

is a sort of wooden gun to the people themselves. But it is not the less necessary for this; for the people must have some complicated machinery or other, and hear its din, to satisfy that idea of government which they have. Governments show thus how successfully men can be imposed upon, even impose on themselves, for their own advantage. It is excellent, we must all allow. Yet this government never of itself furthered any enterprise, but by the alacrity with which it got out of its way. It does not keep the country free. It does not settle the West. It does not educate. The character inherent in the American people has done all that has been accomplished; and it would have done somewhat more, if the government had not sometimes got in its way. For government is an expedient, by which men would fain succeed in letting one another alone; and, as has been said, when it is most expedient, the governed are most let alone by it. Trade and commerce, if they were not made of india-rubber, would never manage to bounce over obstacles which legislators are continually putting in their way; and if one were to judge these men wholly by the effects of their actions and not partly by their intentions, they would deserve to be classed and punished with those mischievious persons who put obstructions on the railroads.

But, to speak practically and as a citizen, unlike those who call themselves no-government men, I ask for, not at one no government, but at once a better government. Let every man make known what kind of government would command his respect, and that will be one step toward obtaining it.

After all, the practical reason why, when the power is once in the hands of the people, a majority are permitted, and for a long period continue, to rule is not because they are most likely to be in the right, nor because this seems fairest to the minority, but because they are

来说，政府是杆木头枪，倘若人们真要使用它互相厮杀，它就注定要裂开。不过，尽管如此，它仍然是必不可少的，因为人们需要某种复杂机器之类的玩意儿，需要听它发出的噪音，借此满足他们有关政府的概念。于是，政府的存在表明，为了人民的利益，可以如何成功地利用、欺骗人民，甚至可以使人民利用、欺骗自己。我们大家都必须承认，这真了不起。不过，这种政府从未主动地促进过任何事业，它只是欣然地偏离自己的职能。它没有捍卫国家的自由，它没有解决西部问题，它没有从事教育。迄今为止，所有的成就全都是由美国人民的传统性格完成的，而且，假如政府不曾从中作梗的话，还可能取得更大的成就。因为政府是一种权宜之计，通过它人们可以欣然地不相互来往。而且，如上所说，最便利的政府也就是最不大被治理的人民的政府，商业与贸易，假如不是印度橡胶所造成的刺激，绝无可能跃过议员们没完没了地设置下的路障而得以发展；如果我们完全以议员们行动的效果，而不是以他们行动的意图来评价的话，那么他们就应理所当然地被视作如同在铁路上设路障的恶作剧者，并应受到相应的惩罚。

不过说实在的，作为一个公民，我不像那些自称是无政府主义的人一样，我要求的不是立即取消政府，而是立即要有个好一点的政府。让每一个人都表明能赢得他尊敬的政府是什么样的，这样也就为赢得这种政府迈出了第一步。

毕竟，当权力掌握在人民手中的时候，多数派将有权统治，而且会长期统治，真正的原因不是因为他们极可能是正义的，也不是因为这在少数派看来是最公正的，而是因为他们在物质上是最强大

131

physically the strongest. But a government in which the majority rule in all cases can not be based on justice, even as far as men understand it. Can there not be a government in which the majorities do not virtually decide right and wrong, but conscience? —in which majorities decide only those questions to which the rule of expediency is applicable? Must the citizen ever for a moment, or in the least degree, resign his conscience to the legislator? Why has every man a conscience then? I think that we should be men first, and subjects afterward. It is not desirable to cultivate a respect for the law, so much as for the right. The only obligation which I have a right to assume is to do at any time what I think right.

…

The authority of government, even such as I am willing to submit to — for I will cheerfully obey those who know and can do better than I, and in many things even those who neither know nor can do so well—is still an impure one: to be strictly just, it must have the sanction and consent of the governed. It can have no pure right over my person and property but what I concede to it. The progress from an absolute to a limited monarchy, from a limited monarchy to a democracy, is a progress toward a true respect for the individual. Even the Chinese philosopher was wise enough to regard the individual as the basis of the empire. Is a democracy, such as we know it, the last improvement possible in government? Is it not possible to take a step further towards recognizing and organizing the rights of man? There will never be a really free and enlightened State until the State comes to recognize the individual as a higher and independent power, from

的。但是，一个由多数派做出所有决定的政府，是不可能建立在正义之上的，即使在人们对其有所了解的意义上都办不到。在一个政府中，如果对公正与谬误真正做出决定的不是多数派而是良知，如果多数派仅仅针对那些可以运用便利法则解决的问题作出决定，难道是不可能的吗？公民必须，哪怕是暂时或最低限度地把自己的良知托付给议员吗？那么，为什么每个人还都有良知呢？我认为，我们首先必须做人，其次才是臣民。培养人们像尊重正义那样尊重法律是不可取的。我有权承担的惟一义务是不论何时都从事我认为是正义的事。

……

政府的权威，即使是我乐意服从的权威——因为我很乐于服从比我渊博、比我能干的人，而且在许多事情上，我甚至乐于服从那些不是非常渊博，也不是非常能干的人——这种权威还不是真正的权威。从严格、正义的意义来讲，权威必须获得被治理者的认可或赞成才行，也就是除非我同意，否则它没有任何理由对我的身心和财产行使权力。从君主集权制到君主立宪制，从君主立宪制到民主共和制的进步是朝着真正尊重个人的方向来进步的，甚至智慧的中国哲人都知道个人是一个王国的基础。民主，如同我们所知道的民主，就是政府进步的尽头了吗？再也不可能进一步承认和组织人的权利了吗？除非国家承认个人具有更高的、独立

which all its own power and authority are derived, and treats him
accordingly. I please myself with imagining a State at last which can
afford to be just to all men, and to treat the individual with respect as
a neighbor; which even would not think it inconsistent with its own
repose if a few were to live aloof from it, not meddling with it , nor
embraced by it , who fulfilled all the duties of neighbors and fellow
men. A State which bore this kind of fruit, and suffered it to drop off
as fast as it ripened, would prepare the way for a still more perfect
and glorious State, which I have also imagined, but not yet anywhere
seen.

的权力，而且国家的权力和权威源自于个人的权力，并且在对待个
人权力方面采取相应的措施，否则真正自由开明的国家就不可能出
现。我常常高兴地设想国家的最终形式，它将公正地对待所有的人，
尊重个人就像尊重邻居一样。如果有人履行了邻居和同胞的职责，
但却退避三舍，冷眼旁观，不为其所容纳的话，它就寝食不安。如
果一个国家能够结出这样的果实，并且能让它快速成熟的话，那么
它就为建立一个更加完美、更加辉煌的国家铺平了道路。那是我一
直梦想的，但在任何地方都没有看到过的国家。

The Four Freedoms
论四大自由

Franklin Roosevelt / 富兰克林·罗斯福

...

In the future days, which we seek to make secure, we look forward to a world founded upon four essential human freedoms.

The first is freedom of speech and expression—everywhere in the world.

The second is freedom of every person to worship God in his own way — everywhere in the world.

The third is freedom from want—which, translated into world terms, means economic understandings which will secure to every nation a healthy peace time life for its inhabitants — everywhere in the world.

The fourth is freedom from fear—which, translated into world terms, means a world-wide reduction of armaments to such a point and in such a thorough fashion that no nation will be in a position to commit an act of physical aggression against any neighbor — anywhere in the world.

That is no vision of a distant millennium. It is a definite basis for a kind of world attainable in our own time and generation. That kind of world is the very antithesis of the so-called new order of tyranny which the dictators seek to create with the crash of a bomb.

To that new order we oppose the greater conception—the moral order. A good society is able to face schemes of world domination and foreign revolutions alike without fear.

Since the beginning of our American history we have been engaged in danger — in a perpetual peaceful revolution — a revolution which goes on steadily, quietly adjusting itself to changing conditions—without the concentration camp or the quick —lime in the ditch. The world order which we seek is the cooperation of free countries, working together in a friendly civilized society.

This nation has placed its destiny in the hands and heads and hearts of its millions of free men and women; and its faith in freedom under the guidance of God. Freedom means the supremacy of human rights everywhere. Our support goes to those who struggle to gain those rights or keep them. Our strength is in our unity of purpose.

To that high concept there can be no end save victory.

……

我们期待，在我们尽力确保安定的未来日子里，能够建立一个基于人类不可缺少的四大自由之上的世界。

第一项自由，是世界上无处不在的言论自由。

第二项自由，是在世界上任何地方，任何人都有以自己的方式信奉上帝的自由。

第三项自由，是远离贫困的自由。从全球意义上说，就是达成经济上的谅解，保证在世界上任何地方，任何一个国家的居民都可以过上健康与和平的生活。

第四项自由，是远离恐惧的自由。从全球意义上说，就是进行世界范围的裁军，目的是使在世界任何地方，任何一个国家都没有能力向任何邻国采取侵略行动。

这不是遥遥无期的幻想。这是我们所追求的世界必不可少的基础。在我们这个时代，我们这一代人，有能力让这样的世界成为现实。这样的世界，与独裁者企图用炸弹创造的所谓"新秩序"暴政尖锐对立。

我们用一种更伟大的观念来对抗这种秩序——那就是道德观念。一个好的社会，能够大无畏地直面诸如统治世界或在别国发动叛乱等此类企图和计划。

有史以来，我们美国就致力于变革——致力于持续不断的和平变革。我们从容地、默默地革命着，并调整它使之适应不断变化的外部条件。我们的革命没有集中营，也无须生石灰来填充鸿沟。我们所寻求的世界秩序是自由国家彼此合作，是在友好文明的社会中携手工作。

我们国家的命运掌握在千百万自由的男女公民手中、头脑中和心中，她把对自由的忠诚置于上帝的指引之下。自由意味着无论在何处，人权都有着至高无上的地位。我们的支持将给予一切为得到或者为保有这些权利而奋斗的人们。共同的目标给了我们力量。

这种崇高的思想必将以胜利告终。

137

Spirit of Liberty
自由的精神

Learned Hand／勒尼德·汉德

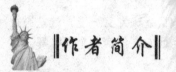

‖作者简介‖

　　勒尼德·汉德(1872~1961)，美国最伟大的法官之一，生于纽约州阿尔伯尼，在哈佛大学完成学业。

　　1909年，勒尼德·汉德被任命为联邦法官，1924年进入美国上诉法院。从1939年到1951年，勒尼德·汉德作为该法院的首席法官，以其才学、智慧和对民主原则的深刻信念成为全国最有影响的法官之一。

　　1944年5月21日，汉德应邀在纽约市中央公园一个大型集会演讲，以这篇纪念"我是一个美国人日"(I Am an American Day)。他在大战关键时期发表的演讲获得很大反响，被收入各种文集。

We have gathered here to affirm a faith, a faith in a common purpose, a common conviction, a common devotion.

Some of us have chosen America as the land of our adoption; the rest have come from those who did the same. For this reason we have some right to consider ourselves a picked group, a group of those who had the courage to break from the past and brave the

感动一个国家的文字

dangers and the loneliness of a strange land. What was the object that nerved us, or those who went before us, to this choice? We sought liberty — freedom from oppression, freedom from want, freedom to be ourselves. This then we sought; this we now believe that we are by way of winning. What do we mean when we say that first of all we seek liberty? I often wonder whether we do not rest our hopes too much upon constitutions, upon laws, and upon courts. These are false hopes; believe me, these are false hopes. Liberty lies in the hearts of men and women; when it dies there, no constitution, no law, no court can save it; no constitution, no law, no court can even do much to help it. While it lies there, it needs no constitution, no law, no court to save it. And what is this liberty which must lie in the hearts of men and women? It is not the ruthless, the unbridled will; it is not freedom to do

我们在这里集会，是为了肯定一种信仰，一种对共同目的、共同信念和共同的献身精神的信仰。

我们中间的一些人已经选择美国作为自己的国家，另外一些人则是做出同样选择者的后代。因此，我们有权把自己看做一个精英群体，它的成员们勇于同过去决裂，勇于面对在一个陌生土地上遇到的危险和孤寂。激励我们或我们的先辈做出这一选择的目标是什么呢？我们追求自由：免遭压迫的自由，远离贫困的自由，独立自主的自由。我们那时努力追求这一目标，而今我们相信自己已经通过奋斗达到了这一目标。当我们说我们首要的目标是追求自由的时候，意旨何在呢？我常常怀疑人们是否对宪法、法律和法庭寄予了过多的希望。这些都是虚幻的希望，请相信我，这些真的是虚幻的希望。自由只存在于人们心中，如果它在人们心中死去，没有任何

as one likes. That is the denial of liberty, and leads straight to its overthrow. A society in which men recognize no check upon their freedom soon becomes a society where freedom is the possession of only a savage few — as we have learned to our sorrow.

What, then, is the spirit of liberty?

I cannot define it; I can only tell you my own faith. The spirit of liberty is the spirit which is not too sure that it is right; the spirit of liberty is the spirit which seeks to understand the minds of those men and women; the spirit of liberty is the spirit which weighs their interest alongside its own without bias; the spirit of liberty remembers that not even a sparrow falls to earth unheeded; the spirit of liberty is the spirit of him who, near two thousand years ago, taught mankind that lesson it has never learned, but has never quite forgotten — that there may be a kingdom where the least shall be heard and considered side-by-side with the greatest. And now in that spirit, that spirit of an American which has never been, and which may never be — nay, which never will be except as the conscience and courage of Americans create it — yet in the spirit of America which lies hidden in some form in the aspirations of us all; in the spirit of that America for which our young men are at this moment fighting and dying; in that spirit of liberty and of America so

宪法、法律或法院能够挽救它，任何宪法、法律或法庭甚至对此无能为力。而当自由存在于人们心中时，没有必要用任何宪法、法律或法庭去挽救它。那么人们心中必须存在的自由是什么呢？它不是冷酷无情，不是恣意放纵的意志，不是为所欲为的自由。这些是对自由的否定，会直接毁灭自由的精神。假如在一个社会中，人们认为不应该对他们的自由加以控制，那么它很快会变成一个只让一小部分凶狠残暴的人拥有自由的社会，这是我们以痛苦的经验换来的一点教训。

什么是自由的精神？

我不能给它准确地定义，只能告诉你们我自己的信念：自由的精神就是反对唯我独尊的精神；自由的精神就是尽量去理解别人的精神；自由的精神就是不带任何偏见地将别人的利益与自己的利益一起考虑的精神；自由的精神就是即使一只麻雀落地也该引起关注的精神；自由的精神也就是基督的精神，他在大约两千年之前教给人类从未学过并且永远难忘的一课：有可能出现一个王国，在那里，人们对最伟大者和最渺小者不分贵贱，一视同仁。现在，这种精神，这种从未存在、或许永不会有的、唯独美国才具有的精神、唯独美国人的良知和勇气才能创造的精神，它以某种形式深藏在大家心中，它让我们的年轻人此刻正为之奋战和牺牲，它让我们看到一个自由、繁荣、安全和富足的美国——如果我们不能把人类所有美好的愿望当做信号、航标和准则，并为之奋斗不已，我们将不能抓住自由精神的真谛，我们将懈怠对

prosperous, and safe, and contented, we shall have failed to grasp its meaning, and shall have been truant to its promise, except as we strive to make it a signal, a beacon, a standard to which the best hopes of mankind will ever turn; in confidence that you share that belief, I now ask you to raise your hand and repeat with me this pledge:

I pledge allegiance to the flag, of the United States of America, and to the republic for which stands — one nation, indevisible, with liberty and justice for all.

自由精神的承诺。为了确定大家共同分享这一信仰，我请求大家举起手跟随我一起宣誓：

我宣誓效忠于星条旗，效忠于美利坚合众国——一个建立在团结、自由与公正之上的联邦国家。

142

不朽的精神殿堂

第三卷

哦，美丽的亚美利加！

长空无垠无际，

金色的麦浪，

雄伟的群山，

富饶的平原。

亚美利加，亚美利加，

愿上帝赐福于你，

为了你的善与美，

让所有的兄弟姐妹都爱你！

哦，美丽的亚美利加！

先辈们的足迹，

迈着坚定、昂扬的步履，

穿过荒山旷野，

开辟自由的天地！

亚美利加！亚美利加！

愿上帝赐福于你，

使你的自制坚定无比，

把你的自由写进法律！

America The Beautiful

美丽的亚美利加

Katharine Lee Bates / 凯瑟琳·李·贝茨

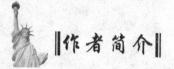 ‖作者简介‖

凯瑟琳·李·贝茨（1850~1929），教育家兼诗人，做过编辑、作家、大学教授。但使她的名字流芳百世的却是诗歌《美丽的亚美利加》，这是一首广为传诵的歌曲，甚至有人建议用它取代现在的美国国歌。

O beautiful for spacious skies,
For amber waves of grain,
For purple mountain majesties
Above the fruited plain!
America! America!
God shed his grace on thee
And crown thy good with brotherhood
From sea to shining sea!

感动一个国家的文字

O beautiful for pilgrim feet
Whose stern, impassioned stress
A thoroughfare for freedom beat
Across the wilderness!
America! America!
God mend thine every flaw,
Confirm thy soul in self-control,
Thy liberty in law!

O beautiful for heroes proved in liberating strife.
Who more than self the country loved
And mercy more than life!
America! America!
May God thy gold refine
Till all success be nobleness
And every gain divine!

哦，美丽的亚美利加！
长空无垠无际，
金色的麦浪，
雄伟的群山，
富饶的平原。
亚美利加，亚美利加，
愿上帝赐福于你，
为了你的善与美，
让所有的兄弟姐妹都爱你！

哦，美丽的亚美利加！
先辈们的足迹，
迈着坚定、昂扬的步履，
穿过荒山旷野，
开辟自由的天地！
亚美利加！亚美利加！
愿上帝赐福于你，
使你的自制坚定无比，
把你的自由写进法律！

O beautiful for patriot dream

That sees beyond the years

Thine alabaster cities gleam

Undimmed by human tears!

America! America!

God shed his grace on thee

And crown thy good with brotherhood

From sea to shining sea!

哦，美丽的亚美利加！
光荣的传奇，
英雄们前赴后继，
为了解放而奋起，
为国献身捐躯！
亚美利加！亚美利加！
愿上帝净化你的财富，
愿你所有的成就都高贵无比，
让每一颗谷粒都完美充实。

哦，美丽的亚美利加！
爱国者的梦想，
憧憬奇妙的岁月，
人类之泪无损于你
圣洁光辉的城市！
亚美利加！亚美利加！
愿上帝赐福于你，
为了你的善与美，
让所有兄弟姐妹都爱你。

感动一个国家的文字

The Star-spangled Banner
灿烂的星条旗

Francis Scott Key/ 弗朗西斯·斯科特·克伊

O say, can you see, by the dawn's early light,
What so proudly we hail'd at the twilight's last gleaming?
Whose broad stripes and bright stars, thro' the perilous fight,
O'er the ramparts we watch'd, were so gallantly streaming?
And the rockets' red glare, the bombs bursting in air,
Gave proof thro' the night that our flag was still there.
O say, does that star-spangled banner yet wave
O'er the land of the free and the home of the brave?

On the shore dimly seen thro' the mists of the deep,
Where the foe's haughty host in dread silence reposes,
What is that which the breeze, o'er the towering steep,
As it fitfully blows, half conceals, half discloses?
Now it catches the gleam of the morning's first beam,
In full glory reflected, now shines on the stream:
'Tis the star-spangled banner: O, long may it wave
O'er the land of the free and the home of the brave!

147

And where is that band who so vauntingly swore

That the havoc of war and the battle's confusion,

A home and a country should leave us no more?

Their blood has wash'd out their foul footsteps' pollution.

No refuge could save the hireling and slave

From the terror of flight or the gloom of the grave:

And the star-spangled banner in triumph doth wave

O'er the land of the free and the home of the brave.

O thus be it ever when free-men shall stand

Between their lov'd home and the war's desolation;

Blest with vict'ry and peace, may the heav'n rescued land

Praise the Powr' that hath made and preserv'd us a nation!

Then conquer we must, when our cause it is just,

And this be our motto: "In God is our trust!"

And the star-spangled banner in triumph shall wave

O'er the land of the free and the home of the brave!

哦！你可看见，透过黎明的曙光，

在暮色将尽时我们纵情欢呼什么？

谁的宽阔条纹、闪亮星徽，冒着连绵不断的炮火，

整夜矗立在要塞上迎风飘扬？

枪火的光芒四射，炸弹在空中轰响，

它们都见证着星条旗的毫发无伤。

啊！那灿烂的星条旗是否仍飘扬在自由的国土，勇士的家乡？

透过朦胧的薄雾，看见

对岸的强敌正在酣睡，四周一片寂静，

轻风时断时续，吹过峭壁之巅，那是什么，

在微风中半隐半现？

它此时映照在水波里，闪闪发亮，

感动一个国家的文字

这是星条旗，哦，愿它永远飘扬，
飘扬在自由的国土，勇士的家乡！

狂妄自大的敌人们，现在何方？
他们吹嘘战争的劫难和纷乱，
会让我们失去家园。
这些奴才和逃兵，已无处躲藏，
逃脱不了被埋葬的下场。
而灿烂的星条旗却高高飘扬，
飘扬在自由的国土，勇士的家乡。

战争的创伤，摆在我们面前，
自由的勇士誓保星条旗永远招展。
祈祷上帝保佑这片土地，赐她胜利与和平，
感谢那创建和保存我们祖国的力量！
我们为正义而战，我们必将凯旋，
"我们信奉上帝"，这誓言永不忘。
灿烂的星条旗将高高飘扬，
飘扬在自由的国土，勇士的家乡！

历史链接……　　1814年，一位名叫弗朗西斯·斯科特·克伊(1779～1843)的青年律师兼诗人，目睹了麦克亨利要塞被一艘停泊在巴尔的摩港的英国旗舰断断续续炮击了25个小时，但被围的要塞军民仍然顽强抵抗。斯科特·克伊灵感激荡，一挥而就，写下这首诗。该诗名为《保卫麦克亨利要塞》，人们配上一首美国人喜爱的祝酒歌曲调演唱它。一个月后，这首歌被重新命名为《灿烂的星条旗》。1889年，美国海军采用了这首爱国歌曲，14年之后，美国陆军也采用了它。1931年，国会立法规定《灿烂的星条旗》为美利坚合众国国歌。

弗朗西斯·斯科特·克伊 ▶

149

O Captain! My Captain!
啊，船长！我的船长！

Walt Whitman/ 沃尔特 · 惠特曼

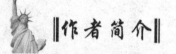 **作者简介**

沃尔特 · 惠特曼(1819~1892)，在纽约市布鲁克林区长大，当过印刷工人、记者、教师和政府职员，主编过好几份报纸。

1855年，惠特曼自费出版了《草叶集》，初印只有900本左右，大部分都送给了朋友。这本薄薄的诗集起初并没引起多少人的注意，但它不押韵和不讲格律的风格最终影响了几代美国诗人。

写于林肯被刺后不久的《啊，船长！我的船长！》是惠特曼广为人知的一首诗。

O Captain! My Captain! Our fearful trip is done,

The ship has weather'd every rack, the prize we sought is won,

The port is near, the bells I hear, the people all exulting,

While follow eyes the steady keel, the vessel grim and daring;

But O heart! Heart! Heart!

O the bleeding drops of red!

Where on the deck my Captain lies,

Fallen cold and dead.

感动一个国家的文字......

O Captain! My Captain! Rise up and hear the bells;
Rise up — for you the flag is flung — for you the bugle trills,
For you bouquets and ribbon'd wreaths — for you the shores
crowding,
For you they call, the swaying mass, their eager faces turning;
Here, Captain! Dear father!
This arm beneath your head!
It is some dream that on the deck
You've fallen cold and dead.

啊，船长！我的船长！可怕的航程已经结束，
我们的船已安然渡过惊涛骇浪，我们所追求的奖赏也已经得到，
港口近了，我已听见钟声，听到了人们的欢呼，
千万只眼睛都在注视着我们的船从容返航，它是那样威严和勇敢，
可是，心啊！心啊！心啊！
啊，鲜红的血滴，
在那甲板上，我的船长躺下了，
他已冰冷，死去。

啊，船长！我的船长！起来听听这钟声，
起来吧——旌旗在为你招展——号角在为你吹响，
为你，岸上挤满了人群——为你，人们准备了无数的花束和花环，
为你，这雀跃的人群在欢呼，他们在急切地望着你；
这里，船长，亲爱的父亲！
让你的头枕着我的手臂！
真像是梦，躺在甲板上，
你已冰冷，死去。

My Captain does not answer, his lips are pale and still,

My father does not feel my arm, he has no pulse nor will;

The ship is anchor'd safe and sound, its voyage closed and done,

From fearful trip the victor ship comes in with object won;

Exult, O shores! And ring, O bells!

But I, with mournful tread,

Walk the deck my Captain lies,

Fallen cold and dead.

我的船长没有回应，他的嘴唇惨白，寂静，

我的父亲感觉不到我的手臂，他已经没有脉搏，也没有了意志，

我们的船已安全地停泊，它的航程已经结束，

从可怕的航程归来，这胜利的船，已经到达目的地；

啊，海岸欢呼，钟声长鸣！

可我却踏着沉痛的脚步，

在甲板上，那里躺着我的船长，

他已冰冷，死去。

Grass 草

Carl Sandburg/卡尔·桑德伯格

‖作者简介‖

卡尔·桑德堡（1878～1967），美国诗人。他的传记作品《亚伯拉罕·林肯：战争年代》1940年获普利策历史奖，《诗作全集》1951年获普利策诗作奖。桑德堡的诗充满名言、逸闻趣事，他的《草》是关于第一次世界大战最感人、最令人难忘的一首诗歌。

Pile the bodies high at Austerlitz and Waterloo.
Shovel them under and let me work —
I am the grass; I cover all.

And pile them high at Gettysburg
And pile them high at Ypres and Verdun.
Shovel them under and let me work.

Two years, ten years, and passengers ask the conductor:
What place is this?
Where are we now?

I am the grass.
Let me work.

将尸体堆砌在奥斯特里茨和滑铁卢，
将它们铲到坑里，然后让我来做——
我是草，我覆盖一切。

将尸体堆砌在葛底斯堡，
将尸体堆砌在伊普尔和凡尔登，
将它们铲到坑里，然后让我来做。

两年、十年之后，旅客问乘务员：
这是什么地方？
我们现在在哪里？

我是草，
让我来做。

瓦尔登湖 Walden

Henry David Thoreau／亨利·大卫·梭罗

‖作者简介‖

亨利·大卫·梭罗(1817~1862)是拉尔夫·沃尔多·爱默生的信徒，1845年，时年二十八岁的他，下决心撇开金钱的羁绊，决定以作诗和论述自然作为终生的事业。在征得爱默生的同意后，他在爱默生拥有的离康科德两英里的瓦尔登湖边建了一座小屋，并在那里写下了著名的《瓦尔登湖》一书，记录他的观察、思维、理想和信念。本文即选自此书。

...

Men frequently say to me, "I should think you would feel lonesome down there, and want to be nearer to folks, rainy and snowy days and nights especially. " I am tempted to reply to such — this whole earth which we inhabit is but a point in space. How far apart, think you, dwell the two most distant inhabitants of yonder star, the breadth of whose disk cannot be appreciated by our instruments? Why should I feel lonely? Is not our planet in the Milky Way? This which you put seems to me not to be the most important question. What sort of space is that which separates a man from his fellows and makes him solitary? I have found that no exertion of the legs can bring two minds much nearer to one another.

......

I find it wholesome to be alone the greater part of the time. To be in company, even with the best, is soon wearisome and dissipating. I love to be alone. I never found the companion that was so companionable as solitude. We are for the most part more lonely when we go abroad among men than when we stay in our chambers. A man thinking or working is always alone, let him be where he will. Solitude is not measured by the miles of space that intervene between a man and his fellows. The really diligent student in one of the crowded hives of Cambridge College is as solitary as a dervish in the desert. The farmer can work alone in the field or the woods all day, hoeing or

......

常有人对我说："我想你住在那里一定很寂寞，总想着和其他的人接触一下吧，尤其是在下雨下雪的日子和夜晚。"这个问题诱使我想作这样一番解释——我们居住的整个地球，在宇宙中也不过是一个小点罢了。而别的星球，我们用天文仪器还不能测其大小，你想象一下它上面两个相隔最远的居民间的距离又是多远呢？我怎么会感到寂寞呢？我们的地球不是在银河之中吗？在我看来，你提出的是一个最无关紧要的问题。人和人群要被怎样的空间分开才会感到寂寞呢？我已经找到了，人腿再努力也只能让人们走在一起，却无法使他们的心彼此靠近。

......

大部分的时间里，我都觉得独处是对健康有益的。有了同伴，哪怕是最好的同伴，不久也会让人心生厌烦，变得很糟糕。我喜欢独处。我没有遇见过比孤独更好的伙伴了。当我们到国外，跻身于人群当中时，也许会比一个人待在室内更感到寂寞。一个人正在思想或正在工作时总是孤独的，让他该怎样就怎样吧。不能以一个人离开他的同伴有几英里远来计算他是不是孤独。真正勤奋的学生，如果在剑桥学院最拥挤的蜂房里，只会感觉孤独得像沙漠上的一个伊

chopping, and not feel lonesome, because he is employed; but when he comes home at night he cannot sit down in a room alone, at the mercy of his thoughts, but must be where he can "see the folks " and recreate, and, as he thinks, remunerate himself for his day's solitude; and hence he wonders how the student can sit alone in the house all night and most of the day without ennui and "the blues"; but he does not realize that the student, though in the house, is still at work in his field, and chopping in his woods, as the farmer in his, and in turn seeks the same recreation and society that the latter does, though it may be a more condensed form of it.

Society is commonly too cheap. We meet at very short intervals, not having had time to acquire any new value for each other. We meet at meals three times a day, and give each other a new taste of that old musty cheese that we are. We have had to agree on a certain set of rules, called etiquette and politeness, to make this frequent meeting tolerable and that we need not come to open war. We meet at the post-office, and at the sociable, and about the fireside every night; we live thick and are in each other's way, and stumble over one another, and I think that we thus lose some respect for one another. Certainly less frequency would suffice for all important and hearty communications. Consider the girls in a factory—never alone, hardly in their dreams. It would be better if there were but one inhabitant to a square mile, as where I live. The value of a man is not in his skin, that we should touch him.

...

感动一个国家的文字

斯兰教托钵僧一样。农夫可以一整天独自待在田地上，或者在森林中工作、耕地或伐木，却不觉得寂寞，因为他有活儿干。可是当晚上回到家里，他却不能独自坐在房间里思考问题，而必须到能"看见人群"的地方消遣一下，按他的理解，这样做是为了补偿他一天的寂寞，因此他觉得很奇怪，为什么学生们可以一天到晚地待在教室里而不觉得无聊和"郁闷"。但是他没有意识到，学生坐在教室里学习，就像他在森林中采伐，像农夫在田地里或是在森林里劳作一样，过后学生也会去消遣，也需要进行社交，尽管那种形式可能更简练一些。

社交往往是很廉价的，我们相聚的时间是如此短暂，以至于来不及让彼此获得任何新的有价值的东西。我们在一日三餐的时间里见面。大家重新相互品尝我们这些陈腐乳酪的味道。我们必须一致同意若干礼节习俗，这些是我们所谓的礼尚往来，能够使大家平安无事地相处，避免有失风度的争吵。我们在邮局碰面，在各种社交场合碰面，在每晚的火炉边碰面；我们的生活太拥挤，相互干扰，彼此牵扯到一起，因此我认为，我们之间已经太缺乏相互尊重了。当然，也有重要而热忱的聚会，次数少一点也就足够了。想想工厂中的女工们，生活中永远不会有自己独立的空间，甚至连做梦都不会是一个人。如果一个人能住上一平方英里，就像我住的地方一样，那情况就会好得多。人们交往的价值不在于有肌肤之亲，所以我们没有必要整日地待在一起。

......

I have a great deal of company in my house; especially in the morning, when nobody calls. Let me suggest a few comparisons, that some one may convey an idea of my situation. I am no more lonely than the loon in the pond that laughs so loud, or than Walden Pond itself. What company has that lonely lake, I pray. And yet it has not the blue devils, but the blue angels in it, in the azure tint of its waters. The sun is alone, except in thick weather, when there sometimes appear to be two, but one is a mock sun. God is alone—but the devil, he is far from being alone; he sees a great deal of company; he is legion. I am no more lonely than a single mullein or dandelion in a pasture, or a bean leaf, or sorrel, or a horse — fly or a bumblebee. I am no more lonely than the Mill Brook, or a weathercock, or the north star, or the south wind, or an April shower, or a January thaw, or the first spider in a new house.

...

　　我的房里有我很多伴儿，特别是早上没有人来访的时候。让我举例说明吧——也许用这种方式更能清楚地表达我的状况。我并不比湖中纵声高叫的潜水鸟更寂寞，也不比瓦尔登湖本身更寂寞。我倒是想获知有谁与这孤独的湖做伴？在它湛蓝的水波上，存在的不是蓝色的魔鬼，而是蓝色的天使。太阳是孤独的，除非天上布满了乌云，有时候看上去像有两个太阳，但其中一个是假的。上帝是孤独的，但是魔鬼就绝不会孤独：它看到许多同伙；它要拉帮结派。我并不比一朵花蕊或牧场上的一朵蒲公英更孤独，我不比一片豆叶、一枝酢酱草，或一只马蝇、一只大黄蜂更孤独，还有密尔溪、风信鸟、北极星或者南风、四月的雨、正月的雪，或者新屋里的第一只蜘蛛——所有这一切的一切，我都不比它们更孤独、更寂寞！

……

作者自述

The Author's Account of Himself

Washington Irving/ 华盛顿·欧文

‖作者简介‖

华盛顿·欧文(1738～1859),19世纪美国最伟大的散文家之一,生于纽约城,他是家里 11 个孩子中最小的。欧文自幼聪颖,19 岁时攻读法律,1804 年至 1806 年间游历欧洲,回国后取得律师资格。但是他对当律师不感兴趣,而且身体不太好,因此,他改变兴趣,进入文学领域,取得很大成就,在美国文学史上占据不可或缺的地位。

I was always fond of visiting new scene, and observing strange characters and manners. Even when a mere child I began my travels, and made many tours of discovery into foreign parts and unknown regions of my native city, to the frequent alarm of my parents, and the emolument of the town-crier. As I grew into boyhood I extended my range of observations. My holiday afternoons were spent in ramble about the surrounding country I made myself familiar with all its places famous in history or fable. I knew every spot where a murder or robbery had been committed, or a ghost seen. I visited the neighboring villages, and added greatly to my stock of knowledge, by noting their habits and customs, and conversing with their sages and great men. I even journeyed one long summer's day to the summit of the most distant hill, where I stretched my eye over many a mile of terra incognita, and was astonished to find how vast a globe I inhabited.

This rambling propensity strengthened with years. Books of voyages and travels became my passion, and in devouring their contents I neglected the regular exercises of the schools. How wistfully would I wander about the pier-heads in fine weather, and watch the parting ships bound to distant climes—with what longing eyes would I gaze after their lessening sails, and waft myself in imagination to the ends of the earth!

Further reading and thinking, though they brought this vague inclination into more reasonable bounds, only served to make it more decided. I visited various parts of my own country; and had I been merely a lover of fine scenery, I should have felt litter desire to seek elsewhere its gratification, for on no country have the charms of nature been more prodigally lavished. Her mighty lakes like oceans of liquid silver; her mountains with their bright aerial tints; her valleys, teeming with wild fertility; her tremendous cataracts, thundering in their solitudes; her boundless plains, waving with spontaneous verdure; her broad deep rivers, rolling in solemn silence to the ocean; her trackless forests, where vegetation puts forth all its magnificence; her skies, kindling with the magic of summer clouds and glorious sunshine, —no never need an American look beyond his own country for the sublime and beautiful of natural scenery.

But Europe held forth the charms of storied and poetical association. There were to be seen the masterpieces of art, the refinement of highly-cultivated society, the quaint peculiarities of ancient and local custom. My native country was full of youthful promise; Europe was rich in the accumulated treasures of age. Her very ruins told the history of times gone by, and every mouldering stone was a chronicle. I longed to wander over the scenes of renowned achievement — to tread, as it were, in the footsteps of antiquity — to loiter about the ruined castle — to meditate on the falling tower — to escape, in short, from the commonplace realities of the present, and lose myself among the shadowy grandeurs of the past.

一直以来，我都很喜欢出游，观察新奇的风土人情。在我还年幼的时候，我便踏上旅程，多次去游历故乡的一些偏僻陌生之地。父母常常为此惊慌，为了找我回家，他们也没少给镇上的地保交一些赏钱。童年时，我扩大了自己的活动地盘。每到假日的下午我总去附近村落转悠，对那里的历史典故和神话传说了如指掌。我熟悉那些凶杀抢掠现场和鬼魂萦绕之地。去邻近村庄的时候，我观察人们的风俗习惯，拜见当地的名人志士并与他们交谈，这大大增长了我的见识。某个夏日，我登上了最远的山岗，从山顶上遥望远处数十英里外的陌生地带，发现我所居住的地区如此辽阔，真让我大大惊叹。

岁月流逝，我出游的兴趣更加浓厚。我特爱游记，如饥似渴的阅读使我无暇顾及学校的正常功课。晴天时，我希望徜徉在码头，看着泊船离岸远去，不禁觉得心神爽朗。点点风帆，消失得无影无踪，我仿佛随着幻觉漂向天边。

细读和深思虽然给模糊的爱好套上理智的约束，但使其变得更为明确和坚定。我游遍祖国山河，如果单是为欣赏优美的风景，那我就犯不着去别处寻找这种欲望的满足感；因为再没有别的国家像美国这样有如此迷人的自然景色了：广阔的湖泊，如银波闪耀的大海；崇山峻岭，铺上空灵爽朗的色彩；深邃的峡谷，繁茂的草木；鸟兽众多，激荡的瀑布在寂静的荒原中轰鸣而下；无边的平原，连绵起伏，葱葱郁郁；深厚宽阔的河流，浩浩荡荡，无声无息地奔流入海；人迹罕至的森林，处处显露着豪爽的景观；夏日的天空，云朵变幻莫测，阳光灿烂——不，一个美国人永远不必去国外寻找宏伟壮丽的美景！

欧洲具有一种迷人的魅力，能让人联想起诗意盎然的典故。那里有杰出的艺术，优雅先进的文明社会，以及古怪离奇的当地风俗。我的祖国朝气蓬勃前途似锦，而欧洲则有着厚重的历史积淀和时代宝藏。那里的废墟记载着岁月的流逝，每块崩碎剥落的石头都是一段编年史。我梦想着漫游名胜古迹——踏着前人的足迹前进；流连在废墟古堡周围——默默地凭吊摇摇欲坠的巍巍高塔。总之，我想逃避俗世的纷纷扰扰，沉醉在昔日辉煌的虚幻中。

I had, beside all this, an earnest desire to see the great men of the earth. We have, it is true, our great men in America: not a city but has an ample share of them. I have mingled among them in my time, and been almost withered by the shade into which they cast me; for there is nothing so baleful to a small man as the shade of a great one, particularly the great man of a city. But I was anxious to see the great men of Europe; for I had read in the works of various philosophers, that all animals degenerated in America, and man among the number. A great man of Europe, thought I, must therefore be as superior to a great man of America, as a peak of the Alps to a highland of Hudson; and in this idea I was confirmed, by observing the comparative importance and swelling magnitude of many English travellers among us, who, I was assured, were very little people in their own county. I will visit this land of wonders, thought I, and see the gigantic race from which I am degenerated.

It has been either my good or evil lot to have my roving passion gratified. I have wandered through different countries, and witnessed many of the shifting scenes of life. I cannot say that I have studied them with the eye of a philosopher；but rather with the sauntering gaze with which humble lovers of the picturesque stroll from the window of one print-shop to another; caught sometimes by the delineations of beauty, sometimes by the distortions of caricature, and sometimes by the loveliness of landscape. As it is the fashion for modern tourists to travel, pencil in hand, and bring home their portfolios filled with sketches, I am disposed to get up a few for the entertainment of my friends. When, however, I look over the hints and memorandums I have taken down for the purpose, my heart almost fails me at finding how my idle humor has led me aside from the great objects studied by every regular traveler who would make a book. I fear I shall give equal disappointment with an unlucky landscape painter, who had traveled on the continent, but, following the bent of his vagrant inclination, had sketched in nooks, and corners, and by-places. His sketch-book was accordingly crowded with cottages, and landscapes, and obscure ruins; but he neglected to paint St.Peter's, or the Colosseum the cascade of Terni, or the bay of Naples; and had not a single glacier or volcano in his whole collection.

　　除此之外，我还迫切渴望拜会当今的伟大人物。我们美国确实也有自己的杰出人物——连一个城镇都会有众多的英雄豪杰。我曾经穿梭在他们中间，可是他们的光芒盖住了我，使我黯然失色。对于小人物而言，最糟糕的莫过于活在大人物——尤其是大城市里的大人物的阴影下。虽然如此，我仍然非常急切地要去探访欧洲的伟人。因为我读过各个哲学流派的作品，它们都认为一切动物到了美国就会退化，包括人在内。我想，欧洲的伟人一定要比美国的优秀，就像阿尔卑斯山的山峰要比哈得逊河流域的高地高许多一样。我这个想法得到了证实。我观察过许多来我们这里的英国游客，我敢断言，在故乡他们只不过是渺小的人物，可是此时此地却显得心高气傲，目空一切。由此我更确定了这一想法。我一定要去那个神奇之地，见识一下已退化成诸如我类的伟大种族。

　　不知幸运与否，我游历的癖好居然得以满足。我转悠了好几个国家，亲眼目睹了许多沧桑变幻。对于这些，称不上拿哲学家的眼光进行过研究，不过确实是以普通文物风光爱好者的身份，畅游在满是图片的橱窗外。有时被造型勾勒出的美感所吸引，有时被漫画夸张的奇特形状所迷惑，有时被明媚动人的景色所诱惑。现在的游客总是随手带着画笔，带回家的都是满满的速描画，时尚如此，所以我也随意凑了几幅，供友人娱乐。当我浏览了那些有心记下的提示和备忘后，常常心生恐慌，我的惰性令一些重大课题束之高阁，而这都是著书立说的游客所要研究的。我担心自己会像一个不幸的风景画家那样使人失望，虽然他曾经游过欧洲大陆，但总是随着自己流浪的嗜好，去犄角旮旯和荒郊野岭里写生。因而，他的写生簿里总有村舍、自然风光和说不上名字的废墟，而没有圣彼得大教堂或者罗马圆剧场，特尼大瀑布或者那不勒斯湾，怎么也找不到一幅冰川或者火山的奇观。

The Ephemera
蜉　蝣

Benjamin Franklin / 本杰明·富兰克林

‖作者简介‖

　　本杰明·富兰克林（1706～1790），18世纪美国最伟大的科学家，著名的政治家和文学家。他生于北美洲的波士顿，幼年家境贫穷，一生只受过两年正式教育。但他自学从未间断过，从自然科学、技术方面的读物到著名科学家的论文以及名家作品无不涉猎。

　　1726年，他出版了《穷理查历书》，当时被译成12种文字，畅销欧美各国，也奠定了他在文学史上的地位。他还是一位杰出的社会活动家，一生用了大量的时间去从事社会活动。从1757到1775年他几次作为北美殖民地代表到英国谈判。独立战争爆发后，他参加了第2届大陆会议和《独立宣言》的起草工作。1776年，70岁高龄的他出使法国，赢得了法国和欧洲人民对北美独立战争的支援。1787年，他积极参加了制定美国宪法的工作，并组织了反对奴役黑人的运动。

　　1790年4月17日，深夜11点，富兰克林溘然长逝。

You may remember, my dear friend, that when we lately spent that happy day in the delightful garden and sweet society of the Moulin Joly, I stopped a little in one of our walks, and stayed some time behind the company. We had been shown numberless skeletons of a kind of little fly, called an ephemera, whose successive generations, we were told, were bred and expired within the day. I happened to see a living company of them on a leaf, who appeared to be engaged

感动一个国家的文字

in conversation. You know I understand all the inferior animal tongues. My too great application to the study of them is the best excuse I can give for the little progress I have made in your charming language. I listened through curiosity to the discourse of these little creatures; but as they in their national vivacity, spoke three or four together, I could make but little of their conversation. I found, however, by some broken expressions that I heard now and then, they were disputing warmly on the merit of two foreign musicians, one a cousin, the other a moscheto; in which dispute they spent their time, seemingly as regardless of the shortness of life as if they had been sure of living a month. Happy people! Thought I; you are certainly under a wise, just, and mild government, since you have no public grievances to complain of, nor any subject of contention but the perfections and imper-

亲爱的朋友，你可记得，上次我们在苟丽磨坊那让人愉快的花园中参加社团活动的那天，我曾在散步时独自停留了一会儿，落在了人群的后面。这是因为有人指给我们看了一种属苍蝇一类的小昆虫的残尸——它叫蜉蝣。据说，它们的生命非常短，在一天时间里，可以生生死死好几代。那天，我碰巧在一片叶子上见到了一群鲜活的蜉蝣，它们看上去正忙着交谈。你是知道的，我几乎能懂得所有低等动物的语言。也许，我对研究它们语言的极大热心却成为我在学习你们美妙语言时少有进步的最好借口了。我好奇地倾听着这些小生物的对话，然而它们却在以自己的方式，三个一群，四个一伙地讨论着，我只能听清其中一部分对话。尽管如此，我还是从那些只言片语中听出，它们正在热烈地争论着两位国外音乐家谁的成就更为杰出。这两位音乐家中一位是蚋先生，另一位是蚊先生。它们热烈地讨论着，似乎忘了生命的短暂，好像可以活一个月之久似的。多么快乐啊！我想：你们一定是在一种贤明公正、宽仁待民的政府之下。因为你们既没有抱怨与牢骚，也没有任何的党派之争，而是

fections of foreign music. I turned my head from them to an old gray-headed one, who was single on another leaf, and talking to himself. Being amused with his soliloquy, I put it down in writing, in hopes it will likewise amuse her to whom I am so much indebted for the most pleasing of all amusements, her delicious company and heavenly harmony.

" It was, " said he, " the opinion of learned philosophers of our race, who lived and flourished long before my time, that this vast world, the Moulin Joly, could not itself subsist more than eighteen hours; and I think there was some foundation for that opinion, since, by the apparent motion of the great luminary that gives life to all nature, and which in my time has evidently declined considerably towards the ocean at the end of our earth, it must then finish its course, be extinguished in the waters that surround us, and leave the world in cold and darkness, necessarily producing universal death and destruction. I have lived seven of those hours, a great age, being no less than four hundred and twenty minutes of time. How very few of us continue so long! I have seen generations born, flouris, and expire. My present friends are the children and grandchildren of the friends of my youth, who are now, alas, no more! And I must soon follow them; for, by the course of nature, though still in health, I cannot expect to live above seven or eight minutes longer. What now avails all my toil and labor in amassing honey-dew on this leaf, which I cannot live to enjoy! What political struggles I have been engaged in for the good of my compatriot inhabitants of this bush of my philo-sophical studies for the benefit of our race in general! For in politics what can laws do without morals? Our present race of ephemerae will in a course of minutes become corrupt, like those of other and older bushes, and consequently as wretched. And in philosophy how

感动一个国家的文字

在颇有闲情地讨论着外国音乐的完美与不完美之处。我将头转向它们中一个白头发的老者，它独自在另一片叶子上自言自语。我觉得它的独白非常有趣，于是记了下来，并且希望这些话同样博她一笑，算做我对她的报答。因为我已受到好友太多的深情厚意，她的清风明月的风度，她的妙音雅奏，一向使我倾倒不已。

老蜉蝣说："这是在很久很久以前，一位著名哲人认为：我们这个世界——即芍丽磨坊，其生存不会超过十八小时。我想，这个观点一定是有所根据的。因为，太阳通过运动赋予了大自然生命，而在我的这个年代里，太阳正在自东往西的移动，明显已经落得很低了；快要沉到我们地球尽头的海洋里去了。太阳必将结束自己的行程，被围绕在我们周围的海水所吞噬，世界变得一片寒冷与黑暗，万物都将死亡与毁灭。我已活过了七个小时，一段看起来不短的时间，足足有四百二十分钟！我们中很少有人能够如此高寿。我目睹了一代又一代人繁衍生息，寿终正寝。我现在的朋友，都是我儿时伙伴的孩子或孙子，而我那些儿时的伙伴却早已不在了。不久，我也会随他们而去，这是自然的规律。虽然目前我还很健康，但是我并不奢望我还能活上个七八分钟。现在我所有的精力都集中在收集这片叶子的蜜露上，虽然我生前已不可能享受了。我一直热心的政治斗争也是为了居住在这个灌木丛中的所有我的同胞们的利益；我所进行的哲学研究同样也是为了我们整个民族共同的利益。可是在政治上，法律没有道德的配合，政治仍旧不能清明。我们现在这一族蜉蝣必须随时警惕，不然在几分钟内，就可能变得像别的、老一些的灌木丛中的蜉蝣那样腐化，万劫不复！在哲学这方面我们的成就是多么渺小啊！唉！艺术是永恒的，而生命则是有限的。我的朋

small our progress! Alas! Art is long, and life is short! My friends would comfort me with the idea of a name they say I shall leave behind me; and they tell me I have lived long enough to nature and to glory. But what will fame be to an ephemera who no longer exists? And what will become of all history in the eighteenth hour, when the world itself, even the whole Moulin Joly, shall come to an end, and be buried in universal ruin? "

To me, after all my eager pursuits, no solid pleasures now remain, but the reflection of a long life spent in meaning well, the sensible conversation of a few good lady ephemerae, and now and then a kind smile and a tune from the ever amiable Brillante.

友们曾这样安慰我，说我活的时间长得足够让我的名字在我死后流芳千古。但是对于一个已死的蜉蝣来说，名声又有什么意义呢？何况到了第十八个小时的时候，整个芍丽磨坊将会消亡，世界末日已来临，还谈得上什么历史呢？”

对我来说，经过了对所有渴望的追求，别无乐趣了，唯有想起世间众生，人虫不分，如能长寿而为大众服务，这是可以引为自慰的；其次则听听蜉蝣太太与蜉蝣小姐们的高谈阔论，或者说偶然从那可爱的白夫人那里，得到巧笑一顾，或者是婉歌一曲，我的暮年也得到安慰了。

撼动一个国家的文字

Beauty 论美

Ralph Waldo Emerson／拉尔夫·沃尔多·爱默生

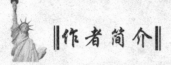

‖作者简介‖

　　拉尔夫·沃尔多·爱默生(1803—1882)，美国思想家、诗人、散文家。生于波士顿牧师家庭，毕业于波士顿拉丁学校和哈佛大学。21岁时成为神职人员，不久便对基督教产生怀疑，1832年辞职远游，遍访欧洲文化名人。曾经深入研究过荷马、柏拉图、但丁、蒙田和莎士比亚。代表作有《论自然》、《美国学者》、《神学院致辞》、《散文选》、《诗集》等。

A nobler want of man is served by nature, namely, the love of Beauty.

The ancient Greeks called the world Κόομος, beauty. Such is the constitution of all things, or such the plastic power of the human eye, that the primary forms, as the sky, the mountain, the tree, the animal, give us a delight in and for themselves; a pleasure arising from outline,

　　大自然除了提供人类衣食所需之外，还满足了一种更高尚的追求——那就是满足了人们的爱美之心。

　　古希腊人把"宇宙"称为"科士谟土"，即美丽之意。万物之本性无比奇妙，或者可以说，人类独具适应性的潜能，能够构形筑影。因而，大自然所有的基本形态，蓝天，山峦，树木，鸟兽，等等，都能使我们惊喜；这种惊喜并不依赖外物，也不因其有任何实用目的，只是就万物的线条、色彩、运动与组合看起来都让人爽心怡性。在

color, motion, and grouping. This seems partly owing to the eye itself. The eye is the best of artists. By the mutual action of its structure and of the laws of light, perspective is produced, which integrates every mass of objects, of what character soever, into a well colored and shaded globe, so that where the particular objects are mean and unaffecting, the landscape which they compose is round and symmetrical. And as the eye is the best composer, so light is the first of painters. There is no object so foul that intense light will not make beautiful. And the stimulus it affords to the sense, and a sort of infinitude which it has, like space and time, make all matter gay. Even the corpse has its own beauty. But besides this general grace diffused over nature, almost all the individual forms are agreeable to the eye, as is proved by our endless imitations of some of them, as the acorn, the grape, the pine-cone, the wheat-ear, the egg, the wings and forms of most birds, the lion's claw, the serpent, the butterfly, sea-shells, flames, clouds, buds, leaves, and the forms of many trees, as the palm.

For better consideration, we may distribute the aspects of Beauty in a threefold manner.

1.First, the simple perception of natural forms is a delight. The influence of the forms and actions in nature is so needful to man, that, in its lowest functions, it seems to lie on the confines of commodity and beauty. To the body and mind, which have been cramped by noxious work or company, nature is medicinal and restores their tone. The tradesman, the attorney comes out of the din and craft of the street and sees the sky and the woods, and is a man again. In their eternal calm, he finds himself. The health of the eye seems to demand a horizon. We are never fired, so long as we can see far enough.

But in other hours, Nature satisfies by its loveliness, and without any mixture of corporeal benefit. I see the spectacle of morning from

某种程度上，这可能由于我们的眼睛自身。眼睛，是世界上最好的画家。眼睛的结构与光学的法则互动，产生出所谓的"透视"，因此任何一组物体，不管它是何种东西，在我们看来都觉得色彩清晰，明暗层次鲜明，井然有序，整体就似乎是一个球；个别的物体或许形态拙劣，了无生趣，但一经组合，就变得对称而完满了。故构图的巧妙，非人的眼睛莫属；而要想把色彩铺设得美妙，则要依赖光线。再丑恶的东西，强光之下，也会产生美。光线不但激活了感官，而且光线好似空间和时间，有着能把一切都覆盖的性质，所以任何东西只要在光明下都是赏心悦目的。即使死尸也有它自己的美。自然界所有事物都在"美"的笼罩之下，几乎所有的个体都这么美好。如橡实、葡萄、松果、麦穗、鸡蛋、形形色色的翅膀以及种类繁多的鸟，如狮爪、蛇、蝴蝶、贝壳、火焰、云朵、蓓蕾、绿叶和如棕榈树似的许多树的树干，我们不断地描摹它们，把它们作为"美"的典范。

为了更进一步地了解，我们可将自然之美，分三方面剖析：

一，倘能抱着单纯的心态去感知自然形态也是一种快乐。自然形态和活动的效用，于人生是必不可缺的。就最基本的作用来说，似乎局限于实用和审美两者之间。俗世纷扰牵绊了人的身心，一旦回到大自然中，自然的医疗妙用就得以发挥，让人们恢复身心健康。走出熙熙攘攘闹市的商人和律师，抬头看见蓝天和树木，就会重新感受到人性的本质。在大自然恒久的天籁中，他领悟到自我真实的一面。如果要保护眼睛的健康，我们的视野一定要宽阔。只要可以看得久远，我们就永远不会倦怠。

但是即使在我们并不觉得劳累的时候，大自然也满足于它的赏心悦目；我们之所以喜欢自然，和我们身体所受的恩惠没有一丝关

the hilltop over against my house, from daybreak to sunrise, with emotions which an angel might share. The long slender bars of cloud float like fishes in the sea of crimson light. From the earth, as a shore, I look out into that silent sea. I seem to partake its rapid transformations; the active enchantment reaches my dust, and I dilate and conspire with the morning wind. How does Nature deify with a few and cheap elements! Give me health and a day, and I will make the pomp of emperors ridiculous. The dawn is my Assyria; the sunset and moon-rise, my Paphos and unimaginable realms of faerie; broad noon shall be my England of the senses and the understanding; the night shall be my Germany of mystic philosophy and dreams.

...

2.The presence of a higher, namely, of the spiritual element is essential to its perfection. The high and divine beauty which can be loved without effeminacy, is that which is found in combination with the human will. Beauty is the mark God sets upon virtue. Every natural action is graceful. Every heroic act is also decent, and causes the place and the bystanders to shine. We are taught by great actions that the universe is the properly of every individual in it. Every rational creature has all nature for his dowry and estate. It is his, if he will. He may divest himself of it; he may creep into a corner, and abdicate his kingdom, as most men do, but he is entitled to the world by his constitution. In proportion to the energy of his thought and will, he lakes up the world into himself.···

3.There is still another aspect under which the beauty of the world may be viewed, namely, as it becomes an object of the intellect. Beside the relation of things to virtue, they have a relation to thought. The intellect searches out the absolute order of things as they stand in the mind of God, and without the colors of affection. The intellectual

系。我常常在屋对面的山顶上眺望晨景，从清晨到日落，心潮澎湃，感受着天使能感受的激情。纤细的云朵畅游在绛色霞光里，就像鱼儿遨游在深海中。我从地面望去，仿佛从海滩上凝视着静谧的大海。海天瞬息万变，我似乎分享着它急速的变幻；这活泼的氤氲侵袭了我的身体，我觉得生命在蔓延，与晨风合为一体。大自然只需来些简单的变幻，就能让我们变得超凡脱俗！给我健康与一天光阴，我将锻造帝王们奢华的浮世绘。绚烂清晨，是我的亚述帝国；夕阳西落，皓月东升，是我的帕福斯和无法想象的超凡景致；泛泛午日，将是我感觉和思维的英格兰；深深黑夜成为我玄妙哲理和梦想的德意志。

……

二，完美无缺的美需要一种更高层的精神元素。高尚神圣之美，与温柔之美不同，是和人类的意志统一的。美是德的标识，这是上帝特定的。凡是顺乎自然规律的行为就是美的，英勇崇高的行为，一定合情合理，它的荣耀甚至恩泽到发生该事的地方和旁观者。圣贤豪杰的伟大行径，都是留给后世的一种教导，我们因此知道：宇宙是属于每个人的基业，每个正常的人都可以把六合之围看成是自己的产业，或者嫁妆。如果他愿意拥有的话，触手可及。他也可以自暴自弃，放弃他的财富；他可以舍弃自己的江山，偏安一隅，苟且偷生。这种不长进的人世界上比比皆是，但根据他素质之高低，他有权拥有自己的世界。权衡自己的思想和意志，拥有属于自己的世界。……

三，从另一种角度也能看出世界之美，即用理智来研究自然界。万物除了与美德相关，还与思想结下不解之缘。万物在上帝灵魂中都有其固有的模式，人们可撇弃情感上的好恶，用理智直接去探究。思维和活动似乎相辅相成，专一的思维产生专一的行为，反之亦然。

and the active powers seem to succeed each other, and the exclusive activity of the one generates the exclusive activity of the other. There is something unfriendly in each to the other, but they are like the alternate periods of feeding and working in animals; each prepares and will be followed by the other. Therefore does beauty, which, in relation to actions, as we have seen, comes unsought, and comes because it is unsought, remain for the apprehension and pursuit of the intellect; and then again, in its turn, of the active power. Nothing divine dies. All good is eternally reproductive. The beauty of nature reforms itself in the mind, and not for barren contemplation, but for new creation.

All men are in some degree impressed by the face of the world; some men even to delight. This love of beauty is Taste. Others have the same love in such excess, that, not content with admiring, they seek to embody it in new forms. The creation of beauty is Art.

The production of a work of art throws a light upon the mystery of humanity. A work of art is an abstract or epitome of the world. It is the result or expression of nature, in miniature. For although the works of nature are innumerable and all different, the result or the expression of them all is similar and single. Nature is a sea of forms radically alike and even unique. A leaf, a sunbeam, a landscape, the ocean, make an analogous impression on the mind. What is common to them all,—that perfectness and harmony, is beauty. The standard of beauty is the entire circuit of nature forms,—the totality of nature; which the Italians expressed by defining beauty " il più nell' uno. " Nothing is quite beautiful alone; nothing but is beautiful in the whole. A single object is only so far beautiful as it suggests this universal grace. The poet, the painter, the sculptor, the musician, the architect, seek each to concentrate this radiance of the world on one point, and each in his

两者之间颇有微词，但它们如动物进食和工作时间相互交迭一样，也为彼此的来临做好准备。美同行为的关系，正如我们所见，不去刻意追求而自然生成，因为它未被寻求所以它来了。然后，保持着美，作为理智思索与追逐的客体；而后，美激活了行动。神圣的东西决不会灭亡，所有的"善"都生生不息。自然之美改善了心灵中的自我，它不是空洞的冥想，而是新创造的起点。

世界的美，人们多多少少都能领略；有些人不仅感受而已，甚至于喜悦。这种爱美之心就是"趣味"。另一些人爱不释手，觉得单是艳美，犹有不足，继而创造新的形式，把美纳入其中，而艺术则就是美的创造。

美术品的创造为人类的传奇揭开一线曙光。美术作品是世界的精髓，是现实的缩影。微观上，它是大自然的产物。尽管自然界的作品难以计数，各不相同，它们的产物却是单纯统一的。大自然海纳百川，但根本上还是如出一辙，可以说是独一无二。一片树叶、一缕阳光、一爿风景、一汪海洋，虽不是同一样景物，但是都可以产生出相同的心灵感受。它们的共同之处在于，完美与和谐才是美。美的标准是自然的全部，是形形色色的大自然的合体。意大利人这样定义美"以一见多"。由此可见，没有什么是独自美丽的，一旦整

several work to satisfy the love of beauty which stimulates him to produce. Thus is Art a nature passed through the alembic of man. Thus in art does Nature work through the will of a man filled with the beauty of her first works.

The world thus exists to the soul to satisfy the desire of beauty. This element I call an ultimate end. No reason can be asked or given why the soul seeks beauty. Beauty, in its largest and profoundest sense, is one expression for the universe. God is the all-fair. Truth, and goodness, and beauty, are but different faces of the same all. But beauty in nature is not ultimate. It is the herald of inward and eternal beauty, and is not alone a solid and satisfactory good. It must stand as a part, and not as yet the last or highest expression of the final cause of Nature.

体观之，没有什么是不美的。单独的物体仅在反射万物之美时才会如此美丽。诗人、画家、雕塑家、音乐家、建筑家，其道虽不同，但只是用不同的形式，将这光辉的世界集于一点；他们各自的作品满足了人们的爱美之心，这又刺激了他们的创作。因而，艺术就是大自然通过人心的净化而形成的。人心有感于万物之美，自然界借助了艺术家才能的发挥，作第二步的创作，即艺术。

因而世界的存在，是为了满足人们灵魂中爱美的需求。这是最终的目标。无人会问，也无人能解释——为什么灵魂需要美。美，从最宏大和最深远的意义上说，是一种对宇宙的表述。上帝是至美的。真善美三者，只是一个本体的三个方面的表现而已。可是自然界的美并非极致。它本身不是完好圆满的"善"，而是为内在的永恒"美"做先导而已。我们可以把它看做整体中的一部分，宇宙另有其根本的原因，其表现的方式也多种多样，自然界的美并不是终极的或最高的体现。

再度游湖

Once More to the Lake

Elwyn Brooks White/埃尔温·布鲁克斯·怀特

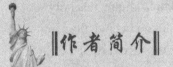

‖作者简介‖

　　埃尔温·布鲁克斯·怀特(1899~1985)，美国著名散文作家、评论家。生于纽约，毕业于康奈尔大学。曾任《纽约人》杂志的编辑和《哈帕斯》的专栏作家，为《纽约人》供职长达12年之久，《纽约人》的成功，他有着不可替代的贡献。同时，怀特在儿童读物的创作上也颇有建树，其代表作是《这就是纽约》。怀特的思想敏感独特，对生活的观察细致入微，文风朴实无华，尤其是一些游记性的文章，被广泛转载于大量的课本与选本之中。其主要作品有散文集《拐角处的第二棵树》、诗集《冷漠的女士》等。

　　One summer, along about 1904, my father rented a camp on a lake in Maine and took us all there for the month of August. We all got ringworm from some kittens and had to rub Pond's Extract on our arms and legs night and morning, and my father rolled over in a canoe with all his clothes on; but outside of that the vacation was a success and from then on none of us ever thought there was any place in the world like that lake in Maine. We returned summer after summer — always on August 1st for one month. I have since become a salt-water man, but sometimes in summer there are days when the restlessness, of the tides and the fearful cold of the sea water and the incessant wind which blow across the afternoon and into the evening make me wish for the placidity of a lake in the woods. A few weeks ago this feeling got so strong I bought myself a couple of bass hooks and a spinner and returned to the lake where we used to go, for a week's fishing and to revisit old haunts.

I took along my son, who had never had any fresh water up his nose and who had seen lily pads only from train windows. On the journey over to the lake I began to wonder what it would be like. I wondered how time would have marred this unique, this holy spot— the coves and streams, the hills that the sun set behind, the camps and the paths behind the camps. I was sure the tarred road would have found it out and I wondered in what other ways it would be desolated. It is strange how much you can remember about places like that once you allow your mind to return into the grooves which lead back, you remember one thing, and that suddenly reminds you of another thing. I guess I remembered clearest of all the early mornings, when the lake was cool and motionless, remembered how the bedroom smelled of the lumber it was made of and of the wet woods whose scent entered through the screen. The partitions in the camp were thin and did not extend clear to the top of the rooms, and as I was always the first up I would dress softly so as not to wake the others, and slide out into the sweet outdoors and start out the canoe, keeping close along the shore in the long shadows of the pines. I remember being very careful never to rub my paddle against the gunwale for fear of disturbing the stillness of the cathedral.

The lake had never been what you would call a wild lake. There were cottages sprinkled around the shores, and it was in farming country although the shore of the lake were quite heavily wooded. Some of the cottages were owned by nearby farmers, and you would live at

大约是在 1904 年的夏季，我父亲在缅因州的一个湖畔租了一间临时住房，把我们都带去了。整个八月，我们都是在那里度过的。我们从一些小猫身上传染了金钱癣，不得不在胳膊和腿上一天到晚都擦满旁氏冷霜；还有一次我父亲从船上掉入水中，当时他西装革履。不过除了这些，我们度过了一个愉快的假期。从那时起，我们大家都公认缅因州的这个湖是世上无与伦比的地方。我们连续几个夏天都在这里度过——通常 8 月 1 日到达，然后过完整个八月。再后来我爱上了海滨生活。但是在夏季的有些日子里，海浪汹涌不息，海水冰凉刺骨，海风从上午到下午吹个不停，这一切让我很是渴望山林中小湖边的清净。几周以前，这种情形愈演愈烈。于是我买了两根鲈鱼钓竿和一些诱饵，重新回到以前我们常去的那个湖畔，准备故地重游，再钓上一个星期的鱼。

　　我带着我儿子一起去。他从没有游过淡水湖，只是透过火车上的玻璃窗看见了漂浮在水面上的莲叶。在驶向湖畔的路上，我开始想象它现在的样子。我猜测岁月会把这片独一无二的圣地破坏成怎样一副模样——那里的海湾和小溪，笼罩在落日里的山峦，还有宿营的小屋和屋后的小路。我相信这条柏油马路已经给了我答案，我还在想象其他哪些地方也被破坏了。很奇怪，一旦你任由思绪回归往日，很多旧地的记忆就会被重新唤醒。你记起了一件事情，就会联想起另一件事情。我想我记得最清楚的是那些爽朗的清晨，清凉的湖水，平静的湖面，卧室里弥漫着木屋的清香，屋子外面，湿润的树林散发的芳香穿透房间的墙板，依稀可嗅。木屋的隔板很薄，而且离房顶有一段距离。我总是第一个起床的人，为了不吵醒别人，我蹑手蹑脚地穿好衣服，悄悄地溜出屋来。外面一片馥郁芬芳，我坐上小船出发，沿着湖岸，在一条长长的松树阴影里划过。我记得当时我总是很谨慎，从来不让我的浆与船舷的上缘碰在一起，以免打破教堂的宁静。

　　这个湖绝不是人们所说的那种荒郊野湖。一些村舍零星地坐落在湖岸边上，尽管湖边都是茂密的树木，但是这里还是农业区；有些村舍是附近农家的，你可以住在湖边，到农舍里用餐——我们一家就是这样。不过，尽管这个湖泊不显得荒凉，可也相当大而且不

the shore and eat your meals at the farmhouse. That's what our family did. But although it wasn't wild, it was a fairly large and undisturbed lake and there were places in it which, to a child at least, seemed infinitely remote and primeval.

I was right about the tar: it led to within half a mile of the shore. But when I got back there, with my boy, and we settled into a camp near a farmhouse and into the kind of summertime I had known, I could tell that it was going to be pretty much the same as it had been before—I knew it, lying in bed the first morning, smelling the bedroom, and hearing the boy sneak quietly out and go off along the shore in a boat. I began to sustain the illusion that he was I, and therefore, by simple transposition, that I was my father. This sensation persisted, kept cropping up all the time we were there. It was not an entirely new feeling, but in this setting it grew much stronger. I seemed to be living a dual existence. I would be in the middle of some simple act, I would be picking up a bait box or laying down a table fork, or I would be saying something, and suddenly it would be not I but my father who was saying the words or making the gesture. It gave me a creepy sensation.

We went fishing the first morning, I felt the same damp moss covering the worms in the bait can, and saw the dragonfly alight on the tip of my rod as it hovered a few inches from the surface of the water, it was the arrival of this fly that convinced me beyond any doubt that everything was as it always had been, that the years were a mirage and there had been no years. The small waves were the same, chucking the rowboat under the chin as we fished at anchor, and the boat was the same boat, the same color green and the ribs broken in the same place, and under the floor, boards the same freshwater leavings and debris—the dead hellgrammite, the wisps of moss, the rusty discarded fishhook, the dried blood from yesterday's catch.

受外界干扰。至少对于一个孩子来说，有些地方确实太过沉静，而且有点原始的味道。

我对柏油马路的猜测是正确的，它把我们带到了离岸边只有半英里的地方。我带着儿子又回到了这里，当我们安顿在一家农舍附近的木屋后，又重新感受到了我所熟悉的那种夏日时光，我知道这一切都和原来一样——我对这一点坚信不疑。第一天早上，我躺在床上，闻着卧室里的清香，听见我的儿子悄悄地溜出房门，乘上一条小船沿着湖岸划去。我突然产生一种错觉，他就是我，而根据最简单的推移法，我就是我父亲了。在那些日子里，这种感觉一直存在，反复地在我头脑中呈现。这种感觉并不是前所未有，但在这个地方，它却变得越来越强烈：我过的似乎是一种双重的生活。有时我做一些简单的活动，比方说捡起一个装鱼饵的盒子，或者放下一只餐叉，或是在说什么话的当儿，就突然有种感觉，好像说话的人或者摆着某个姿势的人不是我，而是我父亲——这真让我感到不寒而栗。

第一天早上我们一起去钓鱼。我感觉那些与往日同样潮湿的苔藓覆盖着罐子里的鱼饵，蜻蜓在离水面几英寸的地方盘旋，接着便落在了我的钓竿头上。正是这只蜻蜓的到来使我更加坚信，所有这一切都和过去一样。岁月就像海市蜃楼一样似乎从来没有存在过。湖面上一如既往地荡漾着微波，在我们暂停垂钓时轻轻地拍打着船头钩的下部；小船还是旧时的那一只，同样的绿色；在同样的位置，有同样的一根肋材断裂了；同样有些淡水中的残渣遗骸停留在船板底下——死了的具角鱼蛉，一团团的苔藓，被人抛弃了的生满锈的钓鱼钩，还有前一天捕鱼时留在那里已经干了的斑斑血迹。我们静

We stared silently at the tips of our rods, at the dragonflies that came and went. I lowered the tip of mine into the water, tentatively, pensively dislodging the fly, which darted two feet away, poised, darted two feet back, and came to rest again a little farther up the rod. There had been no years between the duckling of this dragonfly and the other one — the one that was past of memory. I looked at the boy, who was silently watching his fly, and it was my hands that held his rod, my eyes watching. I felt dizzy and didn't know which rod I was at the end of.

We caught two bass, hauling them in briskly as though they were mackerel, pulling them over the side of the boat in a businesslike manner without any landing net, and stunning them with a blow on the back of the head. When we got back for a swim before lunch, the lake was exactly where we had left it, the same number of inches from the dock, and there was only the merest suggestion of a breeze. This seemed an utterly enchanted sea, this lake you could leave to its own devices for a few hours and come back to, and find that it had not stirred, this constant and trust-worthy body of water. In the shallows, the dark, water-soaked sticks and twigs, smooth and old, were undulating in clusters on the bottom against the clean ribbed sand, and the track of the mussel was plain. A school of minnows swam by, each minnow with its small individual shadow, doubling, the attendance, so clear and sharp in the sunlight. Some of the other campers were in swimming, along the shore, one of them with a cake of soap, and the water felt thin and clear and unsubstantial. Over the years there had been this person with the cake of soap, this cultist, and here he was. There had been no years.

Up to the farmhouse to dinner through the teeming, dusty field, the road under our sneakers was only a two-track road. The middle track was missing, the one with the marks of the hooves and the

静地注视着钓竿的顶头，注视着那些来回飞舞的蜻蜓。我把自己钓竿的顶端伸进水中，试探着不声不响地想把蜻蜓赶走。它迅速地飞离了大约两英尺，平衡了一下身体，然后又飞回两英尺，重新停在钓竿上，不过位子高了一点点。在我的记忆中，这只蜻蜓躲闪的样子和曾经有过的一只一样，在它们中间没有岁月的间隔。我看了看身边的儿子，他正悄无声息地凝视着自己钓竿上的蜻蜓；突然间，他那握住钓竿的手仿佛是我的手，而他注视着蜻蜓的眼睛仿佛是我的眼睛。我感到一阵眩晕，不知道自己的手握着哪根钓竿的一端。

我们钓到了两条鲈鱼，像扯鲐鱼似的轻快地把它们扯上来，也没有用任何鱼网，就这样有条不紊地把它们从船舷上拖进了船舱，然后猛击了一下鱼的脑袋，把它们打晕了。午饭前我们又到湖里游泳了一次，湖水和我们刚才离开时没有什么两样，你仍然可以站在离码头只有几英寸的地方，也只有一点点微风轻拂过的痕迹。这片湖水好像被施了魔法的大海一样，在你离开的几个小时里它可以随心所欲，回来却发现它丝毫没有改变，真可以称得上忠心耿耿值得信赖。在水浅的地方，有一些黝黑光滑的枯枝浸泡在水里，它们一丛一丛地在湖底那些干净的呈波纹状的沙石上随波起伏，而贻贝的痕迹也清晰可见。一群小鲤鱼从这里游过，每一条都投下自己的影子，数量立刻就增加了一倍，在阳光下十分清晰鲜明。有一些游客正沿着湖岸游泳，其中有一个人用了香皂。湖水清澈透明，差不多让人感觉不到它的存在。很多年前，这个用香皂洗浴的人就在这里了，这是一个对湖畔热心崇拜的人，如今他依然在这里。这里的岁月似乎静止未动。

我们穿过了一片繁茂而且弥漫着灰尘的田野到农舍去吃午饭。脚下的这条小路有两条路痕，原来位于中间的那一条没有了，那上面曾经布满了马蹄印和一团团干巴巴的污粪的痕迹。以前这里一直有三条小路可以供人们选择，现在却只剩两条了。有一段时间我根

splotches of dried, flaky manure. There had always been three tracks to choose from in choosing which track to walk in, now the choice was narrowed down to two. For a moment I missed terribly the middle alternative. But the way led past the tennis court; and something about the way it lay there in the sun reassured me, the tape had loosened along the backline, the alleys were green with plantains and other weeds, and the net (installed in June and removed in September) sagged in the dry noon, and the whole place steamed with midday heat and hunger and emptiness. There was a choice of pie for dessert, and one was blueberry and one was apple, and the waitresses were the same country girls, there having been no passage of time, only the illusion of it as in a dropped curtain — the waitresses were still fifteen; their hair had been washed, that was the only difference — they had been to the movies and seen the pretty girls with the clean hair.

Summertime, oh summertime, pattern of life indelible, he fade-proof lake, the woods unshatterable, the pasture with the sweetfern and the juniper forever, and ever, summer without end; this was the background, and the life along the shore was the design, the cottagers with their innocent and tranquil design, their tiny docks with the flagpole and the American flag floating against the white clouds in the bluesky, the little paths over the roots of the trees leading from camp to camp and the paths leading back to the outhouses and the can of lime for sprinking, and at the souvenir counters at the store the miniature birch-bark canoes and the post cards that showed things looking a little better than they looked. This was the American family at play, escaping the city heat, wondering whether the newcomers in the camp at the head of the cove were "common" or "nice", wondering whether it was true that the people who drove up for Sunday dinner at the farmhouse were turned away because there wasn't enough chicken.

本找不到中间的那条路。不过当我们到达网球场附近时，看见了阳光下的某些东西，让我重新确定它曾经确实存在。球场底线旁边的带子已经松懈下垂了，葱绿的车前草和其他杂草在球道上滋生横行；球网（六月份挂上，九月份摘下）在这个闷热的中午也耷拉着；整个球场都弥漫着酷暑正午滚滚的热气，让人感到饥饿、空乏。饭后的甜点可以自己选择黑莓饼或是苹果饼。做服务的人同样是些乡村少女，这里似乎不存在时间的流逝，有的只是舞台的幕帘降落后带给人们的幻觉——这些侍女们依然只是十五岁，她们的头发洗得干干净净，这是唯一改变了的地方——她们看过电影，见过那些有着干净头发的漂亮姑娘。

夏季呀夏季，永恒不变的生活方式，湖水永远不褪色，树木永远不可摧毁；草地上总是长满了香蕨和杜松，夏日的时光永无尽头，这些都是背景，而湖滨沿岸的生活就是其中美妙的图案。村子里的农民们过着恬静的生活；他们小小的码头上立着旗杆，美国国旗在镶嵌着白云的蓝天里飘扬，每棵树下都有一条小径通向一座座木屋，木屋处又有小径通往厕所和树木用的石灰罐；商店里纪念品的柜台上，摆放着用桦树皮制作的独木船的模型，而明信片上的景物也比眼前的真实景物美丽多了。在这里，美国人逃避了城市的酷热喧闹，到这个地方游玩。他们不知道那些新来的住在海湾尽头的居民是"普通老百姓"还是"贵族"，也不知道那些星期天驱车前来农舍吃饭的人，是不是被分量不足的鸡肉打发走了。

It seemed to me, as I kept remembering all this, that those times and those summers had been infinitely precious and worth saving. There had been jollity and peace and goodness. The arriving (at the beginning of August) had been so big a business in itself, at the railway station the farm wagon drawn up, the first smell of the pine-laden air, the first glimpse of the smiling farmer, and the great importance of the trunks and your father's enormous authority in such matters, and the feel of the wagon under you for the long tenmile haul, and at the top of the last long hill catching the first view of the lake after eleven months of not seeing this cherished body of water. The shouts and cries of the other campers when they saw you, and the trunks to be unpacked, to give up their rich burden. (Arriving was less exciting nowadays, when you sneaked up in your car and parked it under a tree near the camp and took out the bags and in five minutes it was all over, no fuss, no loud wonderful fuss about trunks.)

...

我不停地回忆这一切，我似乎感觉那些日子和那些夏日时光的回忆对我而言都是珍贵无比、值得永远珍藏的。那里有快乐，有宁静，还有所有美好的事情。能够在八月就到达那里，这本身就是最重要的：农场的货车停在火车站外，这时又第一回闻到松木散发的清香，第一回见到农民笑容满面的脸庞，宽大的旅行箱气派极了，而父亲在指挥这些事情时显出绝对的权威性；你坐在货车上，享受它拉着你走上十英里的感觉，当到达最后一座小山顶时，一眼就能看见那阔别了十一个月之久的、无比宝贵的一片湖水；其他的游客为你的到来大声欢呼。然后打开大旅行箱，卸下里面准备齐全的物品。（如今再到这里来，已经找不到昔日激动人心的场面了。你所需要做的只是静静地把车开过来，停在木屋旁的树底下，取出行李袋，把一切东西在五分钟内收拾完毕，不会有大声的喧闹，也不会忙着喊着搬行李了。）

……

感动一个国家的文字

Success 成　功

Emily Dickinson/ 艾米莉·狄更生

‖作者简介‖

　　艾米莉·狄更生(1830～1886)生前几乎不为人知,而现在却被公认为是美国最优秀的诗人之一。她的诗大部分都涂写在碎纸片上,有意不让人看,在有生之年所发表的诗作寥寥无几。她在马萨诸塞州的阿姆斯特过着与世隔绝的生活。她在当地的阿姆斯特学校和霍利奥克山女子学院接受教育,极少冒险离开阿姆斯特,甚至没有离开过家。尽管艾米莉·狄更生社会阅历很少,但她的内心世界极为丰富,她的诗集中在爱情、死亡和自然这样的永恒主题上。

Success is counted sweetest
By those who ne'er succeed.
To comprehend a nectar
Requires sorest need.

从未成功的人认为
成功的滋味甜美无比,
必须要有强烈的需求,
方能领会花蜜的美味,

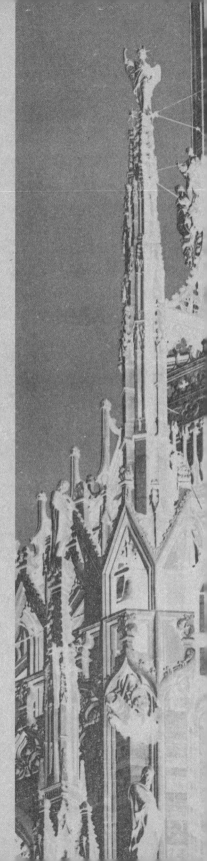

Not one of all the purple Host
Who took the Flag today
Can tell the definition,
So clear, of Victory,

As he, defeated, dying,
On whose forbidden ear
The distant strains of triumph
Break, agonized and clear.

那最显赫的人身着紫衣，
执掌着今日的大旗，
似乎没有人能像他那样
明了胜利的真谛。

当他战败后垂死，
失聪的耳边突然响起
遥远的凯歌旋律，
竟如此的痛苦而清晰。

感动一个国家的文字

未选之路

The Road Not Taken　Robert Frost/ 罗伯特·弗洛斯特

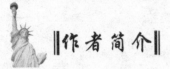

作者简介

　　罗伯特·弗洛斯特(1874～1963),美国最著名的诗人之一。获得诗名之前,弗洛斯特时而务农,时而到中学教希腊语和拉丁语。1913年,他出版了第一部诗集。弗洛斯特的诗歌备受读者喜爱,原因之一是没有受过多少学校教育的人都看得懂,他坚持使用日常语言,描写自己观察入微的日常事件。弗洛斯特的许多诗歌反映了他与大自然的贴近,通过自然来表达一种象征意义。1915年所作的《未选之路》是弗洛斯特最著名的一首诗。

Two roads diverged in a yellow wood,
And sorry I could not travel both
And be one traveler, long I stood
And looked down one as far as I could
To where it bent in the undergrowth;

黄叶林中分出两条小路,
可惜我一人不能同时涉足,
我在路口伫立良久,
向着其中一条翘首极目,
直到它消失在丛林深处。

Then took the other, as just as fair,
And having perhaps the better claim,
Because it was grassy and wanted wear;
Though as for that the passing there
Had worn them really about the same,

And both that morning equally lay
In leaves no step had trodden black.
Oh, I kept the first for another day!
Yet knowing how way leads on to way,
I doubted if I should ever come back.

I shall be telling this with a sigh
Somewhere ages and ages hence:
Two roads diverged in a wood, and I —
I took the one less traveled by,
And that has made all the difference.

但我选择了另一条路，
芳草待踏，分外幽寂，
同样显得诱人、美丽，
虽然这两条路是如此相似，
都几乎没有旅人的足迹。

那天清晨落叶满地，
两条都是未经脚步踩踏的小径，
呵，留下一条路等下次再走，
但我知道路径延绵没有尽头，
恐怕一走就再难回首。

也许多少年后在某地，
我回首往事轻声叹息，
两条道路分散在树林里——
而我选择的那条更少人迹，
从此决定了我人生的迥异。

罗伯特·弗洛斯特

感动一 家 文字

190

Blowing in the Wind
在风中吹响

Bob Dylan / 鲍勃·迪伦

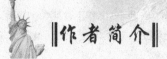

‖作者简介‖

　　鲍勃·迪伦，1941年生于明尼苏达州的德卢斯，在明尼苏达大学学习一年之后，他登上了音乐舞台。他被公认为上个世纪60年代最有影响的歌手，他创作过反战歌曲、爱情歌曲、民歌和摇滚歌曲，他的歌声影响了几代年轻人。《在风中吹响》(1963)是美国民权运动的非正式颂歌，在反越战运动中也很流行。

How many roads must a man walk down
Before you call him a man?
How many seas must a white dove sail
Before she sleeps in the sand?
How many times must the cannon balls fly
Before they're forever banned?
The answer, my friend, is blowing in the wind,
The answer is blowing in the wind.

一个男人要走过多少路，
才能称他是男子汉？
一只白鸽要飞过多少海面，
才能在沙丘安眠？
炮弹要在天空飞翔多少次，
才能永远销声匿迹？
这答案，我的朋友，正在风中吹响，
这答案正在风中吹响。

How many times must a man look up

Before he can see the sky?

How many ears must one man have

Before he can hear people cry?

How many deaths will it take till he knows

That too many people have died?

The answer, my friend, is blowing in the wind,

The answer is blowing in the wind.

How many years can a mountain exist

Before it's washed to the sea?

How many years can some people exist

Before they're allowed to be free?

How many times can a man turn his head,

Pretending he just doesn't see?

The answer, my friend, is blowing in the wind,

The answer is blowing in the wind.

一个人要仰望多少次，
才能看到蓝天？
一个人要有多少只耳朵，
才能听到人们的哭泣？
要有多少死亡才能使他了解，
已有太多的人死去？
这答案，我的朋友，正在风中吹响，
这答案正在风中吹响。

一座山要矗立多少年，
才能被海水冲没？
一些人要生存多少年，
才能被给予自由？
一个人要回头多少次，
才不会假装他什么都没看见？
这答案，我的朋友，正在风中吹响，
这答案正在风中吹响。

192

感动一个国家的文字......

Prologue *Tolerance* 《宽容》序言

Hendrik Willem Van Loon ／ 亨德里克·威廉·房龙

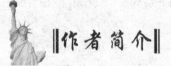 **‖作者简介‖**

　　亨德里克·威廉·房龙(1882～1944)，荷裔美国作家和历史学家。1921年，《人类的故事》的出版使他一举成名，其著作主要是历史和传记，代表作有《人类的故事》、《宽容》、《文明的开端》、《奇迹与人》、《圣经的故事》、《发明的故事》、《人类的家园》及《伦勃朗的人生苦旅》等。

…

Happily lived Mankind in the peaceful Valley of Ignorance.

Out of the darkness crept a man.

The nails of his hands were torn.

His feet were covered with rags, red with the blood of long marches.

He stumbled to the door of the nearest hut and knocked.

Then he fainted. By the light of a frightened candle, he was carried to a cot .

In the morning throughout the village it was known: "He has come back."

The neighbors stood around and shook their heads. They had always known that this was to be the end.

Defeat and surrender awaited those who dared to stroll away from the foot of the mountains.

And in one corner of the village the Old Men shook their heads and whispered burning words.

They did not mean to be cruel, but the Law was the Law. Bitterly this man had sinned against the wishes of Those Who Knew.

As soon as his wounds were healed he must be brought to trial.

They meant to be lenient.

They remembered the strange, burning eyes of his mother. They recalled the tragedy of his father, lost in the desert these thirty years ago.

The Law, however, was the Law; and the Law must be obeyed.

The Men Who Knew would see to that.

They carried the wanderer to the Market Place, and the people stood around in respectful silence.

He was still weak from hunger and thirst and the Elders bade him sit down.

He refused.

They ordered him to be silent.

But he spoke.

……

在这宁静的无知山谷里，人们幸福地生活着。

黑暗中，一个人正在爬行。

他的指甲已经磨破了。

他的脚上缠着破破烂烂的布，由于长途跋涉流出的鲜血已经把布浸透了。

他跌跌撞撞地来到最近的一间草屋，敲了敲门。

感动一个国家的文字

接着他便晕了。借助颤动的烛光，他被抬到一张吊床上。

到了早上，全村的人都相互转告："他回来了。"

邻居们围在他的身边，无奈地摇着头。他们明白，这是早已注定的结局。

那些敢于离开山村的人，等待他的是屈服和失败。

在村子的一个角落，迂腐的老人们摇着头，压低了声音说着恶狠狠的话。

他们并非生来残忍，但法律就是法律。他违背了那些思想陈腐的长辈们的意志，就是犯下了滔天大罪。

他的伤势一旦痊愈，就必须接受判决。

迂腐的长辈们本想慈悲为怀。

他们没有忘记他母亲怪异的、跳跃着光芒的眼眸，也回想起了三十年前他父亲在沙漠失踪的悲剧。

不过法律就是法律，法律是不可违抗的。

而那些思想守旧的老人就是这法律的执行者。

那些迂腐的老人把出游的人抬到闹市区。人们都必恭必敬地在周围站着，鸦雀无声。

出游的人由于饥渴，身体还很虚弱。老人们让他坐下。

他拒绝了。

他们让他闭嘴。

但是他坚持要说。

Upon the Old Men he turned his back and his eyes sought those who but a short time before had been his comrades.

" Listen to me, " he implored. "Listen to me and be rejoiced. I have come back from beyond the mountains. My feet have trod a fresh soil. My hands have felt the touch of other races. My eyes have seen wondrous sights.

" When I was a child, my world was the garden of my father.

" To the west and to the east, to the south and to the north lay the ranges from the Beginning of Time.

"When I asked what they were hiding, there was a hush and a hasty shaking of heads. When I insisted, I was taken to the rocks and shown the bleached bones of those who had dared to defy the Gods.

" When I cried out and said, 'It is a lie! The Gods love those who are brave!' The Men Who Knew came and read to me from their sacred books. The Law, they explained had ordained all things of Heaven and Earth. The Valley was ours to have and to hold. The animals and the flowers, the fruit and the fishes were ours, to do our bidding. But the mountains were of the Gods. What lay beyond was to remain unknown until the End of Time.

" So they spoke, and they lied. They lied to me, even as they have lied to you.

" There are pastures in those hills. Meadows too, as rich as any. And men and women of our own flesh and blood. And cities resplendent with the glories of a thousand years of labor.

" I have found the road to a better home. I have seen the promise of a happier life. Follow me and I shall lead you thither. For the smile of the Gods is the same there as here and everywhere. "

He stopped and there went up a great cry of horror.

他转过来背对老人，眼光在人群中搜索不久前还与他志同道合的人。

"听我说，"他恳请道，"请听我说，大家会很高兴的！我刚从山那边回来。我的双脚踏上了一片新鲜的土地，我的手被其他的民族抚摸过，我的双眼见到了奇妙的景象。

"小时候，父亲的花园就是我的整个世界。

"早在上帝创造世界的时候，花园东西南北各个方位的边界就被确定下来了。

"只要我问起边界的那一边藏着什么，大家就把头摇个不停，口里发出嘘嘘的声音。但是我非要打破砂锅问到底，于是他们就带我来到这块岩石上，让我看看那些蔑视上帝的人的森森白骨。

"'骗人！'我大声喊道，'上帝偏爱英勇的人。'于是，迂腐的长辈们走过来，为我读他们的圣书。他们说，上帝的旨意已经决定了天地间万物的命运。山谷是我们的，由我们来掌管，飞禽走兽和花朵，还有果实和鱼虾都是属于我们的，我们决定它们的命运。但山是上帝的。我们不应该知道山对面的一切事物，直到世界的末日。

"这就是他们说的，他们在撒谎，他们欺骗了我，就像欺骗了你们一样。

"山的那一边有牧场，有和我们一样的牧草，那里的男女老少有和我们同样的血肉之躯。那历经了一千年的城市，被能工巧匠雕刻得雄壮美丽，光彩闪烁。

"我已经找到了一条大道，可以通往更美好的家园，我已经看到了幸福生活的曙光。跟随我走吧，我带着你们奔向那里。上帝在别处有和在这里一样的微笑。"

他停下来了，人群发出了惊恐的叫喊声。

" Blasphemy! " cried the Old Men. " Blasphemy and sacrilege! A fit punishment for his crime! He has lost his reason. He dares to scoff at the Law as it was written down a thousand years ago. He deserves to die!"

And they took up heavy stones.

And they killed him.

And his body they threw at the foot of the cliffs, that it might lie there as a warning to all who questioned the wisdom of the ancestors.

Then it happened a short time later that there was a great drought. The little Brook of Knowledge ran dry. The cattle died of thirst. The harvest perished in the fields, and there was hunger in the Valley of Ignorance.

The Old Men Who Knew, however, were not disheartened. Everything would all come right in the end, they prophesied, for so it was writ in their most Holy Chapters.

Besides, they themselves needed but little food. They were so very old.

Winter came.

The village was deserted.

More than half of the populace died from sheer want.

The only hope for those who survived lay beyond the mountains.

But the Law said, " No!"

And the Law must be obeyed.

One night there was a rebellion.

Despair gave courage to those whom fear had forced into silence.

Feebly the Old Men protested.

They were pushed aside. They complained of their lot. They be-

"亵渎，这是对神灵的亵渎。"顽固不化的老人大声叫着，"要让他罪有应得！他已经失去理智了，竟敢戏谑一千年前制定下来的法律。他死有余辜！"

人们举起了沉重的石头。

他们杀死了这个出游的人。

人们把他的尸体扔到山崖底下，以此训诫其他胆敢怀疑祖先智慧的人，杀一儆百。

没有多久，一场特大干旱暴发了。湍湍的知识小溪流干枯了，牲畜都干渴而死，田地里的粮食都枯萎了，无知的山谷里到处都是饥渴的呻吟。

不过，那些顽固的老人并没有灰心。他们预言说，所有的一切都会转危为安。至少那些先知先觉的圣书上是这样写的。

而且，他们自己已经很老了，吃不了多少粮食了。

冬天来临了。

村庄里荒无人烟。

饥寒交迫夺去了大多数人的生命。

活着的人把生存的唯一希望寄托在山的那一边。

但是法律却说："不可以！"

法律是必须遵守的。

一天夜晚，叛乱爆发了。

绝望赋予那些由于恐惧而逆来顺受的人们以勇气。

迂腐的老人们无力地抗争着。

他们被推到一边，还在抱怨自己不幸的命运，诅咒儿孙的忘恩

wailed the ingratitude of their children, but when the last wagon pulled out of the village, they stopped the driver and forced him to take them along.

The flight into the unknown had begun.

It was many years since the Wanderer had returned. It was no easy task to discover the road he had mapped out.

Thousands fell a victim to hunger and thirst before the first cairn was found.

From there on the trip was less difficult.

The careful pioneer had blazed a clear trail through the woods and amidst the endless wilderness of rock.

By easy stages it led to the green pastures of the new land.

Silently the people looked at each other.

"He was right after all, " they said. "He was right, and the Old Men were wrong…"

" He spoke the truth, and the Old Men lied…"

" His bones lie rotting at the foot of the cliffs, but the Old Men sit in our carts and chant their ancient lays…"

" He saved us, and we slew him…"

" We are sorry that it happened, but of course, if we could have known at the time…"

Then they unharnessed their horses and their oxen and they drove their cows and their goats into the pastures and they built themselves houses and laid out their fields and they lived happily for a long time afterwards.

A few years later an attempt was made to bury the brave pioneer in the fine new edifice which had been erected as a home for the Wise Old Men.

负义。但是当最后一辆马车驶离村落时，他们拦住了它，迫使车夫把他们带走。

就这样，投奔前途未卜的新世界的旅程开始了。

从那个出游者回来到现在已经过了很多年了，所以要找到他开辟的道路，绝不是容易的事情。

成千上万的人在路途上饥渴而亡，人们终于找到了第一座用石子垒起的路标。

从那以后，旅途中的磨难少了一些。

那个细心的开拓者已经用一把火在一望无际的险山乱林中烧出了一条宽阔大道。

沿着这条大道，人们一步步地走到了一个有着绿色牧场的新世界。

人们相顾无言。

"他到底还是对的，"人们说，"正确的是他，错误的是那些冥顽不化的老人……"

"他的话是真实的，那些陈腐的老人在撒谎……"

"他的尸首腐烂在山崖下，可是那些顽固的老人却坐在我们的车里，还唱着那陈旧不堪的歌谣。"

"他救了我们，我们却杀害了他。"

"我们确实对这件事情非常内疚，不过，当时我们如果知道的话，当然就……"

接着，他们为牛马解下套具，把牛羊赶进牧场，建造自己的房屋，规划自己的土地。从此，他们过上了幸福的生活。

几年之后，人们为智慧老人建起了一座崭新的大厦作为住宅，并准备把英勇的先驱者的遗骸埋在里面。

A solemn procession went back to the now deserted valley, but when the spot was reached where his body ought to have been, it was no longer there.

A hungry jackal had dragged it to his lair.

A small stone was then placed at the foot of the trail(now a magnificent highway).It gave the name of the man who had first defied the dark terror of the unknown, that his people might be guided into a new freedom.

And it stated that it had been erected by a grateful posterity.

As it was in the beginning—as it is now—and as some day (so we hope) it shall no longer be.

　　一支庄严的队伍回到了早已荒无人烟的山谷。但是，山崖脚下空空如也，开拓者的尸骨已经无影无踪。

　　饥饿的豺狼早就把尸首拖入了自己的洞穴。

　　人们在开拓者足迹的尽头放上了一块小石头（那里现在已经是一条大道），他们把开拓者的名字刻在石头上——这是第一个挑战未卜世界的黑暗和恐怖的人的名字，是他把人们带向了新的自由。

　　石头上还写着，它是由前来感恩朝拜的后人建造的。

　　这样的事情过去发生过，现在也还在发生，不过将来（我们希望）不要再发生了。

迈向成功之路

第四卷

我相信，个人拥有无上的价值，拥有生存、自由和追求幸福的权利。

我相信，每一项权利都必然包含着责任，每一个机遇都必然包含着义务，每一种获得都必然包含着职责。

我相信，法律为人而制，而非人为法律而生，政府是人民的公仆，而非人民的主人。

我相信，无论体力劳动还是脑力劳动都是高尚的，世界不会让人不劳而获，而会给人一次谋生的机会。

……

Youth 青春

Samuel Ullman / 塞缪尔·乌尔曼

作者简介

塞缪尔·乌尔曼（1840～1920），是位犹太人，出生于德国，1851年随家人移民到美国密西西比，他虽以教育家和社会活动家而闻名于世，但在文学创作方面也很有才华。

太平洋战争打得正酣之时，麦克阿瑟将军常常从繁忙中抬起头，注视着挂在墙上的镜框，镜框里正是这篇名为《青春》的文章，这篇文章一直伴随着他到东京。后来，日本人在东京的美军总部发现了它，《青春》便开始在日本流传。

一位资深的日本问题观察家说，在日本实业界，凡有成就之人，几乎都受过这篇美文的激励，松下电器的创始人松下幸之助就一直把《青春》当做他的座右铭。

Youth is not a time of life; it is a state of mind; it is not a matter of rosy cheeks, red lips and supple knees; it is a matter of the will, a quality of the imagination, a vigor of the emotions; it is the freshness of the deep springs of life.

Youth means a tempera-mental predominance of courage over timidity, of the appetite for adventure over the love of ease. This

感动一个国家的文字

often exists in a man of 60 more than a boy of 20. Nobody grows old merely by a number of years. We grow old by deserting our ideals.

Years may wrinkle the skin, but to give up enthusiasm wrinkles the soul. Worry, fear, self-distrust bows the heart and turns the spring back to dust.

Whether 60 or 16, there is in every human being's heart the lure of wonder, the unfailing childlike appetite of what's next and the joy of the game of living.

In the center of your heart and my heart there is a wireless station: so long as it receives messages of beauty, hope, cheer, courage and power from men and from the infinite, so long are you young.

When the aerials are down, and your spirit is covered with snows of cynicism and the ice of pessimism, then you are grown old, even at 20, but as long as your aerials are up, to catch waves of optimism, there is hope you may die young at 80.

青春不是年华，而是心态；青春不是粉面、红唇、柔膝，而是坚强的意志，恢弘的想象，炙热的恋情；青春是生命深处的自在涌流。

青春气贯长虹，勇锐盖过怯弱，进取压倒苟安。如此锐气，二十后生而有之，六旬男子则更多见。年岁有加，并非垂老，理想丢弃，方堕暮年。

岁月悠悠，衰微只及肌肤；热忱抛却，颓废必致灵魂。忧虑、惶恐、丧失自信，定使灵魂扭曲，意气如灰。

无论年届花甲，抑或二八芳龄，心中皆有生命之欢乐，好奇之冲动，孩童般天真久盛不衰。

你我心中都有一台天线，只要你从天上、人间接受美好、希望、欢乐、勇气和力量的信号，你就会青春永驻，风华常存。

一旦天线坠下，锐气便被冰雪覆盖，玩世不恭、自暴自弃油然而生，即使年方二十，实则垂垂老矣；然而只要竖起天线，捕捉乐观信号，即使八十高龄，行将告别尘寰，你也会觉得年轻依旧，希望永存。

Our Family Creed
家族的信条

John Rockefeller, jr./ 小约翰·洛克菲勒

作者简介

小约翰·洛克菲勒 (1874~1960)，石油大王老洛克菲勒之子，洛克菲勒基金会创办人，曾捐赠联合国总部用地。本篇为 1941 年 7 月 8 日联合服务组织广播节目的一部分，在战争烽火和法西斯势力肆虐之时产生了积极的影响。

They are the principles on which my wife and I have tried to bring up our family. They are the principles in which my father believed and by which he governed his life. They are the principles, many of them, which I learned at my mother's knee.

They point the way to usefulness and happiness in life, to courage and peace in death.

If they mean to you what they mean to me, they may perhaps be helpful also to our sons for their guidance and inspiration.

Let me state them:

I believe in the supreme worth of the individual and in his right to life, liberty and the pursuit of happiness.

I believe that every right implies a responsibility; every opportunity, an obligation; every possession, a duty.

I believe that the law was made for man and not man for the law; that government is the servant of the people and not their master.

I believe in the dignity of labor, whether with head or hand; that the world owes no man a living but that it owes every man an opportunity to make a living.

感动一个国家的文字

I believe that thrift is essential to well-ordered living and that economy is a prime requisite of a sound financial structure, whether in government, business or personal affairs.

I believe that truth and justice are fundamental to an enduring social order.

I believe in the sacredness of a promise, that a man's word should be as good as his bond, that character—not wealth or power or position—is of supreme worth.

这些是我和我太太在教育子女的时候所尽力倚仗的信条，这些是我父亲所深信并以之为人生律条的信条，这些信条中的大部分是我从母亲的膝下秉承而来的。

这些信条告诉人们如何快乐而有所作为地活着，也告诉人们如何勇敢而安详地面对死亡。

假如这些信条于诸位的意义如同它们于我的意义，那么也许它们可以有效地指导和鼓舞我们的儿女们。

让我说出这些信条：

我相信，个人拥有无上的价值，拥有生存、自由和追求幸福的权利。

我相信，每一项权利都必然包含着责任，每一个机遇都必然包含着义务，每一种获得都必然包含着职责。

我相信，法律为人而制，而非人为法律而生，政府是人民的公仆，而非人民的主人。

我相信，无论体力劳动还是脑力劳动都是高尚的，世界不会让人不劳而获，而会给人一次谋生的机会。

我相信，无论在政府、商业还是个人事务中，勤俭节约都是合理安排生活之基本要素，而经济适用是健全的金融机制之必需。

我相信，真理和正义是任何一个长治久安的社会秩序之基础。

我相信，承诺是神圣的；我也相信，假如人的言语能和契约同样可靠，那么这种品质——而非财富、权势与身份地位——就具有至高无上的价值。

I believe that the rendering of useful service is the common duty of mankind and that only in the purifying fire of sacrifice is the dross of selfishness consumed and the greatness of the human soul set free.

I believe in an all-wise and all-loving God, named by whatever name, and that the individual's highest fulfillment, greatest happiness and widest usefulness are to be found in living in harmony with His will.

I believe that love is the greatest thing in the world; that it alone can overcome hate; that right can and will triumph over might.

These are the principles, however formulated, for which all good men and women throughout the world, irrespective of race or creed, education, social position or occupation, are standing, and for which many of them are suffering and dying.

These are the principles upon which alone a new world recognizing the brotherhood of man the fatherhood of God can be established.

我相信，人类共同的职责是有用地服务社会，只有在自我牺牲的炼火中，自私的沉渣才会被焚为灰烬，人类灵魂中的伟大情操才会显现。

我相信，有一位无所不知、大慈大悲的上帝存在——尽管人们对他的称呼各不相同——人们能在与他的意志和谐生活的过程中得到最高的满足感、最大的幸福感，以及最广博的成就感。

我相信，世界上最伟大的事物就是爱，只有爱能够战胜仇恨，而真理能够而且必定能击败强权。

无论怎样表达，以上就是那些信条——世界上所有不计种族、信仰、宗教、地位或职业的善良的人们所代表的信条——而且正是为了这些信条，他们中许多人正在忍受折磨，甚至正在死去。

只有凭借这些信条，人类才能建立起人人如手足、上帝如慈父的新世界。

假如给我三天光明

Three Days to See

Helen Keller／海伦·凯勒

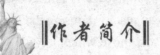

‖作者简介‖

　　海伦·凯勒（1880～1968），美国著名残疾人作家、教育家，生于美国亚拉巴马州。2岁时，一场疾病使她变成了盲、聋、哑人。后来她的父母请来家庭教师莎莉文女士对其进行特殊教育。同时凯勒也通过自身顽强的意志和不懈的努力，1804年毕业于麻省波士顿的瑞地克利夫学院。后来，凯勒专职于写作和残疾人教育事业。她一生共写了19本书，其中《我生活的故事》最为著名，对美国人民及全世界人民起着积极的引导作用。

If, by some miracle, I were granted three seeing days, to be followed by a relapse into darkness, I should divide the period into three parts.

The First Day

...

The first day would be a busy one. I should call to me all my dear friends and look long into their faces, imprinting upon my mind the outward evidences of the beauty that is within them. I should let my eyes rest, too, on the face of a baby, so that I could catch a vision of the eager, innocent beauty which precedes the individual's consciousness of the conflicts which life develops.

And I should like to look into the loyal, trusting eyes of my dogs—the grave, canny little Scottie, Darkie, and the stalwart, understanding Great Dane Helga, whose warm, tender, and playful friendships are so comforting to me.

On that busy first day I should also view the small simple things of my home. I want to see the warm colors in the rugs under my feet, the pictures on the walls, the intimate trifles that transform a house into home. My eyes would rest respectfully on the books in raised type which I have read, but they would be more eagerly interested in the printed books which seeing people can read, for during the long night of my life the books I have read and those which have been read to me have built themselves into a great shining lighthouse, revealing to me the deepest channels of human life and the human spirit.

In the afternoon of that first seeing day, I should take a long walk in the woods and intoxicate my eyes on the beauties of the world of Nature, trying desperately to absorb in a few hours the vast splendor which is constantly unfolding itself to those who can see. On the way home from my woodland jaunt my path would lie near a farm so that I might see the patient horses ploughing in the field (perhaps I should see only a tractor!) and the serene content of men living close to the soil. And I should pray for the glory of a colorful sunset.

When dusk had fallen, I should experience the double delight of being able to see by artificial light which the genius of man has created to extend the power of his sight when Nature decrees darkness.

In the night of that first day of sight, I should not be able to sleep, so full would be my mind of the memories of the day.

The Second Day

...

...my second day of sight, I should try to probe into the soul of man through this art. The things I knew through touch I should now

如果靠某种奇迹我能恢复三天光明，然后又回到黑暗里去的话，我将把这三天分为三个阶段。

第一天

……

　　第一天将是很繁忙的一天。我要把所有的好朋友们都叫来，好好端详他们的面容，将他们外貌下的内在美深深地刻在我的脑海里。我还要看一个婴儿的面孔，这样我就能欣赏到一种充满渴望、天真无邪的美，它是一种没有经历过生活斗争的美。

　　我还应该看看我那群忠诚的、值得信赖的狗的眼睛——严肃而机警的小斯科第·达基和那高大健壮而又善解人意的大戴恩·海尔加，它们热情、温柔而淘气的友谊使我感到惬意。

　　在那紧张的第一天里，我还要仔细观察我家里那些简朴的小东西。看看脚下地毯那热情奔放的颜色，墙上美丽的壁画和那些把一所房屋变成一个家的熟悉的小东西。我会充满敬意地凝视我所读过的那些盲文书，不过我将更热切地盼望看到那些供正常人读的印刷书籍。因为在我那漫长的黑夜生活里，我读过的以及别人读给我听的书已经在我面前筑成一座伟大光明的灯塔，向我揭示人类生命和人类精神的最深源泉。

　　在恢复光明的第一天下午，我将在森林里做一次长时间的散步，让自己的眼睛陶醉在自然界的美丽风景中，我将在这有限的几小时内如痴如狂地享受那永远只能向视力正常人展露的壮观美景。在结束森林散步返家的路旁如果有一个农场，我便能看到耐心的马儿在田间犁地（也许我只能看到拖拉机了）和那些依靠土地生存的人们那宁静满足的生活。我还要为绚丽多彩而又壮观辉煌的日落祈祷。

　　当夜幕降临之后，通过人类天才的发明——人造灯光，我应该体会到双重的快乐。这是大自然当黑夜来临时，为增强自己的视力而发明的。

　　在恢复光明的第一天夜里，我不可能睡着，脑海里满是对白天的回忆。

第二天

……

　　……在我恢复光明的第二天，我就试图通过艺术去刺探人类的

see. More splendid still, the whole magnificent world of painting would be opened to me, from the Italian Primitives, with their serene religious devotion, to the Moderns, with their feverish visions. I should look deep into the canvases of Raphael, Leonardo da Vinci, Titian, Rembrandt.I should want to feast my eyes upon the warm colors of Veronese, study the mysteries of E1 Greco, catch a new vision of Nature from Corot. Oh, there is so much rich meaning and beauty in the art of the ages for you who have eyes to see!

Upon my short visit to this temple of art I should not be able to review a fraction of that great world of art which is open to you. I should be able to get only a superficial impression. Artists tell me that for deep and true appreciation of art one must educated the eye. One must learn through experience to weight he merits of line, of composition,of form and color. If I had eyes,how happily would I embark upon so fascinating a study! Yet I am told that, to many of you who have eyes to see,the world of art is a dark night, unexplored and unilluminated.It would be with extreme reluctance that I should leave the Metropolitan Museum, which contains the key to beauty — a beauty so neglected. Seeing persons, however, do not need a metropolitan to find this key to beauty. The same key lies waiting in smaller museums, and in books on the shelves of even small libraries. But naturally, in my limited time of imaginary sight, I should choose the place where the key unlocks the greatest treasures in the shortest time.

The evening of my second day of sight I should spend at a theatre or at the movies. Even now I often attend theatrical performances of all sorts, but the action of the play must be spelled into my hand by a companion. But how I should like to see with my own eyes the fascinating figure of Hamlet, or the gusty Falstaff amid colorful Elizabethan trappings! How I should like to follow each movement of the graceful Hamlet, each strut of the hearty Falstaff ! And since I could

灵魂。通过触摸可以了解的东西现在可以用眼睛来看了。宏伟而壮观的绘画世界将在我的面前展开，从带有宁静宗教奉献色彩的意大利原始艺术到具有狂热想象意味的现代派艺术。我要细细观察拉斐尔、列奥纳多·达·芬奇、提香、伦布朗的油画，也想让眼睛享受一下委罗涅塞那绚丽的色彩，研究一下艾尔·格里柯的神秘，并从柯罗那里体会自然的新意。啊，这么多世纪以来的艺术为视力正常的人们提供了多少绚丽的美和深广的意义啊！

　　凭着对这艺术圣殿的短暂造访，我不可能把那只向你们打开的伟大艺术世界里的每个部分都考虑得很清楚，我得到的只能是一个表面肤浅的印象。艺术家们告诉我，如果想真实而深刻地评价艺术，就必须培养自己的眼睛，一个人必须从品评线条、构图、形式和色彩的经历中去学习。如果我能看见东西的话，我是多么乐意去着手这件令人着迷的研究啊！然而我被告知，对于你们大多数视力正常者来说，艺术世界是一个沉沉的黑夜，无法探索也难以找到光明。我无可奈何不情愿地离开大都会博物馆，那儿收藏着发现美的钥匙——这种美已经被人们所忽略。然而视力正常的人并不需要从大都会博物馆里去寻找发现美的钥匙。人们在较小的博物馆里，甚至在那些小图书馆书架上的书本里也能找到同样的钥匙。当然了，在我想象中能看见东西的有限时光里，我将选择这样一个地方，在那里，发现美的钥匙可以在最短的时间内打开最伟大的宝库。

　　第二个恢复光明的夜晚我想去戏院看一场电影。虽然我现在也经常出席各种戏剧表演，可剧情却得让一位陪同拼写在我的手上。我多想用自己的眼睛看一看哈姆雷特那迷人的形象，或者穿梭于绚丽多彩的伊丽莎白式服装的人物之中的福斯泰夫。我多么想模仿优雅的哈姆雷特的每一个动作和健壮的福斯泰夫的每一个昂首阔步。

see only one play, I should be confronted by a many-horned dilemma, for there are scores of plays I should want to see. You who have eyes can see any you like. How many of you, I wonder, when you gaze at a play, a movie, or any spectacle, realize and give thanks for the miracle of sight which enables you to enjoy its color, grace, and movement?

I cannot enjoy the beauty of rhythmic movement except in a sphere restricted to the touch of my hands. I can vision only dimly the grace of a Pavlowa, although I know something of the delight of rhythm, for often I can sense the beat of music as it vibrates through the floor. I can well imagine that cadenced motion must be one of the most pleasing sights in the world. I have been able to gather something of this by tracing with my fingers the lines in sculptured marble; if this static grace can be so lovely, how much more acute must be the thrill of seeing grace in motion.

One of my dearest memories is of the time when Joseph Jefferson allowed me to touch his face and hands as he went through some of the gestures and speeches of his beloved Rip Van Winkle. I was able to catch thus a meager glimpse of the world of drama, and I shall never forget the delight of that moment. But, oh, how much I must miss, and how much pleasure you seeing ones can derive from watching and hearing the interplay of speech and movement in the unfolding of a dramatic performance! If I could see only one play, I should know how to picture in my mind the action of a hundred plays which I have read or had transferred to me through the medium of the manual alphabet.

So, through the evening of my second imaginary day of sight, the great fingers of dramatic literature would crowd sleep from my eyes.

The Third Day

The following morning, I should again greet the dawn, anxious to

感动一个国家的文字

因为我只能看一场戏，这使我进退两难，但是我想看的戏实在太多了。你们视力正常的人可以看你们想看的任何戏，不过我怀疑你们之中究竟有多少人在全神贯注于一场戏、一部电影或别的壮观景象的时候，是否意识到并感激那让你享受其色彩、优美和动作的视力的奇迹呢？

除了在触摸的有限范围内，我无法享受节奏感动作的美。尽管我明白节奏欢快的奥妙，因为我经常通过地板的颤动去感受音乐的节拍，但是我也只能模糊地领略巴甫洛瓦的魅力。我可以想象出那富于节奏感的动作，一定是世间最赏心悦目的奇景之一。我可以通过手指去触摸大理石雕像的线条来感悟这一点。如果静止的美可以如此可爱，那么看到运动中的美肯定更令人振奋和激动！

我最深切的回忆之一是在排练可爱的瑞普·凡·温克尔，约瑟夫·杰弗逊做着动作讲着台词的时候，他允许我触摸他的脸和手。这使我对戏剧世界有了贫乏的一瞥，我将永远不会忘记那一刻的兴奋和欢乐。但是，我肯定还遗漏了许多东西。你们视力正常的人能从戏剧表演中通过看动作和听台词而获得多高的享受啊。就算我只能看一场戏，我也能明白我读过或通过手语字母而进入我脑海的一百场戏的情节。

所以，我想象中恢复光明的第二天的夜晚，戏剧文学中的许多伟大形象将挤进我的梦想。

第三天

下一天的清晨，我将再次去迎接那初升的旭日，希望发现新的欢乐。因为我确信，那些能真正看到东西的人肯定会发现，每个黎明都充满了千姿百态、变幻无穷的美。

215

discover new delights, for I am sure that, for those who have eyes which really see, the dawn of each day must be a perpetually new revelation of beauty.

This, according to the terms of my imagined miracle, is to be my third and last day of sight. I shall have no time to waste in regrets or longings; there is too much to see.The first day I devoted to my friends, animate and inanimate. The second revealed to me the history of man and Nature. Today I shall spend in the workaday world of the present, amid the haunts of men going about the business of life. And where can one find so many activities and conditions of men as in New York? So the city becomes my destination.

I start from my home in the quiet little suburb of Forest Hills, Long Island . Here, surrounded by green lawns, trees, and flowers, are neat little houses,happy with the voices and movements of wives and children,havens of peaceful rest for men who toil in the city. I drive across the lacy structure of steel which spans the East River,and I get a new and startling vision of the power and ingenuity of the mind of man.Busy boasts chug and scurry about the river racy speed boat, stolid, snorting tugs. If I had long days of sight ahead, I should spend many of them watching the delightful activity upon the river.

I look ahead, and before me rise the fantastic towers of New York, a city that seems to have stepped from the pages of a fairy story.What an awe-inspiring sight,these glittering spires.These vast banks of stone and steel-structures such as the gods might build for themselves! This animated picture is a part of the lives of millions of people every day. How many, I wonder, give it so much as a seconds glance? Very few, I fear. Their eyes are blind to this magnificent sight because it is so familiar to them.

I hurry to the top of one of those gigantic structures, the Empire State Building, for there, a short time ago, I "saw" the city below through the eyes of my secretary.I am anxious to compare my fancy

根据我想象中奇迹的日期，这是我恢复光明的第三天，也是最后一天。我没有时间去遗憾或渴望了，那儿有太多的东西要去看。我把第一天给了我的朋友，给了那些有生命和没有生命的人间万物，第二天展现在我面前的是人类和自然的历史。今天我要在现实世界里，在从事日常生活的人们中间度过。除了纽约，你还能在别的什么地方发现人类这么多的活动和这样纷繁的情景呢？于是纽约成为我的目的地。

　　我从位于安谧的长岛森林山郊区的家中出发。许多整洁的小屋在绿地、树木、鲜花的拥抱中，充满妇女儿童说笑走动的欢乐声音在四周回荡，这里真是城市劳动者安静的休息场所。当我驱车穿越横跨东河的钢式网状桥时，感觉到了新的激动，感受到人类内心的智慧和力量。河上千帆竞发，百舸争流。如果我以前能看见东西的话，我将用很多时间来欣赏河上的热闹活动。

　　举目前望，面前耸立着奇异的纽约塔，这城市就像是从神话故事的书页中跳出来似的。这是多么令人激动敬畏的奇景啊！这些闪闪发光的尖塔，这些钢和石块构筑的巨大堤岸，就像神为自己修建的一样。这幅有生气的画卷是千百万人每日生活的一部分，我担心很少有人能够注意这些。他们眼睛经常无视这些壮丽景观的存在，因为他们对这些已经太熟悉了。

　　我匆匆忙忙登上那些大型建筑之一——帝国大厦的顶层，就在不久前，我在那里通过秘书的眼睛"看到"了脚下的城市。我急于把我的想象和真实世界做一次比较。我坚信展现在我面前的这幅画

with reality. I am sure I should not be disappointed in the panorama spread out before me, for to me it would be a vision of another world.

Now I begin my rounds of the city. First, I stand at a busy corner, merely looking at people, trying by sight of them to understand something of their live. I see smiles, and I am happy. I see serious determination, and I am proud, I see suffering, and I am compassionate.

I stroll down Fifth Avenue. I throw my eyes out of focus, so that I see no particular object but only a seething kaleidoscope of colors. I am certain that the colors of women's dresses moving in a throng must be a gorgeous spectacle of which I should never tire. But perhaps if I had sight I should be like most other women — too interested in styles and the cut of individual dresses to give much attention to the splendor of color in the mass. And I am convinced, too, that I should become an inveterate window shopper, for it must be a delight to the eye to view the myriad articles of beauty on display.

From Fifth Avenue I make a tour of the city — to Park Avenue, to the slums, to factories, to parks where children play. I take a stay-at-home trip abroad by visiting the foreign quarters. Always my eyes are open wide to all the sights of both happiness and misery so that I may probe deep and add to my understanding of how people work and live. My heart is full of the images of people and things. My eye passes lightly over no single trifle; it strives to touch and hold closely each thing its gaze rests upon. Some sights are pleasant, filling the heart with happiness; but some are miserably pathetic. To these latter I do not shut my eyes, f or they, too, are part of life. To close the eye on them is to close the heart and mind.

My third day of sight is drawing to an end. Perhaps there are many serious pursuits to which I should devote the few remaining hours, but I am afraid that on the evening of that last day I should again run away to the theater, to a hilariously funny play, so that I might appreciate the overtones of comedy in the human spirit.

卷绝不会使我失望，因为对于我来说它将是另一个世界的景况。

现在我开始周游这个城市。首先我站在繁忙的一隅，只是看来往的人群，试着从观察中去了解他们生活中的一些东西。看到他们微笑，我也开心；看到他们如此果断，我感到骄傲；看到他们遭受痛苦，我深感同情。

我漫游到第五大道，将视野从聚精会神的注视中解放出来，以便不留意特殊的事物而只看一看瞬息万变的色彩。我相信人流中妇女衣着的色彩，肯定是我最看不厌的灿烂奇观。不过，假如我能看见的话，可能我也会像大多数妇女一样，过分地注重服装的个性化风格和个性化的剪裁式样而忽略宏观色彩的壮美。我还确信我会变成一个橱窗前的常客，因为去观看橱窗中五光十色的美丽商品一定会令眼睛愉悦。

从第五大道开始游览整个城市——我要到花园大街去，到贫民区去，到工厂去，到孩子们嬉戏的公园去。通过访问外国居民我做了一次不离本土的境外旅行。对于开心和伤痛等一切东西我都是睁大眼睛去关心，以便能深刻探索和进一步了解人们是如何工作和生活的。我的心里充满了对人和物的想象，我的目光将轻轻地滑过但不漏下任何一个细小的东西，它力图紧紧抓住它所凝视的每一件事物。有些场景是令人愉快的，内心充满了喜悦，可有些情景却使人感到悲哀和忧郁。我不会对后者闭上眼睛，因为它们也是生活的一部分，对它们闭上眼睛就等于关闭了心灵，禁锢了思想。

我恢复光明的第三天就要结束了，可能我应该把这剩下的几小时用于许多重要的探索上，可是我担心在这最后一夜，我会再次跑到剧院去看一出狂喜的滑稽戏，以便能欣赏人类精神世界里喜剧的弦外之音。

到午夜，刚刚从盲人痛苦中得到的临时解脱就要结束了，永久的黑暗将重新回到我的身边。很自然短暂的三天时间，不可能让我

At midnight my temporary respite from blindness would cease, and permanent night would close in on me again. Naturally in those three short days I should not have seen all I wanted to see. Only when darkness had again descended upon me should I realize how much I had left unseen. But my mind would be so crowded with glorious memories that I should have little time for regrets. Thereafter the touch of every object would bring a glowing memory of how that object looked.

Perhaps this short outline of how I should spend three days of sight does not agree with the program you would set for yourself if you knew that you were about to be stricken blind. I am,however, sure that if you actually faced that fate your eyes would open to things you had never seen before,storing up memories for the long night ahead.You would use your eyes as never before.Everything you saw would become dear to you.Your eyes would touch and embrace every object that came within your range of vision.Then, at last,you would really see,and a new world of beauty would open itself before you.

I who am blind can give one hint to those who see—one admonition to those who would make full use of the gift of sight: use your eyes as if tomorrow you would be stricken blind. And the same method can be applied to the other senses. Hear the music of voices, the song of a bird, the mighty strains of an orchestra, as if you would be stricken deaf tomorrow. Touch each object you want to touch as if tomorrow your tactile sense would fail. Smell the perfume of flowers, taste with relish each morsel, as if tomorrow you could never smell and taste again. Make the most of every sense: glory in all the facets of pleasure and beauty which the world reveals to you through the several means of contact which Nature provides. But of all the senses, I am sure that sight must be the most delightful.

感动一个国家的文字

看完我要看的全部事物，只有当黑暗重新降临在我的身上时，我才会感到我没有看到的东西实在太多了。不过我的脑海中已经被那壮丽的回忆塞满了，很少有时间去遗憾。今后无论摸到什么物体都会给我带来它是什么形状的鲜明回忆。

如果有朝一日你也将变成一个盲人的话，你或许对我这如何度过三天可见时光的简短提纲提出异议并做出自己的安排。但是，我相信，如果你真的面临如此命运的话，你的眼睛将会向以前从不注意的事物睁开，为即将到来的漫漫黑夜储存记忆。你将会一反常态地去利用自己的眼睛，你所看到的东西都是那么的亲切，你的目光将捕捉和拥抱任何你视野所及的东西，最后你会真正看到一个美丽的新世界在你面前打开。

我作为一个盲人，给你们视力正常的人们一个暗示，给那些充分利用眼睛的人提一个忠告：好好使用你的眼睛就好像明天你就会突然变瞎。这样的办法也可使用于别的官能：好好地去聆听各种声响，鸟儿的鸣唱，管弦乐队铿锵的旋律，就好像你明天有可能变成聋子；去抚摸你想触及的那一切吧，就像明天你的触觉神经就要失灵一样；去嗅闻所有鲜花的芬芳，品尝每一口食物的滋味吧，如同明天你就再也不能闻也不能尝一样。充分发挥每一种官能的最大作用，为这个世界向你展示的多种多样的欢乐和美而高兴吧，这些美是通过大自然提供的各种接触的途径所获得的。不过在所有的官能中，我敢保证视力是最令人兴奋高兴的。

The Way to Wealth

致富之道

Benjamin Franklin／本杰明·富兰克林

Courteous Reader,

I have heard that nothing gives an author so great pleasure, as to find his works respectfully quoted by other learned authors. This pleasure I have seldom enjoyed; for though I have been, if I may say it without vanity, an eminent author of almanacs annually now a full quarter of a century, my brother authors in the same way, for what reason I know not, have ever been very sparing in their applause, and no other author has taken the least notice of me, so that did not my writings produce me some solid pudding, the great deficiency of praise would have quite discouraged me.

I concluded at length, that the people were the best judges of my merit; for they buy my works; and besides, in my rambles, where I am not personally known, I have frequently heard one or other of my adages repeated with" as Poor Richard says "at the end on't; this gave me some satisfaction, as it showed not only that my instructions were regarded, but discovered likewise some respect for my authority; and I own, that to encourage the practice of remembering and repeating those wise sentences, I have sometimes quoted myself with great gravity.

Judge, then, how much I must have been gratified by an incident I am going to relate to you. I stopped my horse lately where a great number of people were collected at a vendue of merchant goods. The hour of sale not being come, they were conversing on the badness of the times and one of the company called to a plain clean old man, with white locks,"Pray, Father Abraham, what think you of the times? Won't these heavy taxes quite ruin the country? How shall we be ever able to pay them? What would you advise us to?" Father Abraham stood up, and replied, "If you'd have my advice, I'll give it to you in short, for *a word to the wise is enough, and many words won't fill a bushel*, as Poor Richard says."They joined in desiring

善解人意的读者：

　　我听说一个作家的作品被其他博学的作家充满敬意地引用是他最大的快乐。这种快乐我很少有过，虽然整整25年来，我年年都是历书的知名作家——如果我没有自夸的话——可不知为什么，跟我同道的作家们却一直都很吝啬他们的掌声，甚至没有一个作家丝毫注意过我，虽然我的作品带给我很多实惠，但掌声太少实在是件很让人泄气的事情。

　　最后我得出了结论，人民是判定我的价值的最好法官，因为我的书都是他们买的。而且，我在没有人认识的地方散步时，经常听见有人重复我的一两句格言，结尾时总有"穷理查说"这样的句子。这让我感到某种满足，因为它不仅表明我的教导受到重视，而且反映了人们对我的权威给予了一定的尊重。我本人为了鼓励大家都来背诵和运用那些充满智慧的句子，也不时引用自己的话。

　　那么，请看下面我要讲的这件事，它让我感到了很大的满足。最近，我在一个人山人海的商品拍卖会上停下来。交易还没有开始，人们谈论着严峻的时势。其中一个人对一个相貌平平、衣着整洁、留着几缕白发的老人叫道："亚伯拉罕神父，请问您怎么看这世道？这么重的税不是简直要亡国了吗？怎么才能交得起税呢？您有什么建议吗？"亚伯拉罕神父站起来回答说："你想听我的建议，我就简单地给你说说，因为'智者听一句话足够，多了也装不满一桶'，这

him to speak his mind, and gathering round him, he proceeded as follows:

"Friends,"says he, "and neighbors, the taxes are indeed very heavy, and if those laid on by the government were the only ones we had to pay, we might more easily discharge them; but we have many others, and much more grievous to some of us. We are taxed twice as much by our idleness, three times as much by our pride, and four times as much by our folly; and from these taxes the commissioners cannot ease or deliver us by allowing an abatement. However, let us hearken to good advice, and something may be done for us; *God helps them that help themselves*, as Poor Richard says, in his Almanack of 1733.

"It would be thought a hard government that should tax its people one-tenth part of their time, to be employed in its service. But idleness taxes many of us much more, if we reckon all that is spent in absolute sloth, or doing of nothing, with that which is spent in idle employments, or amusements, that amount to nothing. Sloth, by bringing on diseases, absolutely shortens life. *Sloth, like rust, consumes faster than labor wears; while the used key is always bright*, as Poor Richard says. But *dost thou love life, then do not squander time, for that's the stuff life is made of*, as Poor Richard says. How much more than is necessary do we spend in sleep, forgetting that *the sleeping fox catches no poultry and that there will be sleeping enough in the grave*, as Poor Richard says.

"*If time be of all things the most precious, wasting time must be,* as Poor Richard says, *the greatest prodigality; since, as he elsewhere tells us, lost time is never found again; and what we call time enough, always proves little enough. Let us then up and be doing, and doing to the purpose; so by diligence shall we do more with less perplexity. Sloth makes all things difficult, but industry all easy,* as Poor Richard says; *and he that riseth late must trot all day, and shall scarce overtake his business at night; while*

感动一个国家的文字 . . . . . .

是穷理查说的。"人们认为他讲得很好,把他围了起来,都想听他谈谈自己的看法。他就开始讲了:

"朋友们,乡邻们,"他说,"税确实很重,如果我们仅仅缴纳政府摊派的税,那就会容易一些。但我们还要缴很多别的税,这些税对有些人来说比缴给政府的税要重得多。懒散征的税是两倍,骄傲征的税是三倍,愚蠢征的税是四倍;当官的可以让我们少缴些税,却没有办法使我们免缴或少缴这些恶习的税。但是,让我们来听听更好的建议,也许能对大家有所启发,因为穷理查在他的《1733 年历书》中说:'天助自助者。'

"如果政府征用人民十分之一的时间为它效力,人民会认为这是苛政。但懒散征用我们的时间更多,想想极度懒散、无所事事所花去的时间吧,再想想干活松松垮垮,只图快活,最终一事无成所耗费的时间吧。懒散引起疾病,必然减短寿命。'懒散像铁锈,比劳作更容易消耗生命',而'常用的钥匙总是亮的',穷理查这样说。但'如果你热爱生命,那么不要浪费时间,因为时间是组成生命的材料',穷理查这样说。我们用于睡觉的不必要的时间是如此之多,别忘了穷理查说的'贪睡的狐狸逮不着鸡','坟墓里可以睡个够'。

"'如果时间是最宝贵的东西,浪费时间必定是最大的浪费。'穷理查这样说,他还告诉我们,'逝去的时间再也无法找回','我们说时间很多,结果时间总是很少。'那么让我们振作起来努力吧,朝着目标努力;勤奋努力,少些困惑,我们会取得更大的成绩。'人懒万事难,人勤万事易',穷理查说,'起床晚的人必须成天赶路,到了晚上活也忙不完','懒惰走得很慢,贫穷很快就能赶上',我们在

225

laziness travels so slowly, that poverty soon overtakes him, as we read in Poor Richard, *who adds, drive thy business, let not that drive thee, and early to bed, and early to rise, makes a man healthy, wealthy, and wise.*

"So what signifies wishing and hoping for better times. We may make these times better, if we bestir ourselves. Industry need not wish, as Poor Richard says, *and he that lives upon hope will die fasting. There are no gains without pains; then help hands, for I have no lands,* or if I have, they are smartly taxed. And, as Poor Richard likewise observes, *he that hath a trade hath an estate; and he that hath a calling, hath an office of profit and honor;* but then the trade must be worked at, and the calling well followed, or neither the estate nor the office will enable us to pay our taxes. If we are industrious, we shall never starve; for, as Poor Richard says, *at the workingman's house hunger looks in, but dares not enter.* Nor will the bailiff or the constable enter, for *industry pays debts, while despair increaseth them,* says Poor Richard. What though you have found no treasure, nor has any rich relation left you a legacy, *diligence is the mother of good luck,* as Poor Richard says, and *God gives all things to industry.* Then *plow deep, while sluggards sleep, and you shall have corn to sell and to keep,* says Poor Dick. Work while it is called today, for you know not how much you may be hindered tomorrow, which makes Poor Richard says, *one today is worth two tomorrows,* and farther, *have you somewhat to do tomorrow, do it today.* If you were a servant, would you not be ashamed that a good master should catch you idle? Are you then your own master, *be ashamed to catch yourself idle,* as Poor Dick says. When there is so much to be done for yourself, your family, your country, and your gracious king, be up by peep of day; *let not the sun look down and say, inglorious here he lies.* Handle your tools without mittens; remember that *the cat in gloves catches no mice,* as Poor

感动一个国家的文字

Richard says. 'Tis true there is much to be done, and perhaps you are weakhanded, but stick to it steadily; and you will see great effects, for *constant dropping wears away stones, and by diligence and patience the mouse ate in two the cable; and little strokes fell great oaks*, as Poor Richard says in his Almanack, the year I cannot just now remember.

"Methinks I hear some of you say,'must a man afford himself no

《穷理查历书》中读到过。穷理查还说，'驱赶你的活儿，不要叫它驱赶你'，'早睡早起使人健康、富有、聪明'。

"所以重要的是希望和向往好的时代。如果我们行动起来，我们可以让眼前这个时代好起来。'勤奋不需要愿望'，穷理查说，'靠希望生活的人会饿死'，'不下苦功无所得'，'学好手艺，因为我们没有土地'，如果有，会缴纳重税。穷理查还说，'有手艺的人就有财产'，'有职业的人就有名利双收的公司'；但是手艺必须做好，职业必须认真从事，否则即使有财产和公司，我们也缴不起税。人勤奋永远不挨饿，因为穷理查说，'勤劳者的家，饥饿会朝里看但不敢进。'法警和警官也不会进，因为'勤奋能还债，绝望添新债'，穷理查说。如果你没有财富，也没有富亲戚留给你遗产怎么办？'勤奋是好运之母'，穷理查说，'上帝把一切交给勤奋'，'懒汉睡时你深耕，自有玉米卖和存。'穷理查说。今天要干的活今天干，因为你不知道明天会遇到多大的阻力，所以穷理查说，'一个今天顶两个明天'，还说，'明天要做的事今天就做。'如果你是仆人，好主人发现你不干活你不惭愧吗？如果你是自己的主人，'发现自己不干活应当感到惭愧'，穷理查说。既然有那么多事要为自己做，为国家做，为仁慈的国王做，天一亮就起床，'不要让太阳向下一看，说，他无耻地躺在这里。'不要戴着手套用工具，'戴手套的猫逮不住老鼠'，穷理查说。确实有许多事要做，也许你力量不大，但只要坚持下去，就会发现卓有成效，因为'水滴石穿'，'有了勤奋和耐心，老鼠可以把缆绳咬成两半'，'一下下轻轻地砍可以砍倒大橡树'，穷理查在他的《历书》中说，我现在记不得是哪一年了。

"我好像听见有人说：'一个人就不能给自己留点儿闲暇吗？'朋

227

leisure?' I will tell thee, my friend, what Poor Richard says, *employ thy time well, if thou meanest to gain leisure*; and, *since thou art not sure of a minute, throw not away an hour*. Leisure is time for doing something useful; this leisure the diligent man will obtain, but the lazy man never; so that, as Poor Richard says *a life of leisure and a life of laziness are two things*. Do you imagine that sloth will afford you more comfort than labour? No, for as Poor Richard says, *trouble springs from idleness, and grievous toil from needless ease. Many without labor, would live by their wits only, but they break for want of stock*. Whereas industry gives comfort, and plenty, and respect: *fly pleasures, and they'll follow you; The diligent spinner has a large shift; and now I have a sheep and a cow, everybody bids me good morrow*; all of which is well said by Poor Richard."

友，我要告诉你穷理查说的话，'好好利用时间，如果你想有闲暇'，'既然你不能把握一分钟，就不要扔掉一小时。'闲暇是拿来做有用的事的时间，这种闲暇勤奋的人会得到，但懒人永远得不到，因此穷理查说'闲暇的生活和懒惰的生活是两码事'。你认为懒散会比勤劳带给你更多的舒适吗？不，因为穷理查说'麻烦源于懒散，痛苦的劳作源于不必要的舒适。''那些不劳动的人只能靠智力生活，但他们会因为缺少粮食储备而崩溃。'而勤劳则带来舒适、富裕和尊敬，'逃避快乐，快乐会跟着你'，'勤奋的纺纱工衣服多'，'现在我有一只羊一头奶牛，人人向我道早安'，穷理查说的这些话都是至理名言。"

感动一个国家的文字

The Road to Success 成功之路

Andrew Carnegie／安德鲁·卡内基

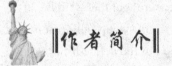

作者简介

安德鲁·卡内基(1835~1919)，美国钢铁大王，幼时家贫，靠个人奋斗发迹，是"美国梦"的典型。晚年捐巨资兴办图书馆事业。本篇是他1885年6月23日对柯里商业学院毕业生的讲话节录。

It is well that young men should begin at the beginning and occupy the most subordinate positions.Many of the leading businessmen of Pittsburgh had a serious responsibility thrust upon then at the very threshold of their career. They were introduced to the broom,

年轻人应该从头开始，从底层做起，这是很好的一件事情。匹兹堡许多出类拔萃的企业家在刚入行时，都承担过一个重要的职责：他们手持扫帚，在清扫办公室中开始了他们的创业生涯。我注意到，现在的办公室都配置了工友，我们的年轻人很不幸地失去了企业教育中有益的一环。但是，假如某一天早上，专职的清洁工偶尔没来，那么具有未来合伙人潜质的小伙子就会毫不犹豫地拿起扫帚。有一次，密

and spent the first hours of their business lives sweeping out the office. I notice we have janitors and janitresses now in offices, and our young men unfortunately miss that salutary branch of a business education. But if by chance the professional sweeper is absent any morning, the boy who has the genius of the future partner in him will not hesitate to try his hand at the broom. The other day a fond fashionable mother in Michigan asked a young man whether he had ever seen a young lady sweep in a room so grandly as her Priscilla. He said no, he never had, and the mother was gratified beyond measure, but then said he, after a pause,"What I should like to see her do is sweep out a room." It does not hurt the newest comer to sweep out the office if necessary. I was one of those sweepers myself.

Assuming that you have all obtained employment and are fairly started, my advice to you is "aim high" I would not give a fig for the young man who does not already see himself the partner or the head of an important firm. Do not rest content for a moment in your thoughts as head clerk, or foreman, or general manager in any concern, no matter how extensive. Say to yourself, "My place is at the top." Be king in your dreams.

And here is the prime condition of success, the great secret: concentrate your energy, thought, and capital exclusively upon the business in which you are engaged. Having begun in one line, resolve to fight it out on that line, to lead in it, adopt every improvement, have the best machinery, and know the most about it.

The concerns which fail are those which have scattered their capital, which means that they have scattered their brains also. They have investments in this, or that, or the other, here, there, and everywhere."Don't put all your eggs in one basket." is all wrong. I tell you "put all your eggs in one basket, and then watch that basket." Look round you and take notice, men who do that not often fail. It is easy to watch and carry the one basket. It is trying to carry too many

歇根一位溺爱孩子并非常时髦的母亲问一个年轻人，是否见过有哪个年轻女士像她的普里茜拉那样潇洒地在屋子里扫地。年轻人回答说从来没有见过，那位母亲高兴坏了。可是他停了一下又说："我想见到的是她在屋子外头打扫。"必要时，让新来的员工在办公室外扫扫地对他们并没有坏处。我自己就曾经是那些扫地人中的一员。

当确定你获得录用并有了一个公平的起点时，我的忠告是："确定远大的目标。"对于那些还未把自己看成大公司的未来的合伙人或者老板的人们，我是无话可说的。不管公司有多大，永远把自己看成这家公司的首席雇员、领班或者总经理。告诉自己："我的位置在最高层。"在你的梦想中，你应该是一流的。

通往成功之路的基本条件和重大秘密是：把你的精力、思想和资本全部集中于你所从事的事业之上。投身于哪一行，就得决心在这一行做出一番事业，做这一行的领导人物，采纳每一点建议，采用最好的设备，尽力精通专业知识。

一些公司的失败，就在于其资金的分散，以及因此而导致的精力的分散。他们这也投资，那也投资，到处投资。"不要把所有的鸡蛋放在同一个篮子里"这句话大错特错了。我要告诉你们的是："把所有的鸡蛋都放在同一个篮子里，然后看紧它。"观察周围并仔细留神，做到了这一点，你就不会失败。照管和携带一个篮子是很简单的。就是因为人们总是试图提很多的篮子，从而打破了这个国家大部分的鸡蛋。一次提着三个篮子的人，就得把一个篮子顶在头上，这个篮子很容易掉下来并把他绊倒。美国商人的一个缺点就是不够

baskets that breaks most eggs in this country. He who carries three baskets must put one on his head, which is apt to tumble and trip him up. One fault of the American businessman is lack of concentration.

To summarize what I have said: Aim for the highest, never enter a bar room; do not touch liquor, or if at all only at meals; never speculate; never indorse beyond your surplus cash fund; make the firm's interest yours; break orders always to save owners; concentrate; put all your eggs in one basket, and watch that basket; expenditure always within revenue; lastly be not impatient, for as Emers on says,"no one can cheat you out of ultimate success but yourselves."

专注一事。

我所说的话总结起来就是：要目标远大；不要涉足酒吧；不要喝酒，或者仅在用餐时喝一点；不要做投机买卖；不要签署支付超过储备的现金利润的款项；把公司的利益看成是你自己的；只有基于帮助货主的目的才能取消定单；要专注；要把所有的鸡蛋放在同一个篮子里，并且照管好它；消费永远小于收入；最后，要保持耐心，因为正如爱默生所说："只有你们自己，才能消蚀掉你们本来能够达到的最终的成功。"

A Message to Garcia
致加西亚的信

Elbert Hubbard／阿尔伯特·哈伯德

In all this Cuban business there is one man stands out on the horizon of my memory like Mars at perihelion.

When war broke out between Spain and the United States, it was very necessary to communicate quickly with the leader of the Insurgents. Garcia was somewhere in the mountain fastnesses of Cuba — no one knew where. No mail or telegraph message could reach him. The President must secure his co-coperation, and quickly. What to do!

Some said to the President,"There's a fellow by the name of Rowan who will find Garcia for you, if anybody can."

Rowan was sent for and given a letter to be delivered to Garcia. How the "fellow by the name of Rowan" took the letter, sealed it up

在所有与古巴有关的事情中，有一个人常常令我无法忘怀。

美西战争爆发以后，美国必须马上与反抗军首领加西亚将军取得联系。加西亚将军隐藏在古巴辽阔的崇山峻岭中——没有人知道确切的地点，因而无法送信给他。但是，美国总统必须尽快地与他建立合作关系。怎么办呢？

有人对总统推荐说：“有一个名叫罗文的人，如果有人能找到加西亚将军，那个人一定就是他。”

于是，他们将罗文找来，交给他一封信——写给加西亚的信。关

in an oilskin pouch, strapped it over his heart, in four days landed by night off the coast of Cuba from an open boat, disappeared into the jungle, and in three weeks came out on the other side of the Island, having traversed a hostile country on foot and delivered his letter to Garcia—are things I have no special desire now to tell in detail. The point that I wish to make is this: McKinley gave Rowan a letter to be delivered to Garcia; Rowan took the letter and did not ask, "Where is he at?"

By the Eternal! There is a man whose form should be cast in deathless bronze and the statue placed in every college of the land. It is not book-learning young men need, nor instruction about this and that, but a stiffening of the vertebrae which will cause them to be loyal to a trust, to act promptly, concentrate their energies: do the thing — "Carry a message to Garcia."

General Garcia is dead now, but there are other Garcias. No man who has endeavored to carry out an enterprise where many hands were needed, but has been well-nigh appalled at times by the imbecility of the average man—the inability or unwillingness to concentrate on a thing and do it.

Slipshod assistance, foolish inattention, dowdy indifference, and half-hearted work seem the rule; and no man succeeds, unless by hook or crook or threat he forces or bribes other men to assist him; or mayhap, God in His goodness performs a miracle, and sends him an Angel of Light for an assistant.

...

We have recently been hearing much maudlin sympathy expressed for the "downtrodden denizens of the sweat-shop" and the "homeless wanderer searching for honest employment", and with it all often go many hard words for the men in power.

感动一个国家的文字

于那个名叫罗文的人，如何拿了信，将它装进一个油纸袋里，打封，吊在胸口藏好，如何用 4 天的时间乘坐一条敞口船连夜抵达古巴海岸，穿入丛林，如何在 3 个星期之后，徒步穿越一个危机四伏的国家，将信交到加西亚手上——这些细节都不是我想说明的，我要强调的重点是：美国总统将一封写给加西亚的信交给了罗文，罗文接过信后，并没有问："他在哪里？"

像罗文这样的人，我们应该为他塑造一座不朽的雕像，放在每一所大学里。年轻人所需要的不仅仅是学习书本上的知识，也不仅仅是聆听他人的种种教诲，更需要的是一种敬业精神，能够立即采取行动，全心全意去完成任务——把信送给加西亚。

加西亚将军已不在人世，但现在还有其他的"加西亚"。没有人能经营好这样的企业——虽然需要众多人手，但是令人吃惊的是，其中大部分人碌碌无为，他们要么没有能力，要么根本不用心。

懒懒散散、漠不关心、马马虎虎的工作态度，对于许多人来说似乎已经变成常态。除非苦口婆心、威逼利诱地强迫他们做事，或者，请上帝创造奇迹，派一名天使相助，否则，这些人什么也做不了。

……

最近，我们经常听到许多人对那些"收入微薄而毫无出头之日"以及"但求温饱却无家可归"的人表示同情，同时将那些雇主骂得体无完肤。

Nothing is said about the employer who grows old before his time in a vain attempt to get frowsy ne'er-do-wells to do intelligent work; and his long, patient striving after "help" that does nothing but loaf when his back is turned.

In every store and factory there is a constant weeding-out process going on. The employer is constantly sending away "help" that have shown their incapacity to further the interests of the business, and others are being taken on. No matter how good times are, this sorting continues ; only, if times are hard and work is scarce, the sorting is done finer — but out and forever out the incompetent and unworthy go. It is the survival of the fittest. Self-interest prompts every employer to keep the best — those who can carry a message to Garcia.

I know one man of really brilliant parts who has not the ability to manage a business of his own, and yet who is absolutely worthless to anyone else, because he carries with him constantly the insane suspicion that his employer is oppressing, or intending to oppress him. He cannot give orders, and he will not receive them. Should a message be given him to take to Garcia, his answer would probably be,"Take it yourself!" Of course, I know that one so morally deformed is no less to be pitied than a physical cripple; but in our pitying let us drop a tear, too, for the men who are striving to carry on a great enterprise, whose working hours are not limited by the whistle, and whose hair is fast turning white through the struggle to hold in line dowdy indifference, slipshod imbecility, and the heartless ingratitude which, but for their enterprise, would be both hungry and homeless.

　　但是，从没有人提到，有些老板如何一直到白发苍苍，都无法使那些不求上进的懒虫勤奋起来；也没有人谈及，有些雇主如何持久而耐心地希望感动那些当他一转身就投机取巧、敷衍了事的员工，使他们能振作起来。

　　在每家商店和工厂，都有一些常规性的调整过程。公司负责人经常送走那些无法对公司有所贡献的员工，同时也吸纳新的成员。无论业务如何繁忙，这种整顿一直在进行着。只有当经济不景气，就业机会不多的时候，这种整顿才会有明显的效果——那些无法胜任工作、缺乏才干的人，都被摈弃在工厂的大门之外，只有那些最能干的人，才会被留下来。为了自己的利益，每个老板只会留住那些最优秀的职员——那些能"把信送给加西亚"的人。

　　我认识一个十分聪明的人，但是却缺乏自己独立创业的能力，对他人来说也没有丝毫价值，因为他总是偏执地怀疑自己的老板在压榨他，或者有压榨他的意图。他既没有能力指挥他人，也没有勇气接受他人的指挥。如果你让他"送封信给加西亚"，他的回答极有可能是："你自己去吧。"我知道，与那些四肢残缺的人相比，这种思想不健全的人是不值得同情的。相反，我们应该对那些用毕生精力去经营一家大企业的人表示同情和敬意：他们不会因为下班的铃声而放下工作；他们因为努力去使那些漫不经心、拖拖拉拉、被动偷懒和不知感恩的员工有一份工作而日增白发。许多员工不愿意想一想，如果没有老板们付出的努力和心血，他们将挨饿和无家可归。

Have I put the matter too strongly? Possibly I have; but when all the world has gone a-slumming I wish to speak a word of sympathy for the man who succeeds — the man who, against great odds, has directed the efforts of others, and having succeeded, finds there's nothing in it: nothing but bare board and clothes. I have carried a dinner-pail and worked for day's wages, and I have also been an employer of labor, and I know there is something to be said on both sides. There is no excellence, perse, in poverty; rags are no recommendation; and all employers are not rapacious and high-handed, any more than all poor men are virtuous. My heart goes out to the man who does his work when the "boss" is away, as well as when he is at home. And the man who, when given a letter for Garcia, quietly takes the missive, without asking any idiotic questions, and with no lurking intention of chucking it into the nearest sewer, or of doing aught else but deliver it, never gets "laid off", nor has to go on a strike for higher wages.

Civilization is one long, anxious search for just such individuals.

Anything such a man asks shall be granted. He is wanted in every city, town and village—in every office, shop, store and factory. The world cries out for such, he is needed and needed badly — the man who can "Carry a Message to Garcia".

So who will send a letter to Garcia?

我是否说得太严重了？不过，即使整个世界变成一座贫民窟，我也要为成功者说几句公道话——他们承受了巨大的压力，引导众人的力量，终于取得了成功。但是他们从成功中又得到了什么呢？一片空虚，除了食物和衣服以外，一无所有。我曾为了一日三餐而为他人工作，也曾当过老板，我深知两方面的种种酸甜苦辣。贫穷是不好的，贫苦是不值得赞美的，衣衫褴褛更不值得骄傲；但并非所有的老板都是贪婪者、专横者，就像并非所有的穷人都是善良者一样。我钦佩那些无论老板是否在办公室都努力工作的人，我敬佩那些能够把信交给加西亚的人。他们静静地把信拿去，不会提任何愚笨的问题，更不会随手把信丢进水沟里，而是全力以赴地将信送到。这种人永远不会被解雇，也永远不必为了要求加薪而罢工。

　　文明，就是孜孜不倦地寻找这种人才的一段长久过程。

　　这种人无论有什么样的愿望都能够实现。在每个城市、村庄、乡镇，以及每个办公室、商店、工厂，他们都会受到欢迎。世界上急需这种人才，这种能够把信送给加西亚的人。

　　谁将把信送给加西亚？

历史链接

　　一百多年前的一个傍晚，出版家阿尔伯特·哈伯德与家人喝茶时受儿子的启发，创作了一篇名为《致加西亚的信》的文章，刊登在《菲士利人》的杂志上。

　　杂志很快就告罄，纽约中心铁路局的乔治·丹尼尔一次要求订购10万册以书籍方式印刷的《致加西亚的信》，用来在车站发放。到1915年作者逝世为止，《致加西亚的信》的印数高达40,000,000册，创造了一个作家有生之年单本图书销售量的历史记录。

239

勤奋的生活

The Strenuous Life

Theodore Roosevelt／西奥多·罗斯福

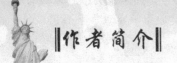

‖作者简介‖

西奥多·罗斯福（1858～1919），共和党人，美国总统，毕业于哈佛大学。曾组织志愿骑兵团参加美西战争，1900年任副总统，次年麦金利总统遇刺身亡，继任总统，时年42岁。任期内推出多项改革，以"改革家"面貌治国，对外则实行"大棒"政策。本文是1899年4月10日发表于芝加哥的一次著名演说节录。19世纪末美国骄奢淫逸、贪图享乐之风盛行，罗斯福特意对共和党俱乐部成员发表了《勤奋的生活》这一演说，旨在遏制当时的腐败之风。

Gentlemen,

In speaking to you, men of the greatest city of the West, men of the State which gave to the country Lincoln and Grant, men who preeminently and distinctly embody all that is most American in the American character, I wish to preach not the doctrine of ignoble ease but the doctrine of the strenuous life; the life of toil and effort; of labor and strife; to preach that highest form of success which comes not to the man who desires mere easy peace but to the man who does not shrink from danger, from hardship, of from bitter toil, and who out of these wins the splendid ultimate triumph.

感动一个国家的文字

The timid man, the lazy man, the man who distrusts his country, the overcivilized man, who has lost the great fighting, masterful virtues, the ignorant man and the man of dull mind, whose soul is incapable of feeling the mighty lift that thrills "stern men with empires in their brains" — all these, of course, shrink from seeing the nation undertake its new duties; shrink from seeing us build a navy and army adequate to our needs; shrink from seeing us do our share of the world's work by bringing order out of chaos in the great, fair tropic islands from which the valor of our soldiers and sailors has driven the Spanish flag. These are the men who fear the strenuous life, who fear the only national life which is really worth leading. They believe in that cloistered life which saps the hardy virtues in a nation, as it saps them in the individual; or else they are wedded to that base spirit of gain and greed which recognizes in commercialism the be-all and end-all of national life, instead of realizing that, though an indispensable element, it is after all but one of the many elements that go to make up true national greatness. No

先生们：

在向你们——西部最大城市的公民，为国家培育了林肯和格兰特的国家的公民，最能体现美国精神的公民——讲话时，我想谈的不是贪图安逸的人生哲学，而是要向你们宣讲勤奋生活论——即过勤奋苦干的生活，过忙碌奋斗的生活。我想说，成功的最高境界不属于满足安逸的人们，而是属于那些在艰难险阻面前从不畏惧终获辉煌的人们。

凡怯懦、懒惰、不相信祖国的人，谨小慎微丧失坚强斗志的"文明过头"的人，混沌无知的人，思想僵化的人，不能像刚毅有抱负的人那样被鼓舞振奋的人——总之，当看到国家有新的责任要承担，当看到祖国正在建立足以应付需要的海陆军，当看到英勇的士兵和水手在美丽的热带岛屿上驱逐西班牙势力，承担起应尽的世界责任，恢复当地秩序——当看到这一切时，所有这些人都退缩了。就是这样一些人，他们害怕过勤奋的生活，害怕过真正值得过的国民的生

country can long endure if its foundations are not laid deep in the material prosperity which comes from hard unsparing effort in the fields of industrial activity; but neither was any nation ever yet truly great if it relied upon material prosperity alone. All honor must be paid to the architects of our material prosperity; to the great captains of industry who have built our factories and our railroads; to the strong men who toil for wealth with brain or hand; for great is the debt of the nation to these and their kind. But our debt is yet greater to the men whose highest type is to be found in a statesman like Lincoln, a soldier like Grant. They showed by their lives that they recognized the law of work, the law of strife; they toiled to win a competence for themselves and those dependent upon them; but they recognized that there were yet other and even loftier duties — duties to the nation and duties to the race.

I preach to you, then, my countrymen, that our country calls not for the life of ease, but for the life of strenuous endeavor.The twentieth century looms before us big with the fate of many nations.If we stand idly by, if we seek merely swollen, slothful ease, and ignoble peace, if we shrink from the hard contests where men must win at hazard of their lives and at the risk of all they hold dear, then the bolder and stronger peoples will pass us by and will win for themselves the domination of the world. Let us therefore boldly face the life of strife, resolute to do our duty well and manfully; resolute to uphold righteousness by deed and by word; resolute to be both honest and brave, to serve high ideals, yet to use practical methods. Above all, let us shrink from no strife, moral or physical, within or without the nation, provided we are certain that the strife is justified; for it is only through strife, through hard and dangerous endeavor, that we shall ultimately win the goal of true national greatness.

感动一个国家的文字

活。他们相信与世隔绝的生活，任由这种生活在侵蚀他们个人吃苦耐劳品德的同时，也侵蚀了一个民族的吃苦耐劳精神。若不然，他们就沉迷于惟利是图、贪得无厌的卑污泥潭而不能自拔，认为国家应一切以商业利益为根本。但他们却不明白，商业利益固然是不可或缺的因素，然而毕竟只是造就真正伟大国家的许多因素之一。诚然，如果一个国家不是深深扎根于其工业活动领域的艰苦努力所带来的繁荣的物质基础之中，那么这个国家也不可能长久地生存下去。但是，如果仅仅依赖于物质财富，任何国家也永远不会成为真正伟大的国家。我们应该向那些创造了物质财富的人们致敬，向那些创建了工厂和铁路的实业巨头们致敬，向那些用勤劳和智慧换取财富的强者们致敬；国家很感激他们以及和他们一样的人。但是，我们更感激另外一些人，他们的最佳楷模就是林肯那样的政治家和格兰特那样的军人。他们的生活轨迹表明，他们清楚工作和斗争的法则，他们含辛茹苦，使自己和依赖他们生活的人们过上了富足的生活，但他们懂得还有更崇高的责任——对国家和民族的责任。

所以同胞们，我要讲的是，我们的国家要求我们不能好逸恶劳，而只能过刻苦勤奋的生活。迫在眉睫的20世纪将决定许多国家的命运。假如我们只是一味地袖手旁观，贪图享乐，苟且偷安，假如我们面临激烈的竞争考验时不是冒着牺牲个人生命和失去亲人的危险去赢得胜利，而是落荒而逃的话，那么，更勇敢坚强的民族就会超越我们，得以统领世界。因此，让我们勇敢地面对充满斗争考验的生活，下定决心卓越而果断地履行我们的职责；下定决心无论在语言还是行动上都坚持正义；下定决心诚实勇敢地以切实可行的方法为崇高的理想服务。最重要的是，无论是精神还是物质的斗争，无论是国内还是国外的斗争，只要我们确定正义在手，我们就绝不能逃避退缩。因为只有通过斗争，通过艰苦和充满危险的努力，我们才能最终达到目标——成为真正伟大的国家。

On His Ninetieth Birthday
当 90 岁来临时

Oliver Wendell Holmes/ 奥利佛·文德尔·霍姆斯

‖作者简介‖

奥利佛·文德尔·霍姆斯以"大反对家"而著称。1902 年，西奥多·罗斯福总统任命他为美国最高法院陪审法官。他任此职时将近 91 岁。本篇是电台为他庆祝 90 寿辰而举办的讨论会上的发言。本文把工作比做赛马，生动形象地说明了作者的观点：工作是人生的重要组成部分，一个人即使取得了很大的成功也不能停止工作，人活着就要工作……

In this symposium, better is it to only sit in silence. To express one's feelings as the end draws near is too intimate a task. That I would mention only one thought that comes to me as a listener-in: the riders in a race do not stop short when they reach the goal, there is a little finishing canter before coming to a standstill, there is time to hear the kind voice of friends, and to say to oneself, the work is done. But just as one says that, the answer comes the race is over but the work never is done while the power to work remains. The canter that brings you to a standstill need not be only coming to rest; it cannot be while you still live. But to live is to function, that is all there is in living. So I end with a word from a Latin voice who had heard the message more than fifteen hundred years ago — Death, death, clutch my ear, and says, "live, I am coming."

在这个讨论会上，保持沉默才是最好的选择。在行将就木之时，表达自己的感受太彻底了。现在我只想谈谈我作为一名听众的想法。赛马的骑手并不是一到终点就马上停步，在站稳之前他还会有一段慢步缓冲的过程。在这段时间内，他倾听朋友的欢呼，并告诉自己任务已经完成。但正像有人说的：比赛的结果出来了，但只要工作的能力尚在，任务就永远没有完成的时刻。慢步缓冲并不意味着就此安歇，只要生命尚存便不能如此。活着就要工作，这就是生命的全部。因此，我以1500多年前的一句拉丁格言作为结束语：死神不至，生命不息。

沉思中的奥利佛·文德尔·霍姆斯

A Fireside Chat
炉边谈话

Franklin Roosevelt/ 富兰克林·罗斯福

My friend,

This is not a fireside chat on war. It is a talk on national security; because the nub of the whole urpose of your president is to keep you now, and your children later, and your grandchildren much later, out of a last-ditch war for the preservation of American independence and all of the things that American independence means to you and to me and to ours.

Tonight, in the presence of a world crisis, my mind goes back eight years to a night in the midst of a domestic crisis. It was a time when the wheels of American industry were grinding to a full stop, when the whole banking system of our country had ceased to function.

I well remembered that while I sat in my study in the White House, preparing to talk with the people of the United States, I had before my eyes the picture of all those Americans with whom I was talking. I saw the workmen in the mills, the mines, the factories; the girl behind the counter; the small shopkeeper; the farmer doing his Spring plowing; the widows and the old men wondering about their life's savings.

I tried to convey to the great mass of American people what the banking crisis to them in their daily lives.

Tonight I want to do the same thing, with the same people, in this new crisis, which faces America.

We met the issue of 1933 with courage and realism. We face this new crisis--this new threat to the security of our nation — with the same courage and realism.

Never before since Jamestown and Plymouth Rock has our American civilization been in such danger as now.

我的朋友：

这次炉边谈话的内容不是关于战争，而是关于国家安全保障，因为你们的总统所有目的的核心，就是想让你们，你们的孩子，你们的子孙后代，不需要再通过拼死抵抗来维护美国的独立，以及美国的独立赋予你我、我们大家的一切。

今晚，面对着世界危机的来临，我的思绪回到了八年前国内危机中期的一个夜晚。当时，美国工业的车轮完全停滞了，我们国家的整个银行系统停止了运转。

我记得很清楚，当我坐在白宫的书房里，准备向合众国人民演讲的时候，我眼前浮现出他们所有人的样子。我看到制造厂、矿井和工厂里的工人们；我看见柜台后的女招待；我看见小商店老板；我看到春耕的农民；我还看到担心着自己毕生积蓄的寡妇和老人们。

我努力让无数的美国人民明白，银行危机对他们的日常生活来说意味着什么。

今晚，在美国面临这场新危机的时候，我想对同样的人们做同样的一件事。

1933 年，我们以勇气和现实的精神迎接了那一场危机；今天，我们以同样的勇气和现实精神来迎接这一场新的危机。

自美利坚文明在詹姆斯敦和普利茅斯岩诞生以来，我们还未遭遇过像今天这么严峻的危机。

For on Sept. 27, 1940 — this year — by an agreement signed in Berlin, three powerful nations, two in Europe and one in Asia, joined themselves together in the threat that if the United States of America interfered with or blocked the expansion program of these three nations — a program aimed at world control — they would unite in ultimate action against the United States.

The Nazi masters of Germany have made it clear that they intend not only to dominate all life and thought in their own country, but also to enslave the whole of Europe, and then to use the resources of Europe to dominate the rest of the world.

In other words, the Axis not merely admits but the Axis proclaims that there can be no ultimate peace between their philosophy — their philosophy of government—and our philosophy of government.

In view of the nature of this undeniable threat, it can be asserted, properly and categorically, that the United States has no right or reason to encourage talk of peace until the day shall come when there is a clear intention on the part of the aggressor nations to abandon all thought of dominating or conquering the world.

At this moment the forces of the States that are leagued against all peoples who live in freedom are being held away from our shores. The Germans and the Italians are being blocked on the other side of the Atlantic by the British and by the Greeks, and by thousands of soldiers and sailors who were able to escape from subjugated countries. In Asia the Japanese are being engaged by the Chinese nation in another great defense.

In the Pacific Ocean is our fleet.

…

Thinking in terms of today and tomorrow, I make the direct statement to the American people that there is far less chance of the United States getting into war if we do all we can now to support the

感动一个国家的文字 . . . . . .

因为在 1940 年 9 月 27 日——就是今年——两个欧洲强国和一个亚洲强国在柏林签署了和约。它们勾结起来威胁我们：如果美国干预或阻止这三个国家旨在控制全世界的扩张行动，它们最终将针对美国采取联合行动。

德国的纳粹头目们的野心已经昭然于世。他们不仅企图征服他们本国人民的思想和生命，还企图奴役整个欧洲，然后利用欧洲的资源来征服世界其他地方。

仅在三周前，他们的头子宣称："世界上有两个势如水火的阵营。"然后在回答对手时，他挑衅地叫嚣道："如果有人说'有这伙人在，我们就永不得安宁'，那他说对了。我们可以摧毁世界上任何异己的力量。"纳粹头子就是这么说的。

换句话说，轴心国不只是承认，他们还公开声明，在他们的政治哲学和我们的政治哲学之间永无调和的可能。

就这个不可否认的威胁的性质而言，我们可以明确果断地宣布：只要这些侵略国一天不明确表示放弃统治或征服世界的全部企图，美国就一天没有权利也没有理由提倡和平谈判。

此时，那些与生活在和平之中的所有人民为敌而结盟的国家的军队，已经被赶离我们的海岸；在大西洋的另一端，德国人和意大利人被英国人、希腊人，还有成千上万从沦陷国中逃出的士兵和水手们所拦截。在亚洲，在另一个伟大的保卫战中日本正受到中华民族的抵抗。

我们的舰队正巡逻在太平洋上。

……

考虑到今天和未来，我直截了当地告诉美国人民：如果我们今天尽全力去支援正在反击轴

249

nations defending themselves against attack by the Axis than if we acquiesce in their defeat, submit tamely to an Axis victory, and wait our turn to be the object of attack in another war later on.

If we are to be completely honest with ourselves, we must admit that there is risk in any course we may take. But I deeply believe that the great majority of our people agree that the course that I advocate involves the least risk now and the greatest hope for world peace in the future.

The people of Europe who are defending themselves do not ask us to do their fighting. They ask us for the implements of war, the planes, the tanks, the guns, the freighters which will enable them to fight for their liberty and for our security. Emphatically we must get these weapons to them, get them to them in sufficient volume and quickly enough so that we and our children will be saved the agony and suffering of war which others have had to endure.

...

We must be the great arsenal of democracy. For us this is an emergency as war itself. We must apply ourselves to our task with the same resolution, the same sense of urgency, the same spirit of patriotism and sacrifice as we would show were we at war.

We have furnished the British great material support and we will furnish far more in the future.

There will be no "bottlenecks" in our determination to aid Great Britain. No dictator, no combination of dictators, will weaken that determination by threats of how they will construe that determination.

The British have received invaluable military support from the heroic Greek Army and from the forces of all the governments in exile. Their strength is growing. It is the strength of men and women who value their freedom more highly than they value their lives.

感动一个国家的文字 . . . . . .

心国进攻的国家，那么合众国卷入战争的可能性就小得多；而如果我们默许他们的失败，屈从于轴心国的胜利，那么我们必将成为下一阶段战争中的攻击对象。

如果我们足够坦诚，那么我们就必须承认无论做何选择都是要承担风险的。但是，我深信，我们绝大多数人民都会同意，我所提倡的方案意味着现阶段最小的风险，却预示着未来世界和平最大的希望。

正在自卫的欧洲人民并没有要求我们替他们作战。他们要求的只是战争的装备，飞机、坦克、枪支和运输机。这些武器能够帮助他们为自己的自由以及我们的安全而战。我们必须当机立断并且尽可能多、尽可能快地把这些武器送给他们，这样，我们和我们的孩子们就能免受战争的痛苦与折磨，而其他人已不得不承受这样的痛苦与折磨。

……

我们必须成为民主的伟大武器库。对我们来说，这与战争同样紧急。我们应该以同样的决心、同样的紧迫感、同样的爱国主义和牺牲精神，来完成我们的任务，就像我们已经亲临战场。

我们已经向不列颠提供了大量的物质支援，未来还将提供更多。

在我们援助大不列颠的决心中没有"瓶颈"。无论独裁者或者独裁联盟威胁说要如何对我们的决心进行解释，都不能削弱我们这个决心。

不列颠已经得到了英勇的希腊军队以及所有流亡政府武装的难以估量的军事支持。他们的力量渐渐强大，这力量来自于视自由重于生命的人们。

I believe that the Axis powers are not going to win this war. I base that belief on the latest and best of information.

We have no excuse for defeatism. We have every good reason for hope — hope for peace, yes, and hope for the defense of our civilization and for the building of a better civilization in the future.

I have the profound conviction that the American people are now determined to put forth a mightier effort than they have ever yet made to increase our production of all the implements of defense, to meet the threat to our democratic faith.

As president of the United States, I call for that national effort. I call for it in the name of this nation which we love and honor and which we are privileged and proud to serve. I call upon our people with absolute confidence that our common cause will greatly succeed.

最新、最有价值的情报给了我一个信念，那就是：轴心国势力绝不会赢得这场战争。

我们没有借口倡导失败主义，我们有无数个充足的理由满怀希望——满怀和平的希望，是的，还有保卫我们的文明以及在未来创造更美好的文明的希望。

我坚信，此刻，美国人民正决心以前所未有的努力去提高各种防御物资的产量，用以对抗我们民主信念所面临的威胁。

作为合众国的总统，我号召全民行动起来。我以国家的名义号召你们，因为我们热爱她、尊敬她，并以能对她有所贡献而深感荣幸与骄傲。我以我们共同事业必胜的坚定信心来号召我们的人民。

历
史
链
接
：《炉边谈话》是富兰克林·罗斯福在第二次世界大战中通过广播向国民发表的家常式讲话，也是他最为著名的演讲。

感动一个国家的文字······

数百年前，一群欧洲移民来到广袤、荒凉的北美大陆，寻求自由与繁荣的梦想；数百年后，他们的民族成为世界上最强壮的民族之一，他们的国家成为世界上最强大的国家之一，他们的文明成为世界上最有影响力的文明之一……